Praise for *Belonging to the World*

"*Belonging to the World* is much more than the story of the tragic loss of a spouse or stepping foot in every country. It is the joy of connecting to the familiar as well as the gratification of learning cultures and fellowship with our broader sense of humanity. This book is an inspiration, a map that leads the reader toward positive affirmation of change."

—Julia Roberts

"In *Belonging to the World*, Barry Hoffner transforms profound personal tragedy into a remarkable journey of meaning and connection. His story resonates deeply with anyone who has seen both the beauty and the brutality of the world and still chooses hope. This book is a testament to resilience, empathy, and the belief that through understanding others, we rediscover ourselves."

—Bill Browder, author of *New York Times* bestsellers *Red Notice* and *Freezing Order*

"Barry reminds us of the beauty of human connection and the power of using grief to reimagine instead of to detach."

—Luke Russert, author of *New York Times* bestseller *Look for Me There*

"This moment in time is our most precious resource. . . . I'm reminded of that this morning by Barry Hoffner, who writes . . . about how, after losing his wife, he decided to spend his time traveling—discovering and rediscovering places—and sharing what he learned along the way.

That's how he chose to spend his time, and I'm so glad he took the time to share his learnings with us."
—Maria Shriver, in her introduction to Hoffner's article in the "I've Been Thinking" column of *The Sunday Paper*

"In *Belonging to the World*, Barry Hoffner takes the transformative nature of travel to a whole other level. He sees travel as a way to connect with others in a profound way, and, as a result, he builds schools where there are none. He builds roads to connect villages and encourages young girls to dream about a future filled with the promise of a better tomorrow. Barry inspires us to make a lasting difference in the lives of others we meet along the way. This book will encourage the reader to view travel in a new and enriching light."
—Margo Bart, president, Travelers Century Club

"In a brave, personal, and deeply emotional memoir, Barry Hoffner succeeds in bringing to life not only a powerful travelogue but also a journey toward meaning that teaches us to be positive and focus on the value of life. *Belonging to the World* is not only an ode to a single personal triumph from a role model in the travel community but also a lesson for anyone who has faced an irrevocable loss in search of an uplifting and inspirational true story."
—Harry Mitsidis, founder of NomadMania and one of the world's most traveled people

"Evoking the romance of their first kiss, Hoffner's *Belonging to the World* is the Taj Mahal of travel books: a masterpiece of a tribute to his late wife, Jackie. He carries her energy to every country in the world like an infinite passport and in doing so, discovers himself."
—Charles Veley, founder of Most Traveled People

"There is too much fear in today's world. Travel is one medicine, but travel with an unselfish purpose, giving more than taking, is what is really important. Barry, through his travels as chronicled in *Belonging to the World*, is a great example."
—Rauli Virtanen, award-winning Finnish journalist and the first person to travel to every country in the world

"After a heartbreaking tragedy, Barry Hoffner set out to visit every country on earth. Along the way finding a path to connection, healing, and hope. A journey we can all learn from."
—Brad Aronson, *Wall Street Journal* and *USA Today* bestselling author of *HumanKind*

"I had the honor of crossing paths with Barry on our shared mission to visit every country, and, out of all the travelers I've met, he is the one who truly embodies the essence of what it means to be a traveler. *Belonging to the World* is a story, one of both tragedy and beauty, offering a message that resonates with anyone searching for belonging and deeper meaning in life."
—Cameron Mofid, youngest person to travel to every country in the world

"This is not a travelogue, although the reader will be introduced to a myriad of exotic landscapes—from Afghanistan to Yemen to Tuvalu and more. This is a love letter to the human race, something we desperately need in this time of dehumanization and division. An ambassador of humanity, Barry Hoffner takes us on a riveting journey of discovery, and, along the way, he finds his own path forward after unimaginable loss."
—Cynthia P. Schneider, former US ambassador to the Netherlands, codirector of the Laboratory for Global Performance and Politics, and adjunct professor of diplomacy, Georgetown University

"*Belonging to the World* is a remarkable book for anyone curious about the world and their place in it. Barry's story isn't just about travel; it's about rediscovering life after loss. Honest, raw, and full of heart, it reminds us why we seek out the unknown."
—Dan Demsky, cofounder, Unbound Merino

"In *Belonging to the World*, Barry Hoffner transforms profound loss into an extraordinary quest across 193 countries. In the process, he discovers that the antidote to grief isn't withdrawal but connection. From the kindness of strangers in war-torn Syria to the grace of refugee families in Lebanon, Hoffner's journey reveals much about our

world, most profoundly that it is a far more welcoming and humane place than it is sometimes portrayed. This book is a moving testament to how travel can heal the deepest wounds, and that in meeting the 'Other,' we might just find ourselves."
—Eamonn Gearon, author of *The Sahara: A Cultural History*

"Barry's story, as told in *Belonging to the World*, is a celebration of humanity. His reflections on Syria highlight his deep care and the warmth and resilience of our culture, reminding readers that true belonging is shared across the world."
—Fadi Assi, CEO, Golden Team Syria

"*Belonging to the World* is a profoundly moving testament to life's redemptive power. Barry Hoffner's journey reminds us that even through loss, destiny finds a way to restore purpose, connection, and the beautiful truth of belonging."
—G A Twum-Barima, cofounder, BT Institute, Accra, Ghana

"*Belonging to the World* is such a wonderful travelogue and memoir that brings together the power of love, longing, and respect throughout a passionate and determined quest to traverse the globe. If this doesn't inspire you, nothing will."
—Gunnar Garfors, Norwegian author, public speaker, and multiple Guinness World Records holder

"Barry is one of those rare souls who leaves a lasting, inspirational impact. Rooted in profound loss, his journey became one of honoring memories, seeking meaning, and reconnecting with humanity. I had the joy of sharing unforgettable days with him in Cairo and Libya, where his determination and zest for life shone brightly. *Belonging to the World* is a powerful testament to resilience, love, and the beauty of human connection—an inspiration for generations to come."
—Ihab Zaki, owner, Spiekermann Travel

"*Belonging to the World* is a powerful testament to resilience and renewal. Barry Hoffner transformed unimaginable loss into a journey of connection across every corner of the globe. As a leader who values the power of global perspective, I find his story both deeply moving and profoundly relevant—a reminder that even in grief, we can rediscover purpose, humanity, and hope."

—Loh Boon Chye, CEO of Singapore Exchange and leading figure in Asia's financial markets

"*Belonging to the World* invites us to trade secondhand narratives for firsthand understanding—an act of courage and compassion in a time when we are too often divided. With piercing vulnerability, honesty, and humor, Barry Hoffner reveals a man unafraid to be afraid, opening his heart as he journeys through love, loss, and the search for meaning. More than a travelogue, this is a tapestry of stories—funny, frightening, heartbreaking, affirming, and full of love. Hoffner reminds us that life's true meaning lies in our relationships: with the world, with others, and with ourselves. *Belonging to the World* is both an adventure and an awakening—a testament to spirit, love, and the enduring human desire to belong."

—Marc Dollinger, professor and Goldman Chair, San Francisco State University

"I have followed Barry Hoffner's journey, as chronicled in *Belonging to the World*, around the world since its inception. His response to the tragedy in his life exposed him to the humanity that abounds in this world, no matter where he went. The journey also led him to create extraordinary additional opportunities for young women in West Africa through his foundation, Caravan to Class. We are proud to support their work empowering women and creating changemakers."

—Naomi Eisenberger, founding executive director, The Good People Fund

"*Belonging to the World* is a profoundly moving and inspiring journey. Barry Hoffner immerses himself in every country on earth—its people, languages, and cultures—while transforming heartbreak into courage. Through grief, love, and loss, he discovers how the world itself can help us find and redefine who we are."

—Nicola Dale, host of *Over the Back Fence* podcast and Australian travel and aviation media personality

"In *Belonging to the World*, Barry's ability to put into words the overwhelming emotions that come with immense grief will capture your heart and leave you wondering how it is possible to heal from such pain. But as his journey evolves, his random connections from around the world turn into moments of healing. It is rare to find people in life—like Barry—who are searching for a bigger meaning, purpose, and feeling. His willingness to embark on this journey, often completely lost, transforms directionless wandering into a pointed and intentional path toward a new chapter in his life."

—Renee Bruns, Guinness World Record holder and world traveler

"Visiting every country in the world is an extraordinary accomplishment—achieved by only about five hundred people out of eight billion. In *Belonging to the World*, Barry Hoffner charts an even more remarkable course within our community of global travelers. His altruistic work in Mali and across West Africa has not only enriched his own journeys but is also transforming the lives of a new generation of West African youth. Beyond his charitable endeavors, Barry has faced and overcome profound personal tragedy, adding depth and resilience to his story. His is not merely a voice among many, but a voice to learn from."

—Ric Gazarian, *Counting Countries* podcast host; cofounder, Extraordinary Travel Festival

"*Belonging to the World* is a remarkable book, a touching, kind, and humble examination of the way that travel can be therapeutic, eye-opening, and rewarding in a way that enriches far beyond simply providing bragging rights and point-scoring. Barry Hoffner tells his story of tragedy, defiance, and a clear-eyed and openhearted commitment to a great passion in an inspiring way. With characters met along the way, ideas to pique the interest of any travel buff or adventure newbie, and, throughout all the globe-trotting, the constant thread of love that is crucial to the genesis of the book and of many of his travels remains alive and evident. A unique and powerful work which can be recommended to anyone interested in travel, grief, moving forward, and where these all intersect."

—Simon Cockerell, general manager, Koryo Tours

"*Belonging to the World* is a beautifully written, deeply personal journey through lands and emotions that many seasoned travelers will recognize—and many more will be inspired by. It's an evocative tapestry of stories, adventures, and reflections that highlight the author's rare ability to connect with people across cultures. This book is a heartfelt invitation to step out, engage deeply, and truly belong to the world."

—Wassim Allache, owner of Algeria Tours 16

Belonging to the World

Belonging to the World

A Journey from Grief to Connection
in Every Country on Earth

Barry Hoffner

GFB

Copyright © 2026 by Barry Hoffner

All rights reserved.

No part of this book may be reproduced, or stored in a retrieval system, or transmitted in any form or by any means, electronic, mechanical, photocopying, recording, or otherwise, without express written permission of the publisher.

Without in any way limiting the author's and publisher's exclusive rights under copyright, any use of this publication to "train" generative artificial intelligence (AI) technologies to generate text is expressly prohibited. The author reserves all rights to license uses of this work for generative AI training and development of machine learning language models.

This is a memoir, and the events and experiences detailed in it have been presented as the author currently remembers them, to the best of his ability.

Some names and identifying details have been changed to protect the privacy of individuals.

Every effort has been made to trace copyright holders and to obtain their permission for the use of copyright material. The publisher apologizes for any errors and would be grateful if notified of any corrections that should be incorporated in future reprints or editions of this book.

Published by GFB™, Seattle
www.girlfridayproductions.com

Produced by Girl Friday Productions

Cover design: Greg Mortimer

Image credits: iStock Photo/Bobbushphoto

IBSN (hardcover): 978-1-967510-45-0
ISBN (paperback): 978-1-964721-41-5
ISBN (ebook): 978-1-967510-21-4

Library of Congress Control Number: 2025921528

First edition

I dedicate Belonging to the World *to two women, both small in stature, yet immense in spirit, who shaped my life in the most profound ways. One, my beloved mother, the greatest source of positivity I've ever known. The other, Jackie, whose grace and goodness felt touched by the divine. To you both, I give my deepest love until my final breath.*

Barry's Bests

1. Best festival experience: Chad (Gerewol)
2. Best wildlife encounter: Rwanda (mountain gorillas)
3. Best landscape: Mongolia (western region)
4. Most beautiful capital: Malta (Valletta)
5. Best natural wonder: Palau (underwater Serengeti)
6. Most striking architecture: Yemen (Manhattan of the desert)
7. Best coffee: Sudan (made with ginger)
8. Best food: Syria (just beats out Lebanese cuisine)
9. Best spiritual experience: Bhutan (land of monks)
10. Best waterfall: Guyana (Kaieteur Falls)
11. Best road trip: Pakistan (the Karakoram Highway)
12. Best antiquities: Algeria (ancient Roman cities)

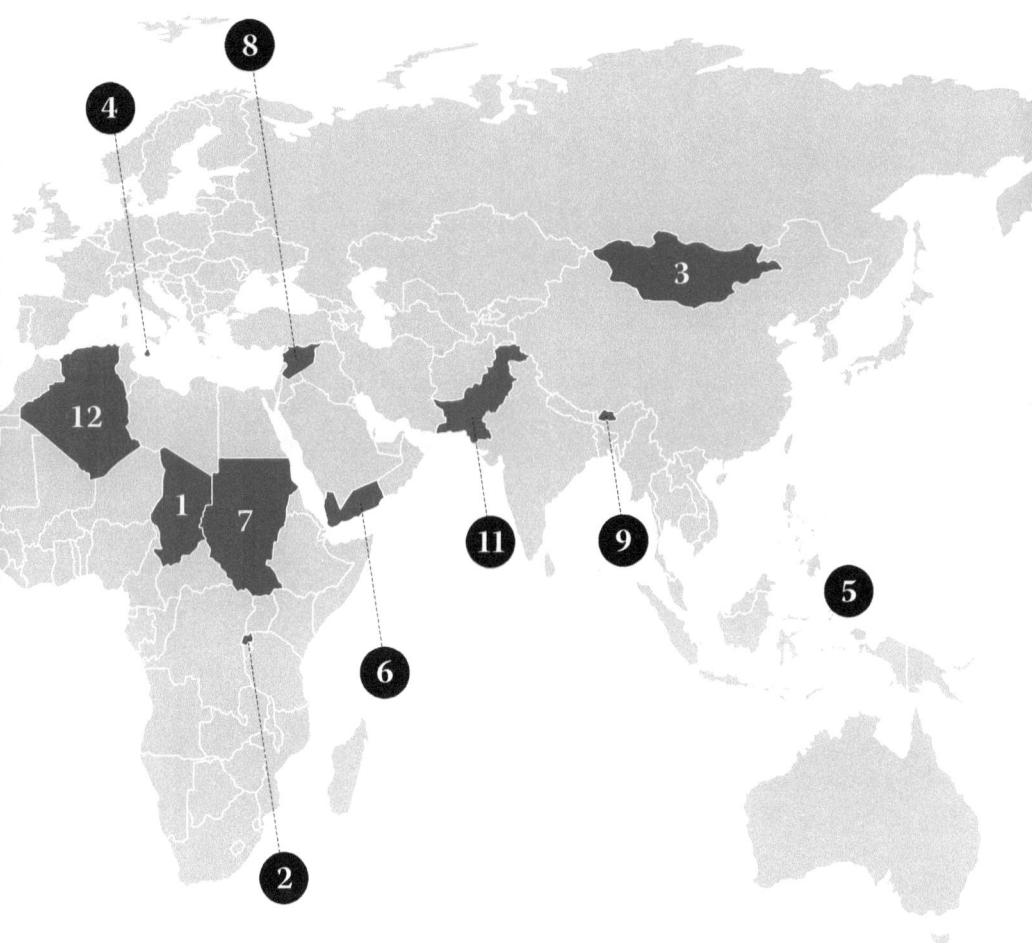

Contents

Foreword by Alvaro Rojas xix
Prologue xxi

PART 1: Everything After

Chapter 1: The Promise of an Empty Nest: Oman 3
Chapter 2: Year Zero: Dubai 9
Chapter 3: Tides of Grief: Jamaica 17

PART 2: The Life We Built

Chapter 4: Finding Uchi: In Search of Home: Japan 27
Chapter 5: In the Shadow of the Taj: India 36
Chapter 6: Bound by a Continent: Africa 42
Chapter 7: Family Life in the Land of the Rus': Russia 48
Chapter 8: Homeward Bound: Mali 56

PART 3: Something Still Calls Me

Chapter 9: The World's Friendliest Half-Marathon: Tajikistan 63
Chapter 10: A Pilgrimage to an Invincible Summer: The Camino 68
Chapter 11: The Power of Connection: Turkmenistan 75
Chapter 12: An Arabic Journey: Jordan 82
Chapter 13: Finding My Place: Suriname 88

PART 4: Project 193: The First Step

Chapter 14: Rapids and Primates: Uganda 99
Chapter 15: Aristotle in the Desert: Saudi Arabia 108
Chapter 16: Where Time Stands Still: Mauritania 114

Chapter 17: A Homecoming of Sorts: Iraq 124
Chapter 18: Roman Antiquity in Africa: Algeria 134

PART 5: Becoming Bolder: Beyond the Comfort Zone

Chapter 19: Taliban Tourism: Afghanistan 143
Chapter 20: Stateless People: Bangladesh 151
Chapter 21: Dancing with AK-47s: Yemen 158
Chapter 22: Never Too Old: Ethiopia 169
Chapter 23: A Birthday to Remember: Syria 179

PART 6: Halfway: The Farther I Go

Chapter 24: Lemurs and Rubicons: Madagascar 205
Chapter 25: A Coca-Cola Celebration: Libya 214
Chapter 26: A Mating Dance: Chad 223
Chapter 27: A Christmas Ride on the Tarmac: Tuvalu 234
Chapter 28: A Visual Desert Treat: Niger 242

PART 7: Full Circle

Chapter 29: Bearing Witness: Sudan 251
Chapter 30: Tranquility in a Buddhist Kingdom: Bhutan 259
Chapter 31: A High-Elevation Highway: Pakistan 268
Chapter 32: The Last African Surprise: Lesotho 274
Chapter 33: The Thundering Hordes: Mongolia 280
Chapter 34: Among a Thousand Tongues: Papua New Guinea 286
Chapter 35: Conflict Borders: Korea 293
Chapter 36: Closure: Botswana 300

Epilogue 311
Author's Note 317
Acknowledgments 319
About the Author 321

Foreword

by Alvaro Rojas (Owner, Wander Expeditions; UN Master, Spain)

It's bad, I thought, replaying his video message over and over. The footage was shaky, the audio drowned by hordes of tourists behind him. I could barely make out what he was saying.

Has this guy really traveled as much as he says he did? I wondered. Why did he want to join a group trip to Uganda? Nothing he said quite made sense. It was a scorching afternoon in Madrid in August 2021, and I was finalizing the selection for one of our expeditions. We had stellar candidates, young, smart, charismatic. So where did this sixty-year-old fit in?

Yet I'd thoroughly enjoyed our earlier one-on-one consultation. Barry had signed up to discuss his journey through the Pacific, his chances of getting an Iranian visa as an American, and to learn more about our trips. Right away, I could tell how sharp he was, always thinking two steps ahead. He had a youthful spark, a dry humor, and surprising wisdom. We even touched on the idea of visiting every country, a natural fit given his travel résumé, but oddly, it hadn't occurred to him. Learning that his mother was born in Baghdad, I told him that he had to go there.

When he applied for the Uganda expedition, it still seemed like an odd choice. With two-thirds of Africa still to go, Uganda was one of the easier countries. Maybe he wanted the group experience? Yet he seemed wary of being the oldest by decades. Usually I'm good at reading people, but this time, I wasn't sure. Still, I'd never seen someone his age, with so many accomplishments, seemingly so eager to prove something to himself. His enthusiasm for travel was contagious.

By October 2021 in Uganda, he'd found his place in the group. It was one of our most vibrant travel "families" ever—loud, funny, full of energy. Barry, more than twice the average age, connected deeply, especially with five women around his sons' age. He opened up to them about Jackie, the love of his life. What began as casual conversation became something raw and healing on long bus rides, over sunset beers, while tracking chimpanzees. Unexpectedly, he found community, even family.

He became the group's funny-punchline guy, offering fatherly advice and sharing his wit. And slowly, he shook off a heaviness. I felt that trip had opened something in him.

Barry kept showing up. In Saudi Arabia that December, we became real friends. He was lighter, cracking spicy jokes, dancing on the roadside, belting out karaoke. Then came Afghanistan and Yemen in 2022, where I saw a more grounded Barry. The still-grieving widower of Uganda had grown into a man who refused to be defined by loss.

It was in Yemen that Barry first mentioned writing a book about healing through travel. As we walked the dusty alleys of Tarim, I thought about how most extreme travelers chase ego or curiosity. Barry's motivation was different. He wasn't alone on this journey, carrying Jackie with him. In every sunset, in every breathtaking view, she was there. His story wasn't just about countries. It was about dealing with grief, being resilient, and finding belonging.

Looking back, I now see why Uganda made sense. It was his return to Africa, to safaris, and to shared adventure. He intuitively knew it was his first step forward.

"You know, you gave me the Elephant Cabin," Barry told me once. At the lodge in Queen Elizabeth National Park, each cabin was named after an animal. He ended up in the Elephant Cabin. At the time, I had no idea what elephants meant to him or the connection to Jackie. One afternoon, a massive wild elephant wandered just a few meters in front of us. Barry didn't retreat or panic. He stood there, but clearly affected, taking in the moment. It wasn't ease I saw, but effort, something rising in him as he faced a living symbol of his loss and maybe a real source of healing.

Prologue

Some journeys we choose. Others choose us.

In late 2017, I received a phone call that shattered my world. My wife, Jackie, my partner in life and in travel, had died suddenly while in Africa. I have replayed that call countless times: the initial shock, the numbness, the weight of grief that followed. Telling our boys their mother was dead was the hardest, most soul-crushing thing imaginable. And yet, that moment, uninvited and irreversible, would eventually steer me toward something else: a path, a pilgrimage, a mission.

I lost Jackie, and nothing can change that. I miss her dearly. It is a hurt that will never go away. But through my healing journey of travel, I have experienced belonging to something much bigger.

Still, it took time to get there. In the aftermath, I stumbled through darkness, unsure of what came next. There's no roadmap for rebuilding a life after loss. And while I don't believe in waiting for hope or faith to transform your life, I do now believe in the power of connection to help guide you on your intended journey.

And it did.

A chance connection with a young Spaniard, an extreme traveler himself, introduced me to a global community of people set on visiting every country in the world. At first, it seemed like a curiosity. Then it became something more. With over 100 countries already behind me, I made a decision: I would visit all 193 of them.

What began as a way to move forward became a way to feel again. I didn't want distraction. I wanted immersion. I wanted to see the world not as headlines, but as people. I wanted to remember what it felt like to be fully alive. As Marcus Aurelius said, "It is not death that a man should fear, but he should fear never beginning to live."

My decision to travel to every country in the world changed everything.

I found meaning in unexpected places: in conversations with strangers in Syria and Sudan, in awe in Bhutan and Bangladesh, in laughter on bumpy bus rides through Papua New Guinea and Pakistan. I didn't travel alone. I carried Jackie with me. And with each country, I came to feel less lost, more connected, not only to others, but to the world and myself.

This wasn't the journey I would have chosen. But it led me back to wonder, to purpose, and perhaps transformation. It gave me a sense of home that spans oceans and cultures.

This book traces that journey, not just across borders, but back to belonging.

Part 1

Everything After

Grief, Silence, and the Weight of Sudden Loss

Chapter 1

The Promise of an Empty Nest

October 2017
Oman

The last time I saw my wife, Jackie, was on a crisp fall morning in 2017, the day after celebrating her fifty-fifth birthday on October 22. I walked her out to the curb in front of our little rental in Georgetown as the Uber pulled up to take her to Dulles Airport. Suspended in time, we held each other longer than usual. Tears pooled silently in the corners of her eyes, so I forced myself to let go. As the car pulled away, I stood there with my heart full, knowing how much this trip meant to her.

We'd be heading off in different directions, Jackie to Africa, to work hands-on with the wildlife she'd grown to love so fiercely, and me to Oman two weeks later, to chase an old dream and explore a good place to learn Arabic. We planned to meet in three weeks in Nairobi to kick off this new chapter of empty-nesting.

Our boys were also starting their own journeys. We had just visited Benjamin early in his first semester at Georgetown University, and

Daniel was far away in Spain, fully immersed in his gap year. We were free again to travel like we did in the old days, just the two of us. At first, I wondered how Jackie would fare with an empty nest. She had often said, "I have the best job in the world as a mom to Benjamin and Daniel." What would she do with all her free time? She wasn't one for idle pastimes or living by convention.

As it happened, she didn't need long to figure it out. She had begun volunteering at WildAid, a nonprofit in San Francisco that fights the demand for exotic animal parts. Jackie was such a bright light that before long, she was hired full time to run WildAid's social media, connecting her with conservationists across Africa. I hadn't seen her this happy and motivated in years, eager to dive deeper into her work just as we entered this next phase of life.

I thought back to the warm summer evening that had set this moment into motion. Jackie asked me to meet her at one of our favorite restaurants in Sausalito, where we lived. She wanted to talk. I had a feeling I knew what it was about. After we toasted with our first glass of Sangiovese, I looked across the table and said, "What's up, Jackie? Let me guess, you want another dog?"

We'd had four up until the previous two years, one more than Marin County's legal limit. Now, for the first time in nearly fifteen years, we were back to only one.

She laughed. "You're funny. I'm quite content with just Annie. Actually, I want to go to Africa. I want to meet the people doing this work that I love. I want to feel it and live it. And maybe include a horse safari in the Okavango Delta."

I smiled. "You have to go."

Her eyes sparkled. "Maybe you can meet me at the end, in Nairobi? We could visit an elephant orphanage together." Nairobi was the place where we first set foot in Africa together, more than twenty years ago.

As I sat across the table, taking in Jackie's magnificent smile, it struck me: I still had a crush on my wife. Jackie and I had been through a lot, including some difficult times in the heat of raising kids. After all our adventures and years parenting the boys overseas, we settled in Sausalito in 2002. There, Jackie created a home for me and the boys, something I hadn't really known before. Now, I would have the best of both worlds: my partner in crime to relaunch the wanderlust we'd shared in our early years, and a home rooted in the familiar comfort of the bay.

"I'll be there," I said. And I meant it.

Muscat, Oman

With Jackie en route to Africa, I boarded a flight to Oman about two weeks later. My dream had always been to study Arabic in Damascus, one of the world's oldest continuously inhabited cities, even mentioned in the Bible. But Syria was still in the throes of civil war, and Baghdad hadn't fully emerged from its own recent violence. My Arabic tutor suggested Oman instead—a Middle Eastern country where bullets weren't flying and a place to safely indulge my curiosity about the Arab world. I went to Oman to see if it was the place I wanted to return to the following year to study Arabic intensively.

My mother, born in Baghdad, had moved to the US at age seven. In my youth, I'd heard her speak Iraqi Arabic with her siblings and my grandmother. She never learned to read or write it, but the sounds stayed with me. Now, I was ready to dive in. And it wasn't just the Arabic language I wanted to understand, but also the culture, the landscapes, and most of all, the people who spoke it.

I'd grown up Jewish, in the long shadow of Middle Eastern wars: 1967, 1973, 1982. We were taught to be wary, to see the region through the lens of trepidation. But what did we really know about the people we were taught to fear?

To this point, my actual "boots on the ground" knowledge of the Arab Middle East amounted to an overnight stop in Dubai, a visit to see the pyramids in Cairo, Egypt, and a two-day stay in Amman, Jordan. I viewed the crossing of the Allenby Bridge from Israel to Jordan as akin to entering a potential danger zone. It was about time I educated myself with real impressions of the Arab world. Oman was the first Arab country to establish friendly relations with Israel in the 1970s, earning the wrath of the Arab League, so it felt like a safe bet.

So I landed in Muscat, and shortly after gave my limited Arabic a try. In the taxi to the Noor Majan Arabic Institute, I greeted the driver with the ubiquitous "Asalam Aleikum." He then rattled something off, speaking too fast. I fumbled, explaining, "Ana min California . . .

shway shway Arabi fukut." (I am from California, only a little Arabic). He laughed, then gave me a thumbs-up. We understood each other, imperfectly. But it was enough.

The institute's area, far from Muscat's charming old port and souq, disappointed me. And my hotel, a sterile Radisson next to a massive mall, felt like a poor trade for ancient alleys and Arabic coffee.

As for coffee, when I'm studying a language in a new country, the location of the nearest coffee spot is *especially* important. For me, drinking coffee and learning a language are inextricably entwined. It's the way I've started my day for years. At the mall, all I found was a Starbucks, not exactly the Arab-coffee vibe I'd hoped for. This was just like being home—well, almost. There was a throng of women holding the veils of their black burqas to the side to drink their coffee, not something I'd ever seen at my local Starbucks. But even here, Arabic gave way to English. *So much for putting my Arabic to use.*

Back at the Radisson at the end of the day, a couple and their young child were walking to the elevator ahead of me. The woman was in a full burqa, and the man had a long beard and wore a *thawb*, the traditional robe-like male attire of the Gulf region. As I started to follow them into the elevator to head down to the lobby, the man held up his arm to block my way and gave me a look that clearly said, *There is no fucking way you're riding in this small elevator with my wife.* As the door closed, I chuckled to myself. No actual Arabic language skill was needed for that translation.

Meanwhile, it had been about three weeks since Jackie left for Africa, and I missed her. We did text a fair amount, so I had her regular updates from South Africa. It was clear she was having an amazing time. "Hey Barry, just wanted to wish you safe travels to Oman and hope you'll enjoy studying Arabic there. Thula Thula is magical," she wrote. "I wish you could see it. I'm headed to Botswana. Can't wait to see you in Kenya." She signed off with a string of emojis: kisses, the heart sign, elephants, rhinos, and other various love icons. Jackie was a fan of emojis.

Hearing from her and knowing she was having a good time left me comforted and ready to delve a bit further into Muscat and other parts of Oman.

Over the next two days, as I ventured beyond the modern malls to explore more of the city, I came to better appreciate its charm. I had been looking to return to the Middle East for a longer trip to spend several months studying Arabic, but Muscat didn't grab me as a place to do this. I was looking for a real Middle Eastern vibe—a place with streets of inner mazes leading to ancient mosques, where vendors with kaffiyehs (the male Arab headdress) sold tasty Arabic delights like baklava and shawarma, and where I was served strong Arabic coffee in little welcoming places surrounded by men smoking their hookahs (waterpipes).

Muscat was nice but not exactly what I was looking for, so it was time to tour a bit more of the country. Unfortunately, I did not have a chance to see the turquoise waters of the Gulf of Oman that I'd heard so much about, but I would experience some of Oman's other natural beauty like its renowned desert. And after that, I would be reuniting with Jackie.

When my guide, Juma, arrived to pick me up for a day of exploring, I cut right to practicing my rudimentary Arabic with him. I had his captive audience for the next day and a half and can only imagine how annoying it must have been to humor me. Fluent in English, he probably wished I'd stay in my lane. As we drove out to the desert, he pointed out sights, in English, and I'd reply with my go-to phrase in Arabic, "Hatha jamil" (That is beautiful). At one point, he shot me a look that said, *You're killing me, dude.*

Eventually, we came to our first stop, a massive grove of graceful palm trees, the vast desert beyond stretching to the horizon. This was the first Arab oasis I'd seen, and it fit the images in my mind perfectly: palm trees, lots of sand, and Arabs in their local dress as they sipped coffee at a nearby table. As we headed for the Wadi Shab, Oman's legendary picturesque canyon with crystal clear waters, we followed a path through a narrow valley bisected by a dry river basin with cliffs on either side and came upon some large rock formations up ahead.

"Are you ready to go swimming?" Juma said, turning to me and grinning like he knew something I didn't. He'd told me to make sure to bring a bathing suit, but given that we were so far from the coast, I wasn't sure he was serious. I'd crammed my swim trunks into my backpack anyway. As we climbed the rocks and saw what was below, I was glad I had. Directly in front of us, a twenty-foot waterfall spilled into a natural Olympic-sized pool of emerald-green water.

My God, so pristine.

Once I caught my breath, I set my backpack down, quickly changed into my swimming trunks, and dove in—*instant euphoria.* This was way beyond anything I'd imagined a desert oasis could be. When I came up for air, Juma told me there was so much water flowing in Wadi Shab at certain times of the year that Red Bull had its annual cliff-diving championships here in 2012. If I couldn't make it to the beaches of the Gulf of Oman, at least I'd immersed myself in *this* gem.

Thoroughly refreshed, I followed Juma back to the car, and he drove us deeper into the heart of the desert for our next stop, Wahiba Sands, known for its miles and miles of towering dunes. We got there just before the sun began to set, and after checking into our camp at the base, we climbed the dune to watch the sun go down the rest of the way. Surrounded by a sea of sand, we spent about an hour in silence. It had been so hectic in the Hoffner household the past months, with so many changes taking place, that I felt grateful for the quiet, inviting me to pause.

The temperature went from hot to warm to cold as I watched the waves of sand deepen from amber to rust red, sitting on what seemed like the top of this majestic desert. As the sun bade its farewell, I finally felt fully present and at peace in the vastness and solitude of the surrounding land. We stayed until the sky completed its transition from sunset to a blanket of stars, an awe-inspiring progression.

As we headed back down in partial darkness, I couldn't have felt more content. I'd just discovered another dazzling corner of the earth. I hadn't heard from Jackie in two days, but she was deep in the Okavango Delta, off the grid, I figured. There was likely not much cell reception. Whatever the case, after the next two days of travel, via Dubai, I was leaving the Arab world. I'd see Jackie's sparkling smile once again, and we'd make the next discovery together in Africa.

Chapter 2

Year Zero

November 2017
Dubai

As the plane touched down in Dubai, I checked my phone for a text from Jackie. There was nothing but a voicemail from an unknown country code. *Probably spam.* Without listening to it, I tucked my cell back into my bag and headed to the airport hotel, Le Meridien, where I'd be spending the night before flying to Nairobi the next morning to meet my wife.

I hadn't been in Dubai in twenty-five years. Curious to see how it had changed, I dropped my bags in the room and set out. My first stop was Ski Dubai, the indoor ski slope at the Mall of the Emirates. It was surreal—skiers under artificial stars and even penguins on a fake hillside. *Real penguins.* Outside again in the ninety-degree heat, I stood gawking at the Burj Khalifa like a tourist on another planet.

Next, I wandered through the massive Dubai Mall, the largest in the world, passing luxury storefronts: Gucci, Armani, Dior. By late afternoon, I'd had enough. Dubai was impressive, but no longer held the intrigue of a place in transition. It had arrived. I returned to the hotel for some things on my to-do list for my trip the next day. Checked in for my Emirates flight, booked a transfer to the Nairobi hotel, and scheduled a wake-up call. Nothing left to do but order room service and try to sleep.

Just as I hung up with the front desk, I got a call from the same area code as the voicemail.

"Hello?"

"Hello, this is Barney . . ." said a garbled voice that I was straining to hear through my cell phone.

Struggling to hear, I pleaded, "Could you please speak more clearly and louder? I can barely hear you."

"This is Barney from Okavango Horse Safaris [OHS] in Botswana. There has been a terrible accident! Jackie was killed by an elephant!"

The words didn't land so much as detonate, like a wrecking ball hitting me at full force, but with my mind racing even as my body went numb with the force of the blow. My heart pounded, and I dropped into a surreal, hyperaware focus as my brain tried to comprehend the incomprehensible.

I spent the next hour talking with a bewildering number of people in Botswana: staff from OHS, the US ambassador to Botswana, the helicopter pilots who flew her to the hospital in the town of Maun, the police in Maun, even the person who handled Jackie's body, Omphile, a man whose voice was oddly soothing.

I was living in two parallel worlds: one shattered, the other focused on the hardest task of all—telling my boys they'd lost their mom. Within minutes, the life I knew before no longer existed.

Still in shock, I wrestled with an impossible choice: *Fly to Botswana or fly to my boys?* If I went to Botswana, I might not be with them for days. But if I didn't, I'd likely never see where Jackie took her last breath.

No, I had to focus on our boys and get to them as soon as possible.

To confirm my instincts, I called my best friend, Neil, a psychologist in Los Angeles, and he helped put to rest the idea of going to Botswana. With Daniel spending a gap year in Seville, Spain, and Benjamin in the middle of his first semester at Georgetown University in DC, it quickly became clear. There wouldn't be time to tell both boys in person. Benjamin would have to be told over the phone. The first call went to Jane, director of Georgetown's Academic Resource Center. "Jane, this is Barry Hoffner, Ben's dad. I have some difficult news and need your help with something." She sprang into action, connecting me with Rabbi Rachel Gartner, whom I'd met on a previous visit. Rachel agreed to be there in person with Benjamin.

A few minutes later, she texted from outside his dorm. I called. "Hi, Dad. Hold on, someone's at the door."

"Benjamin," I said once they were in the room together, "I have some very heartbreaking news. There's been an accident. . . ."

The rest is a blur. At some point, I asked him not to tell anyone for twenty-four hours, until I could reach Daniel. He agreed. "Benjamin, I'll be with you as soon as I can. I love you. I love Daniel. And I love Mom." Words escaped me from there. I had no idea what else to say.

I held it together until I couldn't. As I sat at the hotel table, head in hands, the dam broke, and a tidal wave of sorrow overwhelmed me. I wasn't just sobbing; I was unraveling. I'd never known such pain, raw, unrelenting, absolute.

Eventually, I pulled myself together. There was no choice. I called Daniel's host family in Spain and booked the first available flight to Madrid. It left the next morning. When this was done, I put on some Norah Jones music and tried to rest. *No chance.* Just after midnight, I made my way to the airport and sat in a daze at a café until boarding.

I felt like I was watching the world from behind glass. It no longer included me. I occasionally looked up and noticed other travelers coming and felt no common link to them, and in one piercing moment, it dawned on me: *I was not part of their world anymore.*

· · ·

I don't remember much of the train ride from the Madrid airport to Seville. What I do recall is the taxi ride to Daniel's host home, which I spent rehearsing over and over how I would tell him.

Manuel opened the door and pulled me into a hug. No words. He pointed down the hall to Daniel's room. I knocked, and after a brief pause, Daniel opened the door, his face registering clear surprise.

"Dad, what are you doing here?"

"Daniel, please sit down. I have terrible news. . . . Mom has died. She was killed by . . ."

He let out an anguished primal scream before collapsing into my arms.

Later, I returned to my hotel. The calls—Jackie's parents, her sister, my family, close friends—each one replaying the nightmare. Then came the email to everyone else. I hated the impersonality of it but couldn't bear more phone calls. And so, I poured my heart out one more time, in writing.

> I am sorry to have to give you this terrible news, particularly via email. My beloved Jackie passed away yesterday, on November 14, in Botswana. There will be a time to get into more details, but Jackie was killed in a tragic elephant accident. . . . It seems almost too unreal to be writing this given her love and strong advocacy for elephants. My focus right now is on my boys. No parent should ever have to tell their still-too-young children that they have lost a beloved mother. While I am obviously crushed by this loss, I am even more devastated for my boys. Their loss of Jackie's female caring, support, and love is a great one. Only time can make sense of this tragedy. We will find the time and place to commemorate Jackie's life. What helps most is picturing Jackie's sweet face, feeling her spirit, and knowing that because of her, I have the most wonderful, kind, and considerate boys any parent could ever ask for.
> Love, Barry

. . .

I often think about the phrase "year zero." I first heard it on *The Late Show* a few years ago, listening to Anderson Cooper and Stephen Colbert talk about the loss of their respective fathers at the age of ten. At that young age, Colbert lost not only his dad but also his two older brothers in a plane crash. He said his "year zero" began the next day.

I didn't know it yet, but my "year zero" had just begun. It's hard to describe the anguish of holding something you know will change your children's and other loved ones' lives forever. Holding this loss inside until I told both my boys took its toll. I couldn't stop thinking about those soul-crushing conversations. Now, with this devastating news out, a new reality began: *my year zero.*

Only two difficult days later, less than one week before Thanksgiving, Daniel and I boarded a plane bound for DC. Daniel slept next to me, both of us emotionally exhausted. As the flight took off, I was hit by a tidal wave of memories, all the memories I had of Jackie and all of us as a family, literally thousands of dreamlike recollections. Though I muffled my sobbing so Daniel could keep sleeping, the memories buoyed me with vivid images of a blessed life together before having kids and our life as a family. I felt a sense of gratitude that was as powerful as it was indescribable. It was a sacred place I hadn't known existed until that moment.

I also realized something else that gave me a strange kind of strength. I'd just endured the worst two days I would ever go through. As surreal as it sounds, that thought brought a flicker of clarity. Though I'd done the most difficult thing I would ever do that crushed my soul to no end, somehow, I was still standing.

Reuniting with Benjamin in DC was as heartbreaking as I'd imagined. Jackie and I had already planned to spend Thanksgiving there with her family. Despite everything, we stuck to that plan. The boys and I stayed in a small room at the Georgetown Inn. I couldn't stop crying; their smallest gestures undid me.

One night, Benjamin awoke around midnight. "What are you doing, sweetheart?" I said.

"I'm going out."

"Benjamin, it's after midnight, and it's freezing outside."

"I'm going to buy sandwiches at the twenty-four-hour store and give them to the homeless people on the street."

Speechless, I broke down yet again. His empathy, even in grief, was pure Jackie. I was starting to wonder how many times the human heart could break.

I remembered little of that Thanksgiving, but the "firsts" had begun: first night, first holiday, first week without her. Life with Jackie was now a defined and significant period of our lives, and now, life without her, our year zero, was here, not having given us a choice.

. . .

Once back in Sausalito, I had more trying things to attend to, most significantly the planning of Jackie's celebration of life. The gravity and significance of the event were not lost on me. I was powerfully motivated, knowing I would never have a more important task than to honor my wife in a way befitting the exceptional human being she was. So, I threw myself into the preparations, sure she'd have approved of the results. One close friend emailed me afterward: "You and Jackie fell in love at the Taj Mahal; that, my friend, was the Taj Mahal of ceremonies."

Nearly seven hundred people came to the Marin Jewish Community Center. We began with eulogies from me, the boys, and Jackie's parents, followed by an evocative slideshow of our life together. Music was performed by friends, some of them well-known musicians: my dear friend Dave Koz on sax, Livingston Taylor on guitar, my nephew Nate Sparks on piano, and even Jake Shimabukuro on ukulele, playing "Somewhere Over the Rainbow." After the music, the video continued with moving tributes to Jackie in numerous languages from friends all around the world.

By the end of the two-hour ceremony, I was spent. Not just from organizing the event, but from the emotional toll of giving Jackie the send-off she deserved. I had swung from deep sorrow to gratitude for the outpouring of emotion for Jackie and us from the community. I was so profoundly proud and full of love for my boys, who spoke about their dear mother with such grace, feeling, and eloquence. But it all worked its way to numbing exhaustion. The hardest part was then attending to everyone who wanted to extend their condolences. What do you say the hundredth time someone says, "I'm so sorry for your loss," and still sound sincere? I appreciated the graciousness behind their words, but I just wanted to be alone to process everything, yet there was still the reception following the ceremony.

In the days that followed, although I was still in the early stages of grief and shock, somehow, my heart was full. Full of love for Jackie and my boys. It seemed strange to feel this way, but I couldn't deny it. The usual noise in my mind was gone. In its place was love, intense, palpable, resting in my chest. Jackie's ceremony had been so full of love, and it seemed to have attached itself to me. I carried it around just like I carried around the image of the hundreds of sunflowers that had adorned the main hall of the Marin Jewish Community Center; the sunflower was Jackie's favorite flower (she had one tattooed on her arm) and one that seemed to reflect her brilliant spirit best. Reading messages from friends and family after the ceremony also lifted my spirits during that very dark time. One, from someone we didn't know well, read as follows:

> I was deeply honored to attend Friday's service and feel privileged to have known Jackie, even briefly. It's clear how profoundly she impacted so many lives. You, your boys, and Jackie's family are in my heart and thoughts and will be for a long time. Over the holidays, I'll be dedicating quiet time and reflection to her memory; there's so much she can still teach me about the art of living and being a better person.

What I saw at her celebration of life also profoundly impacted me. Also, Jackie's focus on kindness had a visible ripple effect all through our community. Though her time was cut way too short, she had lived a very worthy life. As for me, I spent most of my existence trying to achieve a bewildering number of concrete goals. Maybe I was missing the big picture? I couldn't yet see what came next, but the day's images had already settled deep inside.

As time passed, it became more and more clear that I was heading into some great unknown. I recalled a message that Omphile from Maun in Botswana had sent me while we worked together on coordinating some difficult tasks: "The Bible says, 'We should never walk with fear of what we may lose or have lost, rather we walk with love and faith when we are going through hard times.'" I'm not religious; I don't even believe in God these days, but I do have faith—faith in the love and kindness we each carry within us. I witnessed it firsthand in those days after Jackie's death, and I am not sure how I could have survived without it. The empathy displayed to me and the boys was magnified a hundred times in the rawness of our grief.

Yes, the weight of what we lost, a wife, a mother, a best friend, was crushing. And yet, even in the vastness of that absence, something else was ever present—not peace, but gratitude.

Enough to take a step. Still grieving, still broken, but knowing that I would need to push forward for my boys, if nothing else.

Chapter 3

Tides of Grief

January 2018
Jamaica

Everyone grieves differently. Benjamin's way was to throw himself into his studies, taking a full second semester's worth of classes while also making up for incompletes from his first semester. Daniel's way was to study and learn how to save people by getting his Emergency Medical Training (EMT). And my way was to be alone. But in the tight-knit community Jackie and I had built over the years in Marin County, solitude was hard to come by. Every walk through the neighborhood or trip to Whole Foods brought a familiar face, someone asking gently, "How are you doing?" or, harder still, offering only a blank stare, unsure of what to say. I realized I needed anonymity, a place where I could disappear, if only for a while. I needed space to grieve and make sense of what had shattered my world.

So, in early January, I temporarily moved to Georgetown, Washington, DC, and rented the same house at 1043 Cecil Street where we had celebrated Jackie's last birthday. Benjamin moved in with me. Daniel stayed home to pursue EMT training.

Before Jackie's passing, my days were packed with ranch work, investments, real estate, sports, boards, and my foundation work. But now, I abandoned all of this except the work of my foundation. Losing Jackie, and in such a surreal, incomprehensible way, was a rupture I couldn't begin to process. It felt like I had stepped outside of my own life, like I was watching it unfold from a distance. Later, I would learn there was a word for this eerie detachment I felt from my body, thoughts, and feelings; it is called "depersonalization." As Benjamin insightfully put it, "I feel like I'm in a movie, playing the role of a son who just lost his mom in a tragic accident."

Man, I was lonely for Jackie's company. In Georgetown, I only saw Benjamin for a few minutes each morning and during the evening. I am not the type to bury a problem, even something as difficult as the loss. Being more of a fixer-type, I knew there was no quick fix here. There really was no choice other than to take it head-on, *to lean into it*. I didn't know what healing looked like, but I was clear that it wouldn't come through planning or productivity. Maybe presence was the only place to start.

I started this search by reading the Stoics, including the great philosopher Seneca, who talked about "having pity on the person who never went through anything deep, who had not been knocked down or bloodied in the ring." This stuck with me, and I began to see my grief as something I had to go through that would somehow make me a better, more enlightened person once out the other side.

There was no desire to see most people, no interest in laughing with friends or making small talk. The loneliness wasn't about missing social time; it came from the sudden absence of a powerful presence. In its place had emerged a kind of tranquility, something not easily surrendered. Disciplined rituals became anchors: coffee and Arabic at 5:30 a.m., breakfast, meditation, grocery runs, reading, and dinner. A regimented routine gave me the illusion of control over a life that had spun out of control. Evenings also brought a focused nighttime ritual.

I'd read a passage of *Healing After Loss: 365 Daily Meditations for Working Through Grief*, by Martha Whitmore Hickman, then a bit about meditation in general in Robert Wright's *Why Buddhism Is*

True and Marcus Aurelius's *Meditations*. It amazed me that he wrote it while on campaign against the Germanic tribes. After a day's battle, he would retire to his tent and write his reflections, under candlelight, about how to live with purpose and die with dignity. These weren't just intellectual pursuits; they were lifelines, or possibilities for who I might become or how I would transform without Jackie.

I also needed some levity in my routine. After Jackie died, the boys heard me laughing at *Meet the Fockers*. "Dad, watch *The Office*," they said. It became my nightly balm. At first, laughter felt foreign. But *The Office* brought brief joy before sleep, a reminder that the path to healing wasn't a leap, but a slow return.

I was usually fast asleep by 9:00 p.m. Sleep was the only real respite from my incessant thoughts and heartache. There, I could escape into the subconscious world, where Jackie might appear in a dream, allowing me to feel a moment of comfort when I woke. In one vivid dream, Jackie and I were taking a hike and saw a couple in a canyon struggling with a horse. We stopped to help them, and afterward, the woman asked Jackie, "How do you put up your hair so beautifully?" Jackie took the rubber band out of her hair and styled the woman's hair like hers. The woman smiled. It felt so real. Jackie loved horses, and I often heard her stories about riding Rosie.

During the day, I studied Arabic with Zahraa, a Syrian refugee from Aleppo. She had survived Assad's bombardment and had lost close family in the war. Her resilience moved me, and we bonded quickly, particularly after I told her in Arabic, "I promise you that I will visit Aleppo one day, inshallah." She often brought delicious Syrian dishes: fatteh, kibbeh, fattoush—all welcome upgrades to my cooking that Benjamin was grateful for.

As the months passed, I felt a very subtle shift. Daily meditation revealed quiet truths about the nature of my mind. I began to see that suffering, mine and others', can feel lighter when we recognize it as part of being human, something that comes and goes rather than something that defines us. Maybe it could even help me, if I stopped resisting it. Over time, I started to feel that this hard chapter might lead to a deeper connection with myself and with the world around me.

Rereading Harari's *Sapiens* deepened my understanding of grief and the stories we tell to make sense of it. Some narratives bind us through shared meaning; others simply protect the ego, shielding us from the parts of ourselves we're not ready to face.

As I began to detach from this old self, I saw clearly for the first time the games my mind had been playing with me: the business goals, the drive for financial comfort, the need to see my sons succeed, all illusions of success I once felt the need to chase. In recognizing this, I also realized that I could find a new, different way of living, and I knew I needed to be on a path to doing just that. I knew that being older meant learning to accept my place in the world with greater humility and clarity. Now, retired and no longer feeling the need to build my status, I turned toward seeking out deeper virtues and began to wonder if I could love the way Jackie had, without agenda, with kindness at the center.

As time passed, I realized I would eventually need to restart my life. I didn't know what that life would look like, but I knew I would need to find my new place in the world apart from the empty-nesting life I had envisioned with Jackie. While the loss of Jackie will always be the biggest earth-shattering event in my life, I didn't want to live my life focused on that tragedy. Having it change me was fine, but I would not be the guy who made people say, "I feel so bad for him losing his wife the way he did." It wasn't about Jackie's death defining me but rather deepening me.

There was rarely an hour in a given day when I didn't think of her, sometimes in a comforting way, sometimes mournfully. I knew I'd given Jackie a good life with our adventures around the world, my love and unwavering commitment to our family, and the ability to make her dream of raising our kids full time a reality. As part of the grieving process, though, I also felt the need to apologize to her: for the times we argued, the times I could have demonstrated my love more, the nights I could have stayed up with her to watch a movie but didn't, the life events she was going to miss. I didn't feel I was a bad husband, but loss makes us reflect on all the ways we could have been better. I guess this is called the "bargaining stage" of grief.

Grief felt less like a process and more like something I carried. A way of holding Jackie close. When I'd read a passage from *Healing After Loss*, I almost always teared up, and occasionally much more than that. But sometimes, I *wanted* that to happen, to go there on purpose. It was part of *my* grief, part of what kept Jackie close to me. At times, I was consciously awaiting that song, that thought, the sight of a dog, or of a mother with her beautiful child or an elderly couple holding hands that would *take me to my grief.*

After a few months, feeling a budding new outlook taking hold on my life, I felt it was time to at least consider reentering the world. I once heard Anderson Cooper talking about his own healing journey and about how burying grief mutes the ability to feel joy. It wasn't yet about feeling joy, but I knew that any return had to be different, no slipping back into old patterns. I had no idea when the grieving might end, but I did start to see the possibility that grief might transform me into a better version of myself.

I wasn't unkind, but I'd spent too much of my life leading from the head instead of the heart. Now, I wanted kindness to guide me more. Did life have to be a series of transactions or an existence driven by agenda? Nothing could fill the hole Jackie left—not plans, not work, not ambition. I needed to get out there and *do stuff.* On the one hand, there would be no decisions to make if I had a job I had to go to every day or kids I had to take care of. But I also knew that I was incredibly fortunate to have the freedom to choose my grieving path. Soon, a thought came, so obvious I was surprised it hadn't come sooner: What about taking a trip somewhere? After all, travel was what Jackie and I had planned to do in our empty-nesting years. It had always been a vital part of who I was, before Jackie and with her.

After passing his EMT, Daniel told me that he wanted to take a trip to the US Virgin Islands with Tom, a survivalist mentor and family friend. Initially, I was not really excited about the idea. I'd first met Tom when we hired him to spend a weekend camping at our ranch with Daniel and some of his friends to teach them survival skills: build a shelter, make fire without matches, trap animals, and make tools. Petite Jackie had joked with towering Tom, "No accidents, or you'll answer to me." Eventually agreeing to let Daniel go, I decided to at least fly with him to Miami and see him off. This was also the perfect opportunity to take that trip I'd been thinking about. Jamaica was an easy flight from Miami; I could escape the winter cold of DC, and it was an easy country to visit. I told myself that I needed a rest, a change of scenery. But beneath that was a growing awareness that travel, the old balm, might rescue me again. Being somewhere else might let me forget where I was. Could it be the start of a new, different path?

Jamaica

Earlier in 2017, I had traveled to the Dominican Republic, staying at a nice boutique hotel in the old section of the capital, Santo Domingo. I enjoyed it. The sweeping views of the harbor, the old Spanish colonial architecture, the friendly Latin-vibe, and, of course, the coffee. Jamaica was a neighboring country to the Dominican Republic. Why not check it out? Yes, it had a different history of colonization (the British), but it was a Caribbean Island country with beautiful landscapes and a vibrant culture. How different could it be? I booked a room at an all-inclusive resort in Ocho Rios, thinking I'd have a few days of tranquility on the beach, with nothing but the sound of soft waves and palm tree leaves swaying in the breeze. The warm sun and salt air would do me good, I thought. But I quickly realized that was not the trip I had signed up for.

Everywhere I turned, from the beach to the lobby to the bathrooms, had music blaring. People were partying, dancing, and doing shots as they spoke to one another in that loud way one speaks when they have no clue how drunk they really are. There was even a full bar in my room with tequila, rum, and vodka *on tap*; you could just open the spigot and drink yourself into oblivion. I could have chosen to numb out with alcohol during such a difficult time, and no one would probably have faulted me. But I couldn't do that: to myself, to my boys, or to Jackie's memory. By choosing this resort in Jamaica, I hadn't thought through what kind of environment I really needed. I was far too fragile to be here. *Lesson learned.*

On day three, I checked out, forfeiting what I'd paid for the rest of my stay, and moved to a small, less-crowded guesthouse for the remaining few days. Even in my new place, it wasn't working for me. The beach was as postcard-perfect as ever, but I couldn't feel it. The sunsets came and went, but none of it touched me. Sure, it felt okay to relax by the ocean, swim a bit, do some reading. But I still judged this trip by my first days at the all-inclusive resort.

I had been an avid traveler for over forty years and rarely had a bad trip, but I had to admit that this was not a success. My first attempt to reenter normal life felt more like an assault on my senses. In the end, I thought I could outrun the sadness. I'd traveled my way into new chapters before. But this grief wasn't going anywhere. It came with me, tucked inside my suitcase. And with this, I began to feel a sense of dread and anxiety rising within me. Some of my life's best moments came through travel: my first trip abroad, falling in love with Jackie, raising our boys across continents.

I flew home, more tired than when I left. Whatever I'd been seeking, it wasn't waiting in Jamaica. If healing was out there, it would demand more of me, more presence, more purpose. I just didn't know what that meant yet. I began to second-guess travel itself. Already having lost so much, had I lost my passion for travel too? Was I just running out the clock now? Or was there still something more waiting for me, and if so, how would I find it?

Somewhere inside, I knew: To move forward, I had to return to the part of myself shaped by movement and curiosity. Travel couldn't be an escape for me but rather the path to reclaiming the belief that, even after loss, my life and the world still held wonder. And maybe, in rediscovering that wonder, I could begin to heal. Maybe the key to my year zero wasn't just a simple trip, *but a resurrection.*

Part 2

The Life We Built

Love, Travel, and the Road to Belonging

Chapter 4

Finding Uchi: In Search of Home

June 1978
Japan

I've asked myself for years why some people feel most alive on the road while others never leave home. For me, the urge began early. I didn't feel a strong sense of home, with my parents divorcing when I was a child, but I found freedom in wandering.

My wandering may not be an addiction, but it's close. Maybe it is rooted in a love of language, or just in my DNA. Still, even with roots in Iraq and Eastern Europe, I didn't grow up in a worldly household. Apart from a trip to Tahiti with my mom and sister when I was seven, as part of the "celebration" of her divorce, travel wasn't part of my upbringing.

It was 1978. Apple had just launched its first PC, "Go Your Own Way" played on the radio, and disco fever ruled. My friend Steve and I had been parking cars and pumping gas to save for a summer trip before college. I wanted to surf in Hawaii; he wanted to backpack through Europe. We flipped a coin. Steve won. Not the most strategic way of making decisions, but sometimes fate knows best.

We were two SoCal "valley boys" with Eurail passes and a guidebook, wandering from hostel to hostel, no cell phones or email. One budget-busting night in Barcelona around the lively area called Las Ramblas taught us a hard lesson. A man approached, claiming to have just gotten engaged. "I love Americans," he said in Spanish, inviting us for a celebratory drink. I translated for Steve. What eighteen-year-old says no to that?

We were soon swept into a bar, had a few rounds, and lost track of our "host." As we left, the bartender stopped us: "Tienes que pagar la cuenta." I protested, "Our friend was paying," but no luck. The bill? 400 pesetas, nearly a week's expenses. Apparently, we'd "offered" to buy drinks for the entire bar. Surrounded by some imposing figures, we negotiated it down and got out fast.

I've been wary of free drinks ever since.

To recover financially, we took overnight trains or slept in stations. That first summer—Paris, gelato in Italy, train rides through the Alps, hostels, and midnight adventures—felt like stepping into a living postcard. I wasn't just hooked; I was already scheming my return. That coin flip had changed my life.

That fall, I began university at UC Irvine, determined that first trip wouldn't be my last. The next summer, I jumped on a $199 Qantas deal to Australia with my buddy Neil, my sister, Marci, and her friend. It was my third continent, and I wasn't slowing down. I returned broke but convinced my mom to fund a Spanish program in Barcelona the following summer. She was a practical woman, but went all-in on education for her kids.

I didn't spend much time in class. A week in, two friends invited me to Morocco. I said yes. We took a ferry from Gibraltar and a grimy overnight train to Marrakesh. As we stopped at unknown stations during the night, vendors lined the platform, hawking sweet mint tea, fresh oranges, and handwoven blankets, their calls mingling with the distant call to prayer before we arrived at our destination. Dropping our bags at the hotel, we made a beeline for the souk, with the narrow alleys' twists and turns shaded by faded canvas awnings, alive with vibrant colors. The medina hit all the senses with every corner revealing something unexpected: spices, snake charmers, storytellers, carpets, and chaos. It was thrilling, but not without danger. One afternoon, we were cornered by thuggish touts and called "dirty Jews." We got away safely, but it shook me a touch.

Still, the trip to Morocco wasn't defined by fear but rather by that *dreamy feeling* I get thinking about a foreign land. And just like that, I'd reached my fourth continent at the age of only twenty.

Egypt and Israel

Back at UCI for my final year, I met Jackie at a fraternity party. She was adorable and full of life. There was something disarming about her, the way she laughed, the way she really listened. Being around her just made everything feel lighter. I had a sort-of girlfriend then, but I knew I wanted Jackie in my orbit. Little did I know the road it would take to make that happen.

It had been a few years since Morocco, but I couldn't shake the feeling I had there, the thrill of pushing my boundaries. The need to wander had only grown stronger. So, I deferred admission to Columbia Business School and took a gap year after graduation. After working and saving up, I was off again to Paris (the city that had stolen my heart a few years earlier), Interlaken, Rome, and the Italian coast. But as much as I loved Europe, it had started to feel too comfortable. I needed to get *uncomfortable*.

After fourteen cramped hours on the Magic Bus to Istanbul, a stopover in Greece, and a boat ride through Cyprus and Alexandria, I finally reached Cairo, the "City of a Thousand Minarets." It was loud, chaotic, and gritty, but I loved it. My mom, who had emigrated from the Middle East, wasn't thrilled I was going; she worried about how a Jew would be treated there. But I felt completely at ease among the Egyptians I met.

Egypt had been a dream for years. Unlike Morocco, which I stumbled into, this trip felt like a return to something familiar, the language my mom spoke, the food she cooked, the culture I'd only heard about.

Even the souqs of Marrakesh hadn't prepared me for Cairo's Khan el-Khalili. The colors, smells, and noise were overwhelming. I was drawn to the coffee stalls where men smoked hookahs, played backgammon, and debated politics. A quick coffee turned into an hour. From there, I made my way overland across the Sinai Desert to Tel Aviv. I've always loved overland crossings. In terms of geography, it's a tiny shift. But like the crossing from Egypt to Israel, you often find yourself in another world.

Once in Israel, I stayed with distant relatives and got a firsthand look at the diversity of Jewish life: kibbutzniks on the Sea of Galilee, intellectuals in Tel Aviv, and middle-class families in smaller towns just trying to raise their kids and get by. My cousin's husband, Eli, took me to the Iraqi section of Tel Aviv, where men grilled meat on sidewalk barbecues and sipped thick Arabic coffee while speaking a mix of Arabic and Hebrew.

The highlight, though, was visiting the Western Wall in Jerusalem, Judaism's holiest site. Maybe it was a light version of the "Jerusalem syndrome," defined as "an acute psychotic state observed in tourists and pilgrims who visit Jerusalem." The last remnant of the ancient retaining wall where King Solomon's temple, built around 1000 BC, once stood, it had been in my imagination since Hebrew school. I'd heard about it my whole life, but nothing prepared me for the moment I saw it.

Entering through the Damascus Gate, I wound through the Arab quarter until the Western Wall emerged before me. The sight of the wall gave me chills, its massive stones crammed with folded pieces of paper into the cracks. They were prayers, wishes, and hopes people had written and tucked into the stones. The volume of notes carried thousands of dreams, a reflection of our need to connect with something divine. I tore a page from my notebook and tucked in my own wish: *I want to see the world.* I didn't realize then that this wish had already begun to unfold.

I spent two months in Israel, and for the first time, I felt more grounded in a story much bigger than my own—a story that gave shape to a lineage I'd never fully grasped growing up in California, with my mother's Jewish roots in Baghdad, my father's in Eastern Europe.

New York City

"Why should we hire you?" one of the Lehman Brothers interviewers asked as I sat nervously in their Wall Street office. *Fair question.*

I didn't have a good answer. When I started my MBA at Columbia, I didn't get the memo that I was supposed to know what I wanted to do in finance after just the first month of business school.

One interviewer put it bluntly: "You went to UC Irvine and have no experience. Your classmates are Ivy grads who've already worked on Wall Street." I bombed a few interviews and started wondering if this world was even for me. But eventually, I pulled it together just enough to land a summer offer at JP Morgan, which turned into a full-time job. I accepted without looking elsewhere; it was one of the most international banks, and I was eager to get back overseas.

I stayed in touch with Jackie during my years at Columbia. I'd hang out with her in Haight-Ashbury, near where my sister lived, on my infrequent trips home. During one trip, I made a clumsy pass at her, only to learn she was still with her long-distance boyfriend, Mark. Not one to give up, I invited her to visit me in New York the following year. I was delighted when she said yes and assumed her acceptance meant Mark was no longer in the picture. *Turned out he was.*

When Jackie arrived in New York, she called from a pay phone. "I'm on my way over. You are not going to believe this, but Mark heard I was visiting you and decided to take a trip to New York, *coincidently*. But he has his own place to stay."

Awkward, but fine. Then came the second call, fifteen minutes later. "You're not going to like this. . . . Mark's place fell through. Any chance you have room?"

Somehow, I said yes. In my tiny one-bedroom, Jackie and Mark got the bed; I took the couch. *Yes, that really happened.* I kept telling myself, *Just bad timing.*

Argentina

With a full-time job lined up after graduation, I decided it was time for one last big adventure. For the next two months, I planned to travel overland from Buenos Aires to California, then get myself back to NYC to finally launch my career. Eager to get on the road, I even skipped Columbia's graduation ceremony and boarded a flight to Argentina.

My relatives in Buenos Aires welcomed me warmly. The day after I arrived, my mother's cousin Dorothy hosted a dinner, where, by pure chance, I met Tim, the general manager of JP Morgan Buenos Aires. Near the end of the meal, he casually asked, "Barry, how would you like to work with us for a few months?"

I looked up from my empanadas, stunned. "That would be a dream, but I'm supposed to start the JP Morgan training program soon." Tim said he'd see if they could delay it. If so, I was in.

Life at the JP Morgan Buenos Aires (BA) office was nothing like Wall Street. In NYC, mornings began before sunrise; here in BA, nights stretched into steak dinners, Malbec, and late-night clubs. No one showed up before 9:00 a.m., and even then, work started only after coffee, medialunas, and a chat about football and the peso. It was my first time living and working abroad, and I loved it.

By late fall, I wasn't ready to leave, but it was time to start at JP Morgan in NYC, in the Treasury Department. This was pre-Euro, and the foreign-exchange trading floor buzzed with orders shouted in every major currency: deutsche marks, yen, francs, lira, and sterling. I was hooked, fascinated by the constant fluctuations, the forces behind them, and who was buying and selling.

As luck would have it, the department head, Olivier, was French. I hadn't yet mastered the art of patience and made sure to let him know, often, that I wanted to work in the Paris office someday. I must have worn him down, because one day I got a call from Marcus Meier, the legendary head of the Paris office.

"Hello, Barry, this is Marcus Meier," came the voice in a strong Swiss-German accent. Everyone in JP Morgan's financial markets knew his name. He wouldn't call a junior trader in New York unless it was important. "Olivier mentioned you're interested in Paris. We have a position open."

Just like that, I was off to Paris, this time not just to visit, but to live and work in one of the world's most beautiful cities. Investment banking buzzed in New York, London, and Tokyo. That was where all the action was. But it never occurred to me that I was missing out by being in Paris.

Japan

For the next decade or so, I lived and worked around the world: Paris,

Tokyo, Zurich, Singapore. During this time, I had lost contact somewhat with Jackie, and then, one day, out of nowhere, I got an invitation to her wedding. The realization that a *good one got away* shattered the idea that *it's all about timing*.

After I'd worked a bit less than two years in Paris, my manager, Marcus, was transferred to run JP Morgan's business in Japan and asked me to come work for him. Well, let's just say he wasn't really *asking*. So, while I was not quite ready to give up my Parisian life, I was off on a new adventure. It's one thing to travel to a country with a completely different culture from your own and another to live and work in one. It didn't take long to realize this or learn about the Japanese concept of *uchi*.

Loosely defined as social circles, or even concentric social circles, uchi can be thought of as a kind of nonphysical "home," a kind of place of belonging.

At JP Morgan Tokyo, I had my own uchi—a team of ten Japanese colleagues who worked for me. We often went out together at night and even took a few weekend *"onsen* trips" to remote villages nestled in forests and hills. The onsen is usually part of a *ryokan* (Japanese inn) and features outdoor baths with views of nature. But my colleagues also had their own private circles at home, and those spheres were rarely mixed. I had a strong bond with my team at the office, but it didn't extend into their personal lives.

One day at work, one of my staff, Katsumata-san, seemed quite anxious. He kept eyeing me as if he wanted to speak with me. He finally got up the courage and nervously confided that he liked Honda-san from the next desk. When I asked why, he said, "Because she has a nice atmosphere." I wasn't sure if that was either the funniest description of a woman I ever heard or the most profound. Either way, I guess I had earned a place in his inner circle.

But I also realized that living overseas, with my sister in the Bay Area and my mother in a retirement community in Las Vegas, I was lacking my own home, my own uchi.

. . .

Living in Asia gave me opportunities for real adventure: Vietnam in the 1980s, crossing all of China in the early 1990s, and a return to Morocco for a friend's wedding in Marrakesh while working at JP Morgan Zurich. This time my then-girlfriend Patty came along, and I hoped things would go more smoothly than on my first trip.

On a flight from Zurich to Casablanca, I watched us cross the Mediterranean, then veer east. *Strange,* I thought, before drifting off. Hours later, I woke to the pilot announcing our descent, but outside it was pitch black. The plane stopped with a jolt, no taxiing, no terminal lights.

Then came a chilling announcement in Arabic, which I recognized due to my mother's background. A flight attendant's face said it all as she translated: "All Arab nationals may disembark. Everyone else must stay on board."

I looked back. A man in the aisle was pointing a gun at the attendant.

Holy shit. A hijacking.

My mind raced. I had an Israeli stamp in my passport and a Jewish last name, Hoffner. I grabbed Patty. "We're out of here!"

We bolted down the stairs and off the plane just as armed men stormed aboard. On the tarmac, we were herded onto a bus, taken to a holding room, and met with silence. When I finally asked where we were, an older man leaned over and whispered, "Casablanca. The soldiers were clearly told not to tell us anything."

So much for things going smoothly on my return to Morocco.

Later, I reflected on what scared me most: not the danger, but the fear that I wouldn't rise to the moment. In crisis, things move too fast for fear. You just act. You hope courage shows up.

Looking back, I realized the hijacking hadn't awakened some thrill-seeker in me that craved danger. But it did give me a calm conviction that perhaps it was time to shift gears and live with more intention.

· · ·

My final posting with JP Morgan was in Singapore. And ten years in, despite a really good work-life balance in a city-country I had grown fond of, I requested a sabbatical to study Mandarin in China. I wanted to slow down, learn, explore. I didn't have a detailed plan, and for once, that felt okay.

Out of the blue, Jackie reached out. She was passing through Singapore with her friend Vicki, on their way to India. We had been out of touch for some time when she sent me an invitation to her wedding. Now, less than two years later, her marriage had ended badly, broken by a deceitful man (not Mark). His loss. I was excited to see her.

Showing the two women around Singapore, I once again saw why I liked Jackie so much. She was curious, kind, and, of course, as radiant as ever. She noticed everything, my travel photos, the foods of Singapore. I couldn't help but wonder, *Is this my uchi?*

Then she asked, "Why don't you travel with us to India before you go to China?"

Maybe this sabbatical wouldn't just be about language after all.

Chapter 5

In the Shadow of the Taj

December 1994
India

Our taxi driver was stopped again at yet another military checkpoint as we arrived in Srinagar, the capital of Kashmir in northern India. A territory contested by India, China, and Pakistan, Kashmir was more militarized than we'd realized. We'd chosen the destination on a whim, drawn by its mystique. Now, the airport agent's parting words echoed in my mind: *May God be with you.*

We arrived to a spectacularly beautiful lodging, a shikara, one of the beautiful carved cedar boats on Dal Lake, and a stunning view of the snow-capped Himalayas. But that turned out to be the highlight in Kashmir after the tense military stares and bitter winter cold.

Moving on, a two-day bus ride brought us to Himachal Pradesh, arriving in McLeod Ganj on Christmas Day. Home to the Dalai Lama and many Tibetan refugees, it was a peaceful town of monasteries and mountain views, and Jackie fell for it immediately. "This place clears my mind and makes me reflect on how I want to live more spiritually." Jackie's joy and tranquility were infectious. I hadn't felt this kind of peace in years. After long days in finance, split-second decisions, bottom-line stress, midnight emergencies, I finally felt like I'd come up for air.

In our short time traveling together, Jackie had already proven to be the perfect travel partner, adventurous, upbeat, and always present. With that and her striking blue eyes and golden hair, I began to feel something deeper. I wanted to be around her all the time. Jackie embodied that phrase my Japanese colleague Katsumata-san had used about "having a nice atmosphere."

A few days later, while walking past a Buddhist temple in search of the Dalai Lama's residence, I blurted, "I know you're planning to work in Bangalore, but . . . would you consider continuing to travel with me, at least for a while, once Vicki returns home?"

Jackie's tone was light but positive. "Yeah, sure. That would be fun." Later, I glimpsed a postcard she was writing to her parents: *Barry has made me an offer I cannot refuse . . .*

I played it cool, not ready to confess my feelings. I didn't want to ruin our dynamic, even if I was quietly thrilled.

From that moment, everything shifted. We were going to be traveling together, alone. On the overnight bus to Agra, I barely slept, watching Jackie rest across the aisle. We all know that familiar feeling when we can't stop thinking about someone. When no matter where a thought starts, it comes straight back to them.

In Agra, we visited the Taj Mahal. Emperor Shah Jahan built it in 1632 in memory of his wife, who had died in childbirth. With its symmetrical dome and four minarets of white marble, it's one of the world's most iconic buildings, an eternal symbol of love. After Vicki returned to the hotel, Jackie and I lingered by the reflecting pool, the golden sunset glinting off the dome. She wore a sleeveless white top, her sunflower tattoo peeking through lace, her Doc Martens grounding her. I knew this was the moment.

I leaned in, and this time she didn't pull away. It was a kiss a decade in the making. I'd always found first kisses to be thrilling, but this was different. It was a kiss that said, *I found you.* As Coelho writes in

The Alchemist, "There is only that moment, the incredible certainty that everything under the sun has been written by one hand only. It is the hand that evokes love and creates a twin soul."

Every place we visited after this seemed to put on a show just for us, as if celebrating that Jackie and I had found each other. We journeyed through Rajasthan: Jodhpur, Jaisalmer, and Pushkar. In the last of the three, Jackie woke me on New Year's Day to get a blessing from a Hindu priest for our journey. She was broadening my world far beyond travel.

Burma (Myanmar)

After Vicki flew home to California, Jackie and I went to Bangkok. At night, neon lights buzzed to life, casting an eerie glow over the chaotic and sometimes seedy streets. Go-go bars lined Patpong, the red-light district, each one promising a spectacle, with scantily clad women dancing behind glass to pounding techno music. It was chaotic and slightly sordid. But Jackie, of course, was fascinated. She jokingly insisted we visit for "scientific observation."

Things weren't always perfect between us. A stock market crash had tanked my JP Morgan shares, our travel fund. Jackie made a flippant comment about rich people losing money, and I launched into a defensive rant. It was tense for a day, but Jackie let it go.

With apologies made and accepted on both sides, we were on to Burma (now Myanmar), where we were bowled over by the architecture and the friendliness and beauty of the people, even the men in their longyi, the skirt-like garment most of them wore. The crown jewel in a skyline full of gems was the Shwedagon Pagoda in Yangon, one of the oldest and most sacred in the region, its three-hundred-foot gold stupa rimmed with jewels. I held Jackie in my arms as we watched monks in purple robes sweep by and stared up at the glowing lights of the pagoda.

After a rough overnight ferry to Mandalay, made worse by overflowing toilets, we took a walk to clear our heads and wandered onto the campus of a Buddhist university. Outside a dormitory, a robed monk approached us and gently asked, "What do you want to know?"

"Can we come inside?" I asked.

He nodded and led us to his room, where he showed us his English tapes, poured us tea, and introduced us to a few fellow monks. "My parents sent me, the second son, to a monastery young. Now I study the Buddha's teachings, tend the gardens, cook. We are learning to live a spiritual life."

"It sounds peaceful," I said.

Jackie asked, "Doesn't it get lonely?"

The monk smiled. "Loneliness is part of the human experience. But even silence holds connection if your heart is open."

Jackie and I exchanged a look; his wisdom humbled us. As we left, another monk offered, "May you always be happy in life." Watching Jackie's serene face, I thought, *She's my ticket to happiness.* As we were walking away, she told me, "That moment with the monks was one of the most meaningful of my life."

Laos

Next was Laos. I needed to get to Kunming, China, for my Mandarin studies as part of my sabbatical, and the plan was to travel overland from Vientiane. Thankfully, Jackie had abandoned her idea of working in a biology lab in India. She was with me for the duration. It felt adventurous, especially since the logistics were so uncertain. Would Jackie get a visa at a remote Laos-China crossing? Would mine even work? She was game either way.

We headed north to Luang Prabang, the old capital along the Mekong, and spent a few days among coconut palms, teak trees, and orange-robed monks. Each morning, the monks walked through town, collecting food offerings, a beautiful ritual of humility and grace.

Intent on reaching China, we pressed farther north, taking a thrilling speedboat ride on the Mekong, then a car to the border town of Boten. No phones, no internet. Outdated Lonely Planet guides. At the crossing, I asked about getting Jackie a visa there. I already had a visa for China long before I started my travels. But Jackie had been unable to procure one a few days earlier, upon our arrival in Vientiane, because it was still Chinese New Year. A uniformed officer crossed his arms and said, "Bu ku neng." Without even needing translation, the message was clear: "No fucking way."

Normally, I loved remote overland crossings, but here at this silent post, I regretted dragging Jackie into it. Before I could speak, she cut in. "It's okay. I'll head back to Luang Prabang, fly to Vientiane, get the visa, and meet you in Kunming."

It sounded like a headache. "Jackie, are you sure? I'll go with you."

She placed her hand on my cheek. "I'm fine."

I walked her back across the Laos border. We found a southbound pickup packed with Laotian women in traditional dress, and Jackie climbed in. As I waved goodbye, I felt uneasy. She'd come to Asia expecting a lab job in India, not solo travel in rural Laos. But there she was, disappearing down the road, and I was more in awe of her than ever.

China

Once through immigration and in China, I boarded a bus for the three-day trip to Kunming, hoping Jackie and I would reunite as planned at the Kunming Hotel. We agreed to meet at noon, three days later. If one of us wasn't there, we'd try again the next day.

Unbelievably, our makeshift plan worked. Jackie got her visa, and even arrived a day early. When I walked into the hotel lobby, there she was, smiling. No venting at all as she led me to our room. As we entered, she pointed to the French bread, smoked salmon, and Bordeaux on the table that she had purchased in Vientiane. "Our reunion feast." She beamed and threw her arms around me.

The next day, we checked into our dorm room at Yunnan University. Spartan, with hot water only twice daily, but for ten dollars a day, we couldn't have been happier.

Fifteen years after meeting at UCI, we were back on a college campus, studying, making friends, and taking weekend trips. But this wasn't Newport Beach. We were in China. Our circle included students from Italy, England, Japan, and Korea, most of them still in their teens. One of Jackie's Korean classmates had a pet monkey. The Italians obsessed over improving the local food, which usually meant fried rice with unidentifiable ingredients. Jackie, ever festive, was big on birthdays, something I hadn't grown up with. The two collided on my thirty-fifth birthday.

We'd befriended a Chinese family with a clean and reliable restaurant. Their daughter, Luisa, loved practicing English with us. When I arrived to meet Jackie for lunch, Luisa stood outside, grinning. "Surprise!" Inside, I received birthday wishes in Mandarin, Italian, and Luisa's charming English version: "I am feeling so beautiful today to celebrate your birthday." Jackie had organized it all with the Italian students at our school who promised an "authentic" pasta meal. We drank mugs of local beer, and Jackie stood to toast. "To my hubby, here's to a hundred more." We had to say we were married to share a room at the university.

With only four hours of language class each day, we had time to explore. Jackie volunteered at an orphanage. China's one-child policy had led to many abandoned girls. Who better than Jackie to shower them with love? I found a gig teaching English.

Kunming was a great base for road trips: Dali, Lijiang, and one particularly incredible trip to the dramatic Tiger Leaping Gorge. At the gorge's edge, twelve thousand feet above the Yangtze, Jackie froze. "I forgot to tell you, I have vertigo." I wasn't as sympathetic as I should've been. Still, we crossed landslides and narrow ledges, step by step. We passed Naxi men and mules on ancient trails. Jackie loved that the Naxi culture was matriarchal, and that their writing used pictographs.

Still, daily life in China wore on Jackie. One afternoon, she came back from the orphanage in tears. "A man spit right in front of me just as I tripped and fell. No one helped. I landed in his spit." I had to stifle a laugh, *still learning empathy*, and I could tell she was done. But I nevertheless felt obligated to stay because my Mandarin still wasn't where I wanted it to be. Jackie had come to China for me, with no prior interest and no Mandarin. But she left conversational and full of memories. That night, she told me, "This trip woke me up. China is like no place on Earth. And even with the challenges, I'll miss it, and you, even more."

Three weeks after Jackie left, I couldn't take it anymore. I bought a ticket to San Francisco and walked away from China and my sabbatical. For the first time, I'd abandoned an overseas adventure—for love.

Chapter 6

Bound by a Continent

**September 1995
Africa**

Once I got home from China, Jackie collected her things, most importantly her dog, Gryphen, and drove from Southern California to the Bay Area to be with me. Back from sabbatical, I had some disagreements with JP Morgan about where my next posting would be. One thing led to another, and I had an offer with Chemical Bank as manager director for their Emerging Markets trading business for Eastern Europe, with a focus on Russia.

But a bigger decision and question weighed on me: If I accepted, would Jackie come with me? Now back home, she was contemplating nursing school after her previous breakup had set her career back. I worried that with our relationship still being fairly new, she might say no. I loved working abroad but had found something more important than my next job.

Thankfully, I didn't have to choose between them.

The day after we arrived in London, CNN announced that

Chemical and Chase Manhattan Bank were merging. The news sent shock waves through the company, as layoffs were imminent. My first few months were spent letting go of staff I barely knew. The only bright spot was life outside work, our Chelsea flat, London's bookshops and cafés, Saturday films like Jackie's favorite, *Lawrence of Arabia*, Wagamama noodles, and pints at the Ladbroke Arms in Notting Hill.

But was that bright spot outside of work bright enough? Much as I tried to motivate myself, by Monday morning, my heart wasn't in it. The fact was I missed being on the road with Jackie, making new discoveries of cultures and places. It had been risky enough to take a sabbatical before, but to leave a job after just a few months following a long leave, surely that was a career killer.

I was reflecting on this one evening while Jackie and I were drinking pints and eating fish-and-chips at the Ladbroke Arms, our favorite pub. I noticed the woman sitting next to us had a copy of Lonely Planet's *Africa* on the table in front of her.

"Sweetie, I dread going to work every day. I miss the familiarity of JP Morgan, I miss feeling like I know what I am doing at work, and I miss being on the road with you. I know I can push through this if I need to. But I am not sure I really want to."

By the end of the evening, aided by a few extra beers, we'd hatched a plan in which I'd quit my job, and we'd take what Jackie called a "daring overland trip" through the second-largest continent in the world, Africa. *Thank God for pubs in London.* With only a rough itinerary and some visas for a few African countries for our grand adventure, we said goodbye to new friends and boarded a flight to Kenya.

Africa. Sure, I'd been to the continent before—Morocco, Egypt, a Club Med in Senegal—but this was different. Fifty-four countries, endless terrain, and no real plan, just a vague north-to-south route. It felt like stepping into the unknown. I'd normally had a language hook for my travels: Spanish in Latin America, French in Paris, Mandarin in China. But Africa was pure exploration, and Jackie's warm companionship gave me the courage to take the leap. We walked out of Nairobi airport feeling like marshmallows in a bowl of Lucky Charms, our pale skin from a London winter set against the rich, sun-warmed tones of equatorial Africa. But by the end of our first day, that changed.

We stumbled into a bar near our hotel; turned out it was a spot frequented by some working ladies of the night. Jackie's smile worked its magic, as always. Within minutes, several young women had pulled up chairs. They asked Jackie all the questions they wouldn't ask me: Do men use prostitutes where you live? Do their wives know? Do they cheat? Jackie was in her element: open, empathetic, engaged. And just like that, we felt comfortable.

Our first stop was summiting Mount Kenya, where we camped with Scottish soldiers, a German named Rolf, and our Kikuyu guide, Elijah. I was relearning that, despite her petite frame, Jackie could rough it far better than most.

From there, we experienced the Serengeti: giraffes meandering by our vehicle, zebras and wildebeests in migration. One early evening, a troop of baboons raided our camp. Jackie crouched down to greet a baby baboon, but when it let out a shriek, two large ones came charging over. She leaped behind me in a flash. We couldn't stop laughing about it all night in our little tent. After all, we share 98 percent of their DNA.

Then came Kilimanjaro. At the chaotic Arusha bus station, we got swept up by touts and naively handed over $400 to a man named Clemence Munta, owner of Star Tours. Something felt off. Later, other travelers confirmed our doubts. When we returned to the Star Tours office, it was closed, so we visited the local police. "He's here in lockup," one officer said. Clemence emerged disheveled and sweating. "You're a liar and a cheat," was all I could manage. We got half our money back, and a hard lesson in trusting our gut.

We eventually found a legitimate guide, and I summited Kilimanjaro: We experienced five days of changing landscapes and one small glacier at the top. We were moving south from Livingstonia, Malawi, heading toward Zimbabwe, but with Easter approaching, our transport options were limited. Our solution? Climb into a packed, open-top garbage truck with thirty locals. It was grimy, sweaty, smelly, exhausting. But slowly, we adapted. Jackie looked at me and said, "This is just a story for us, but for them, this is daily life. I marvel at the strength of the human spirit."

Passing through Mozambique into Zimbabwe, we then arrived at Vic Falls. A huge highlight was riding the Class Five rapids down the mighty Zambezi River. Looking out over Victoria Falls as elephants roamed the plateau of pools, plunging hundreds of feet into the river,

I couldn't help but wonder, *Do we ever have to go back?* Was there a way we could just keep traveling in Africa? Yes, the world has beautiful places, but Africa's range—rainforest, alpine, lunar, glacier, all in one Kilimanjaro hike—felt unmatched. Then the turquoise waters off Zanzibar, the ancient Rift Valley, and now one of the world's most spectacular falls complete with animals you can only see in this part of the world.

Finally, we had a long stretch of road directly to either Cape Town or Windhoek, where we planned to celebrate my thirty-sixth birthday. Birthdays were never a big deal to me. I often let them pass without notice. Not Jackie. "I got the Italians to help throw you a party in Kunming last year," she reminded me. "They're not here this time, but you're not getting away without a celebration."

To reach either, we had to pass through Botswana's Ngoma crossing, then traverse Namibia's Caprivi Strip, bordered by Zambia, Angola, and Botswana, before hitching a ride down Namibia. We had no idea how we'd manage it or if anyone would stop.

Class Five rapids and summiting mountains aside, I can't say that Jackie and I were adrenaline junkies or that we were even the boldest of travelers. But the idea of hitchhiking part of the way across Africa would make any parent cringe, especially Jackie's very doting parents. "Please don't tell your parents how we're traveling," I joked. We were learning what we could handle, and how far we'd go for the journey.

We caught our first ride out of Victoria Falls with a kind elderly Zimbabwean man who dropped us at the Ngoma Bridge into Botswana. There, a young couple, Annie and Joshua, picked us up. They were headed to Namibia with their four-month-old daughter after working at a game park for the World Wildlife Fund. They drove us most of the way across the Caprivi Strip before stopping at their home in Popa Falls for a long, home-cooked lunch, which we were more than happy to help finish.

Jackie and I were learning to appreciate Africa's unhurried rhythm. That night, they dropped us at a run-down lodge, where we "feasted" on green beans, canned sardines, biscuits, and beer. As we played cards, Jackie calmly watched a line of spiders climb the ceiling. Most would have been horrified. But Jackie wasn't most people, accepting the discomforts without complaint, as she so often did. That mindset would serve us well in the days ahead.

At sunrise, we had our thumbs out again. Our first goal was reaching the highway to Namibia's capital. After an hour, it looked like we might have to walk the full mile with our packs, until we finally flagged down a truck driver.

Thank God.

Then we saw the bed of the truck. My heart sank. Jackie gave me a look that said, *Please don't make me do this.*

"It's just over a mile," I said. "No idea when the next ride will come."

We climbed in beside a freshly slaughtered cow, holding our noses and backpacks clear of shifting blood as the truck lurched down the road. When we climbed out, Jackie gave me a look and uttered the perfectly reasonable request, "Let's not do that again."

Our next ride came from three African men driving a truck twelve hundred kilometers to Windhoek. Jackie and I sat in the back cab, chatting through the open window. After nine hours, we arrived the night before my thirty-sixth birthday.

As we celebrated, we reflected on how connection makes the unfamiliar feel like home. The men, delivering high school exams, refused any payment. Their generosity reminded us of a truth we'd seen often in Africa: The less people had, the more giving they were.

For the next week, we explored Namibia, with its limitless horizons, stark desert landscapes, and towering sand dunes at least one thousand feet high that flow right into the Atlantic Ocean at Swakopmund. For the last leg of this adventure, we traveled to Cape Town via the Fish River Canyon in southern Namibia, with its iconic landmark, Table Mountain, dominating the skyline and offering a view of the meeting of the Atlantic and Indian Oceans.

Four months and six thousand kilometers after we walked out of Nairobi airport, it was time to go home. While we were traveling, I rarely thought about what I was giving up: financial security, career growth, a rooted family life. But once the motion stopped, those thoughts crept in. Quitting that job had been a leap into the unknown, but it turned out to be one of my better decisions. What we gained, adventures across a vast stretch of Africa, filled with beauty, connection, and meaning, was worth far more than anything I gave up.

We had both grown deeply fond of a continent too often misrepresented as a single, troubled place with the media mostly focusing on poverty and conflict. Sure, there is some of that. But what we also saw was a mosaic of cultures, landscapes, languages, and, above all, a spirit of resilience, joy, and generosity. In many ways, the sense of community and strength we found in Africa surpassed anything we'd known back home. Our experience in Africa very much shattered the general Western notion of what "success" is usually about. It was a realization that you didn't really need as much as you think to be happy.

It was during this Africa trip that I also realized that Jackie wasn't just someone along for the adventure. I can't say that I was thinking about marriage at that point, but neither could I see myself with anyone else. Our adventures weren't always easy, but they brought us closer. From glaciers to deserts, sunrises to crowded bus rides, we were building something lasting.

We planned our return to California, but with an around-the-world ticket, why not use it? "Let's go east," Jackie said. "Australia. I want to see a koala." After spiders and slaughtered cows, she deserved koalas.

We flew to Sydney, then on to Fiji for rest and relaxation, and then on to San Francisco. But one question lingered:

What now?

Chapter 7

Family in the Land of the Rus'

**September 1996
Russia**

Meandering past the pink-hued stone buildings, I zigzagged between camouflaged tanks lining the streets of Yerevan, Armenia, admiring them like a fleet of sports cars. After our return from Africa, Jackie was back in Sausalito settling in, while I was on a consulting assignment for the Barents Group with the country's Central Bank. While I was deciding what to do next with my career, or rather, life, Barents gave me some part-time consulting work that took me to some cool places in the former Soviet Union.

Armenia was going through a disputed presidential election, its first transitional election since the fall of the Soviet Union. My first morning there, I awoke to thousands chanting outside, demanding the president's resignation. The government claimed it was an attempted coup, but the military stayed loyal. Despite the tanks, I felt oddly unconcerned. By week's end, calm had returned, and after finishing work in Yerevan, I decided to explore Georgia's capital, Tbilisi.

On the near-empty flight to Tbilisi, I met Giorgi, a large Georgian man dressed in black, with a strong nose, beard, and piercing blue eyes. We struck up a conversation about culture and wine. As we landed, he asked, "What are you doing tomorrow night?"

"No plans. Just exploring Tbilisi."

"Well, I've organized a special event for my son. Join us. I'll pick you up at your hotel."

It sounded like a once-in-a-lifetime chance to experience Georgian culture up close. I had to say yes.

After an hour driving through the dark countryside, a twinge of anxiety crept in. I was alone at night with a stranger in a place I didn't know. But I recalled our talk about life and family and relaxed. We eventually turned onto a dirt road lined with identical black Mercedes and entered a large room with a long table set for roughly twenty-five men. I'd stumbled upon a *khorovats*, a Georgian feast where guests share grilled meats and the *tamada*, toastmaster, leads rounds of heartfelt toasts.

"This is for my son," Giorgi explained. "He just completed his first big business deal, bought a used Mercedes, drove it through Armenia and Iran, and sold it in Kuwait for a nice profit." Quite the adventure.

We feasted on *khachapuri*, grilled meats, and, of course, Georgian wine. Georgia is considered the "cradle of wine," with eight thousand years of wine-making history. Only a few spoke English, but what I focused on was the deep pride Giorgi had for his son. The way he looked at his boy with such pure love in his eyes stayed with me.

Hungover the next morning, I thought about a recent conversation with Jackie. At thirty-three, she wasn't sure she still wanted kids. Her ambivalence had surprised me, given how caring and nurturing she was. But seeing Giorgi and his son aroused something in me, something unresolved with my own father, and a desire to have a special father-son connection, like Georgi, one day. If Jackie didn't want kids, would love be enough?

. . .

As the 1996 holidays approached, Jackie seemed off, emotional, and low energy.

One night, she emerged from the bathroom in tears. "I'm pregnant."

I froze, then cracked some dumb joke about "getting my checkbook out"—my sense of humor doesn't always fit the occasion—but then reversed course quickly. "That's the best news I've ever received in my entire life." She just fell into my arms, whispering, "I really needed to hear that."

We got married quietly on Valentine's Day 1997 at Café Devino, our favorite spot in Sausalito. Jackie had a trademark way of delivering big news—"Hi, Mom and Dad, are you sitting down? Barry and I were married, and I'm pregnant"—all in one big breath.

Some months later, with Jackie feeling better, we celebrated our wedding on a boat with friends and family in the Bay Area. In just six months, we'd returned from a dream trip to Africa, gotten pregnant, tied the knot, and now, it was probably time for me to get back to serious work.

Benjamin was born on September 9, 1997, and just like that, my indecision about what I needed to do vanished. Holding him brought a deep sense of responsibility. Who doesn't remember the first time they held their firstborn and what that felt like? There are no accurate words for that special feeling. *So, no more part-time gigs, sabbaticals, or wandering.* I had landed a job with ING-Barings, so we were headed back to London with baby Benjamin just a few months old. After I'd been about six months in their London office, the firm offered me an opportunity to transfer to Moscow.

With that, I started studying Russian with Pimsleur tapes but assured Jackie we could stay in London if that felt best for the family. I said this, knowing it would be a dream for me to live and work in Russia. But now came the harder part, selling the possible Moscow move. It wasn't just about Jackie adjusting; we had baby Benjamin. Also, London was starting to feel comfortable again. "Before we decide," I said, "let's take a summer trip to Russia. It's beautiful then."

"Okay." She smiled. "I had a feeling something like this might happen when you started studying Russian."

That summer, we visited Saint Petersburg during the White Nights. Jackie was charmed by the romantic strolls along the Neva, warm twilight skies, music in the streets.

"I love it here," she said. "If you think it's the right job, let's do it."

I had to hand it to Jackie: How many wives are even willing to consider an international move with a young baby to a place like London, let alone to post–Soviet Moscow? It was starting to sink in that I really was the luckiest guy on the planet.

I thought to myself, *Well, that was easy.*

But it felt too easy, until midway through the flight back to London, it hit me: *We are actually doing this.*

Russia

While Jackie and Benjamin were visiting family in California, I started traveling back and forth to Russia, in training for my new gig at ING-Barings Moscow. One night, Jackie called. "Don't get out your checkbook. I'm pregnant."

This time, I answered without a dumb joke and with full sincerity. "I'm as excited as the first time."

I lined up a charming apartment in central Moscow, and before moving in, we stayed at the historic Metropol Hotel while we waited for the apartment to be ready. Directly across the street was the Bolshoi Theatre, and not more than a ten-minute walk away was Red Square, with the visual wonders of Saint Basil's Cathedral nearby and the Moskva River passing behind the Kremlin. The combination of the architectural grandeur and historical significance of Moscow told me we were going to be living in an interesting place at a pivotal time in Russia's history. But at this point, I had no idea *how interesting* the time would be.

About a month before our move, cracks began to show in Russia's so-called miracle transition to capitalism. The country was drowning in debt, much of it funneled out by newly minted oligarchs. Then came the blow: Russia defaulted on its local debt and devalued the ruble, which quickly lost 90 percent of its value. The Central Bank was powerless to stop the collapse.

It didn't take a financial genius to figure out that as we celebrated Benjamin's first birthday with caviar and vodka from room service, it cost practically nothing with the ruble in free fall. Too bad that Benjamin was too young to partake in his own celebration. The financial inconsistencies in Russia were stark: no diapers on the shelves because they were imported, but all the caviar we could want for pennies.

Despite the massive rush to the exit of Russia by a number of foreign investment banks, ING-Barings had a real banking business across the vast country. My job appeared to be safe. During my first week, I got a crash course in Russian-style corruption. Misha, ING-Barings' head of security and a former KGB officer, took me to get my driver's license. At the DMV, he spoke quickly in Russian, then told me to sit at a computer. "Just press any button," he said. My Russian was not yet good enough to understand all the Cyrillic characters on the computer, so I did. He slipped the official a crisp hundred-dollar bill, and moments later, I heard, "Pozdravlayu, Gospodin Hoffner, vi zdali ekzamen." (Congratulations, Mr. Hoffner, you passed the exam.) With a chuckle, I realized this was how things got done in Russia.

Jackie gave birth to Daniel in London on April 8, 1999. He wanted out about ten days earlier than scheduled, meaning that I missed his birth, stuck in Moscow until I could get to London later that evening. With Benjamin still a toddler and Daniel just a week old, Jackie was still planning something for my thirty-ninth birthday, She had succeeded the past few years in China and Namibia, but I put a stop to a celebration in London just a week after Daniel's birth. Still, she left me a sweet note:

> Dearest Barry,
> I know this birthday is overshadowed by Daniel's arrival, but I have a feeling you don't mind the spotlight shifting. My wish for you: many joyful years filled with love, memories, and adventures with me and your two sons and maybe more to come. Love, your Jackie.

Now, with two boys, we moved from our central Moscow apartment to a spacious dacha in Serebryany Bor. The area was a forested island on the Moscow River where locals sunbathed in summer and ice fished in winter, vodka in hand. Our miniclan included Valentina, a former kindergarten teacher turned nanny; Elena, a former engineer, now housekeeper; and Kyril, a retired dancer turned driver, casualties of Russia's economic collapse. Jackie soon added a growing family of pets. When one unruly dog clashed with the others and wrecked the house, I finally said, "Sorry, Jackie, this one's going back." Kyril adopted it. Instant hero.

Jackie made fast friends with a group of women from many different countries and also with Valentina. They had basically invented their own language—some mixture of sign-language, English and Russian without the grammar. As Jackie said about the dreadful Russian grammar, "What's the point?"

Before long, we'd made it through our second Russian winter, and it never got as brutal as we'd feared. Sure, it was very cold. You know it's cold when vodka freezes and when Celsius and Fahrenheit meet at minus forty, but with the sun so bright when we were outside our back fence, walking on the frozen Moscow River on a snowy day, it was so magical that you didn't mind. About two years into my contract, I began traveling *without my family*, another trade-off, as I took responsibility for the company's financial-markets businesses in Eastern Europe and the former Soviet Union. This meant traveling three days a week to places like Kiev, Sofia, Bucharest, Budapest, Warsaw, Bratislava, and Prague. Each trip came with its own world to understand. I did a good bit of work travel within Russia as well. In a country of nine time zones, the trips were often longer, more exhausting, but often more exciting than my Eastern European business trips.

I took one trip with our head of research, Phil, who flew in from London. We were traveling to Krasnoyarsk in Siberia in midwinter to meet and interview General Alexander Lebed, governor of the region. In the run-up to the consequential Russian presidential elections of 2000, General Lebed was seen as a possible alternative to the increasing buffoonery of Yeltsin. There was a serious worry that Yeltsin could lose to the Communists. I had never met with a general before, let alone a Russian general. The guy had the hugest head I had ever seen. Sadly, he was killed in a helicopter crash two years later under mysterious circumstances. *This was Putin's Russia.*

On the return Aeroflot flight, I was asleep against the window when Phil shook my arm. "Barry, wake up. Look at the aisle." Groggy, I opened my eyes to see a four-foot alligator crawling a few rows ahead. *A live alligator.*

The female crew jumped into action. One flight attendant grabbed blankets from the overhead bins, layered them over the gator, and, with help, tied it up using passengers' belts. *Russian women can be particularly tough when the occasion calls for it.* Apparently, a man had bought it in the Far East and was smuggling it to Moscow. *I thought things like this only happened in movies.*

During a trip to Sofia, Bulgaria, on September 11, 2001, running on the treadmill, I was watching a TV monitor tuned to CNN and saw what looked like a plane crashing into one of the Twin Towers. *Why is CNN showing a movie clip?* Then the second plane hit, and the horrifying truth settled in. This wasn't fiction. It was unfolding in real time.

I flew to Bucharest the next day but never left my hotel room. After getting back to Moscow, I started questioning my constant travel. Then, just a month later, while preparing to leave Kiev on another business trip, I was told the airspace had closed. A Ukrainian missile had mistakenly downed a passenger plane. I took the overnight train back to Moscow and realized I was done.

At home that weekend, I looked at Jackie and said, "I think it's time to move back to Sausalito."

"I think so too," she replied, resting her head on my shoulder.

・ ・ ・

I didn't know what I'd do for a living when I got there; I just knew my gut was telling me to go home. I'd always wanted to live somewhere really different, learn the language, absorb the culture, meet some interesting people, and experience a place where you were not always 100 percent sure you were on solid ground. A place that made you feel alive, where you could see something on a given day that you were unlikely to see anyplace else, like the alligator on the flight back from Siberia. Or where you had to be on your game when stopped by the Russian police, taking it as a challenge to negotiate your way out of having to give a bribe. Moscow had been all I'd hoped for: foreign, unpredictable, unforgettable. But now it was time to go home. Jackie and the boys left first. I stayed behind to meet tax requirements and to take one last epic trip: six weeks on the Trans-Siberian Railway, followed by a climb up Mount Elbrus.

Crossing nearly six thousand miles from Vladivostok to Moscow, I encountered a different Russia. In cities like Irkutsk, Novosibirsk, and Yekaterinburg, I glimpsed the country's traditional soul, worlds apart from Moscow's gleaming materialism. Russia, I realized, wasn't becoming Western. It probably never would. As Churchill said, it remained "a riddle wrapped in a mystery inside an enigma."

And so, four years after we first moved here, I stood once more at an airport, this one the Sheremetyevo International Airport, ready to go home, no idea what I'd do next, but this time knowing that I wanted to stay put for a while.

Chapter 8

Homeward Bound

**July 2002
Mali**

While I'd been living overseas for sixteen years, many of my friends from back home had been raising families, serving on school committees, coaching sports, and putting down roots. I instinctively knew that was what the next phase of life needed to look like. Kids don't like being pulled from schools and friends every few years. Jackie knew that well; her father was a Marine colonel, and she moved constantly. We didn't want that for Daniel and Benjamin. So, despite my wandering past, I was back in Sausalito to stay.

At least until my kids were through high school.

I was ready to leave finance, but unsure of what would come next. We weren't rich, but we had saved while living in Russia. By chance, I found an eighty-acre property in the hills above Cloverdale. We were smitten and named it Silverwood Ranch after Serebryany Bor (Silvery Woods), the name of the place where our family had lived in Moscow.

My new "career" was ranching. I had no experience, wasn't handy, and at first, there was no money in it. But Jackie loved animals, so we got a few goats and sheep. Slowly, I began to believe I belonged there.

Our neighbors grew premium grapes, and consultants said our land had potential. So I went for it. There's a saying in the wine world: "How do you make a small fortune in the wine business? Start with a large one."

I took viticulture courses and lined up buyers for our grapes. Slowly, it started to work. And just for fun, we planted two hundred olive trees from four Tuscan cultivars; another adventure had begun.

Silverwood Ranch grew to twelve hundred acres, yielding two hundred tons of grapes a year. Our cabernet went into Francis Ford Coppola Winery's Archimedes wine; our olive oil won gold in New York. Setbacks came: wildfires, pests, cold. We started our own American Viticultural Area (AVA), and I became its first president. The ranch didn't pay like finance, but it grounded me and gave me some belonging.

Jackie's focus at the ranch was, of course, on the animals. We had a menagerie of goats, llamas, miniature donkeys, and even a cow, Norma. But the latest were Babydoll sheep. Jackie brought them in to graze between vines. Somehow, we also came home with two orphaned goats, thanks to the boys. For the first few months, the animals ended up not at the ranch but at our Sausalito home, zoning laws be damned. I was outvoted 3-1.

I figured that was the end of my adventures—at least for a while. But as the years passed and the boys grew, an itch began to return, the kind that no number of goats or zoning violations could quite scratch.

Mali

Approaching fifty, I craved a raw, meaningful adventure. I'd read about the Festival au Désert in Timbuktu, a legendary Sahara music festival that had drawn artists like Bono and Paul Simon. Timbuktu—it sounded mythical, like the edge of the known world. It felt like the perfect response to staving off a midlife crisis.

The festival had begun as a celebration of peace between the Tuareg ethnic group and the Malian government. It wasn't just music; it was a portal into a culture. Bono once called the region "the Big

Bang of everything we love." Jackie, ever supportive, said, "Barry, you have to do that."

My arrival in Bamako was chaotic, with visa bribes and a missing guide. Had it really been almost fifteen years since Jackie and I traveled overland through Africa? I felt uneasy until I heard my name: "Barry Hoffner!" It was Amadou, my guide. "Comment ça va? Je vous souhaite la bienvenue au Mali." After a bit of back-and-forth, I was happy to know that my French was still working.

By nightfall, we reached Djenné, home to the world's largest mud-brick structure, the Great Mosque. The drive there revealed village after village of mud-brick homes and earthen mosques, young girls hauling water, donkeys and camels pulling ropes.

The next day, we boarded a motorized pinnace on the Niger River, headed for Timbuktu. Life unfolded on the riverbanks: kids splashing, women washing clothes, men casting nets. Village children waved at me from every village we passed. It was serene, vivid, deeply human.

By day three, I was ready for solid ground. I could've kissed the sand. The music hit me first: electric guitar, jazz sax, the kora and calabash drums. The vocals, high-pitched and haunting, were sung in Songhai and Tamashek, local ethnic languages. I couldn't understand a word, but I didn't need to. The emotion was unmistakable.

Nomads arrived by camel or 4X4. Here in the desert were sword vendors, camel races, hypnotic dancing, and mint tea in every tent. Reality bent in that desert haze. *I was in another world.*

Before coming, I'd researched the Tuareg, a nomadic matriarchal ethnic tribe whose trade routes vanished with desertification. Forced to settle, many turned to herding or farming. Literacy was low, their language, Tamashek, only officially written since 1967. Education was slipping further out of reach.

On the third day of the festival, I asked Amadou to take me to a Tuareg village. We rode camels to Tedeini, swaying with the desert's rhythm. The chief, Mohammed, welcomed us. I was fascinated to learn from him that the Tuareg were a matriarchal society, with his wife engaging with us as much as he was. She served me tea, three cups, as per the tradition based on a Pakistani proverb: "When you share the first cup of tea, you're a stranger; with the second cup, you are a friend; and with the third cup, you become family." And each successive cup gets increasingly sugary.

Beautiful, another cultural encounter.

Later, we toured the village and came across a makeshift school: Kids were on the sand under a torn canvas. A mother, barely literate, pointed at French words on a chalkboard. Behind them stood the shell of a collapsed mud hut.

"Qu'est-ce que c'est?" I asked.

"C'était l'école," Mohammed said. (That was the school.)

On the ride back, gently rocked by the desert, an idea took hold. I couldn't fix West Africa's literacy crisis, but I could build one school. Here. It was that feeling that comes along a few times in your life, a powerful idea that you must act on. Maybe it was more than chance that brought me to Tedeini. All I knew was that building a school here, now, felt like something I had to do.

Back in the town of Timbuktu, I met a French woman working for an NGO. I shared my idea, and she didn't laugh; instead, she gave me contacts. At home, I began emailing. One name stood out: Hamadou, head of a local nonprofit who knew Tedeini and agreed to visit. A week later, he sent a thorough report with demographics, education needs, and a plan for a path forward. His nephew, Abdoulaye, an Algerian-trained engineer, joined the team. I was all in.

Jackie and I made a sizable gift. Many friends and family chipped in for my fiftieth birthday. Nine months after sipping tea in that tent, I returned to Tedeini. In the midst of mud huts stood a real school: cement, painted, with windows, a solid roof, and a certified teacher.

One morning, I stood in the classroom as a little girl walked to the chalkboard and shyly recited the French alphabet. In that moment, I knew I had to keep going.

Back home, I launched a nonprofit, Caravan to Class, named for the Tuareg caravans that once crossed the desert. By 2017, seven years later, we'd built and supported eleven schools, educating over fifteen hundred children. The need remained immense, more than half of the over nine hundred villages in the Timbuktu region still lacked schools, but at least we were doing our best to make a dent.

That year, Benjamin joined me to inaugurate a new school in the village of Bantam during his gap year before starting at Georgetown University. He opened the doors of the school to ululations and applause. Watching him connect with Hamadou and Abdoulaye, despite the language barrier, was one of my proudest moments. Two worlds I loved, together in celebration.

This was the heart of travel: breaking cultural barriers, forging human connection. A Jewish kid from Marin County and my Muslim friends from the Sahel just simply enjoying being together.

The work challenged me too. Cultural values sometimes clashed, like polygamy. I dined with Hamadou and his first wife one night, then with him and his second wife the next. I couldn't change the culture, but I could keep showing up.

At the same time, Jackie's work through WildAid, protecting elephants, rhinos, and other iconic species, had become central to her. As the summer of 2017 approached, both boys were preparing to leave the coop: Daniel to Spain for a gap year, Benjamin to Georgetown. With our sons launched, we were free to deepen our missions.

Jackie's work focused on East and Southern Africa, mine in West Africa, but our hearts remained rooted in the same continent. Africa had long claimed a part of us.

More than two decades earlier, we had set off into the African unknown with nothing but backpacks and curiosity. Now, Africa was calling, *again.*

Part 3

Something Still Calls Me

The First Signs of Life After Loss

Chapter 9

The World's Friendliest Half-Marathon

April 2018
Tajikistan

I was reflecting on those final months, Jackie heading to Botswana, me to Oman, and our plan to reunite in Nairobi. Though it was now only four months later, those plans of 2017 seemed to belong to a completely different life. After all, it was year zero, the depths of winter 2018.

I was back in Georgetown after Jamaica, my failed attempt to travel again. I was adhering to a scripted routine and trying not to dwell on my misadventures. Maybe travel was no longer for me: the logistics, the long flights, the loneliness without Jackie. Had this constant in my life failed me, or had I failed it?

For these last months, grief consumed me. Beyond caring for my boys, not much else mattered to me. Meditation and spiritual reading kept the disorientation at bay, but I wanted more than just survival. I was searching for something that could carry me toward the doorstep of healing. And in the back of my mind, I knew that travel, despite the Jamaica disaster, was a likely pathway. I needed a destination that felt different, one that awakened something real inside me.

One evening, while sitting at the café next door to our house on Cecil Street, I read that Uzbekistan had just devalued its currency. It reminded me of the trip Jackie and I took there in 2001, just before we departed from Russia. We'd left Benjamin and Daniel, then three and four, with Valentina in Moscow. Did we really do that, travel to Central Asia and leave them in Russia without Mom and Dad? Uzbekistan wasn't objectively dangerous, but it was still the Stans, not long removed from what Reagan once called "the Evil Empire." Still, the promise of adventure and the country's fascinating history—the blue domes of Samarkand, the medieval architecture of Bukhara, and the legacy of Alexander the Great and Genghis Khan—drew us in.

As I thought back on that trip, it hit me. There were only two of the five "Stans" that I hadn't visited yet: Tajikistan and Turkmenistan. *Three down, two to go.* That was when I felt it: that *dreamy feeling* I used to get contemplating a trip to a new place. Before I could worry what my boys might think, I was already typing "Tajikistan tours." The first result was Koryo Tours, a name I recognized and with a tagline that screamed at me: "Be the first foreigner to run in the Dushanbe International Half-Marathon." *Barry, you have to do that.* It used to be Jackie's enthusiasm that helped to push me toward faraway places. Now, I had to find that drive within myself. After the start of a difficult year of solitude, contemplation, and search for meaning, now was a time for action.

Tajikistan was the kind of pull I'd been waiting for, a gravitational pull that perhaps initially didn't make sense, but one that called to my soul and gave me a defined goal. For the first time in a while, I had something clear to work toward.

That night, I decided to talk to the boys. I was nervous about bringing up faraway travel that could put me out of contact. We talked about Jackie often, but it was different asking them to be okay with something that might stir up painful memories, particularly of those devastating phone calls from overseas that continued to scar.

"It's fine, Dad," Benjamin said.

"Do what you need to do." Daniel shrugged, eyes on his phone. Maybe they were ready to see the old me again. Maybe we all were.

・ ・ ・

It wasn't just Tajikistan that interested me; it was the race. Running had been a big part of my life from college until my knees said, "No más." I was never the fastest, but I remembered the sense of agency and control it gave me, something I wanted now more than ever. I wasn't in great shape, but training gave me a target. And I realized I couldn't wait for clarity to come. I had to move, even without certainty. Action itself became my compass.

I had ten weeks to prepare. My first run on the C&O Canal in Georgetown didn't even hit two miles, but slowly, I built up to 13.1. With the serious physical exertion of training, I started sleeping through the night again. And as I trained, my thoughts shifted from grief to anticipation. Less to missing Jackie and more to the buzz of exploring another "Stan." Though, as I grew increasingly comfortable, even excited about the trip, some questions began to nag at me. How would I stay in touch with the boys regularly? Would there be internet? Could this be the place where I would get some clear revelation of the direction my life could take? The questions were still there, but I let them drift past. Maybe I didn't need answers, just the movement.

There was one doubt I could not quiet: Was I ready to travel in a group again? I had come to see solitude not just as beneficial but as essential to my well-being. But ready or not, it was time to try.

Tajikistan

You can always tell the far-flung places by the flight times. My Turkish Airlines flight landed in Dushanbe at 3:00 a.m. Two things struck me right away. First, the street signs: Cyrillic letters I could read but didn't understand. The language was Tajik, close to Farsi, but written in Cyrillic. Second was "the Roof of the World," the Pamir Mountains, massive, snow-covered, and majestic. I could even see them in the background in the dark, and I was instantly captivated.

My guide, Jamshed, met me with an ear-to-ear smile and a Koryo

Tours Welcome sign. I pulled out some of my rusty Russian: "Privet, ochin priyatna." Walking into the hotel side by side with Jamshed, I suddenly felt comfortable that I'd made the right decision, saying to myself, *I am going to like Tajikistan just fine.*

That night at our welcome dinner, I was anxious, but I quickly relaxed. These people *chose* to run a half-marathon in Central Asia; we at least had that in common, right? I was also fascinated by their stories. One guy's long-term goal was running a half or full marathon in every country possible; this would be his sixtieth. *What a cool idea to attach a quest to one's travel interests.* A couple from Belgium had left their young kids at home to do something adventurous. They were like Jackie and me, back on that trip to Uzbekistan. And a reminder to me of what I'd been missing, the joy of meeting people who shared the same strange pull toward the far corners of the world.

I didn't know it at the time, but though I had just arrived, this trip already felt something of a turning point. I was no longer just trying to outrun grief or pretend things were normal like when I was in Jamaica. Tajikistan felt different, like a cautious toe dipped back into the world, not for escape, but maybe, just maybe, for reconnection.

Race day came quickly. Twelve of us joined local runners and elite marathoners as they stretched, set watches, and retied shoes. As we waited for the starting gun, my legs shook with anticipation, and I felt a surge of excitement I hadn't experienced in a long time. When the blast of the gun came, I felt a massive burst of adrenaline as my legs launched into the first race they'd run in nearly twenty years. This was what it meant to feel *alive* again.

This feeling, though, didn't help me burn up the track. I'd just turned fifty-eight, and my legs showed their age as they worked damned hard to keep me in the middle of the pack. But there was a great consolation prize: I couldn't have asked for a nicer bunch of competitors. The Dushanbe International Half-Marathon has the tagline "Run in Remote Central Asia with the Friendliest People We Know," and it turned out to be amazingly accurate. Every time one of the Tajik runners passed me or I them, they'd wave and smile. I'd never seen this in all the years I participated in races.

After the race, the Dushanbe Tourism Association put on a dazzling show of traditional Tajik dance, the performers' colorful costumes vivid against the white-tipped mountains. Sitting beside the Ethiopian who won with a 4:20 mile pace, I laughed at how far I'd come since my 8:00 per-mile jogs along the canal. He was probably showering in his hotel room and had ordered room service by the time I finished.

Back in my own hotel room, dog-tired, I felt like something had shifted. That night, for the first time, I skipped my grief reading ritual and went straight to *The Office*. It was a small decision, but it felt like an exhale. Grief hadn't left, but it was like giving grief the night off.

The next morning, I woke with a lightness I hadn't felt in a long time. I wasn't healed, not even close, but something had definitely changed. We spent the next six days exploring the ruins of the Sogdian Empire, ancient Zoroastrian temples, and narrow mountain roads that snaked past remote villages. On our last day before returning to Dushanbe, we reached a small chalet at Iskanderkul, a secluded lake named for Alexander the Great. The crystalline waters shimmered beneath the high-altitude sun.

That afternoon, I took a walk alone to a thundering waterfall just as the sun dipped behind the snow-capped peaks. To my surprise, I found myself with an unexpected emotion, not from sadness, but from the sheer beauty of it all. It was as if something in me had opened, and I didn't resist it. I welcomed it. What if the moments we feel most alive aren't the ones we plan, but the ones we let break through? For the first time in a long while, I didn't feel the need to hold anything back. Whatever it was, Jackie wouldn't just have approved; she would have been the first to take my hand and walk me toward it.

I knew joy and pain would keep showing up, and I also knew I'd need others beside me to carry both. It wasn't just the grandeur of the mountains or the finish line that stayed with me. It was the connection that I felt with the people I traveled with and the Tajiks I met along the way. The trip hadn't fixed anything, but it reminded me that movement still held meaning. Maybe empowerment wasn't about certainty but the willingness to give it a shot. And maybe, if I kept showing up in the world, taking that first step again and again, some part of me might return to life too.

Chapter 10

A Pilgrimage to an Invincible Summer

**June 2018
The Camino**

By this point, I had accepted, out of necessity, that my empty-nest years weren't going to go as planned. Sure, I could still travel, but not with the sense of grounding or belonging I once hoped for, let alone the companionship. "Home" had never meant much to me until Jackie. After years of wandering, she gave me the chance to settle down. It was the best possible gift I could receive. But now, seven months after losing her, the idea of living full time in Sausalito terrified me.

I was doing my best to climb out of grief, and I feared that staying in that house would only trap me in it. But as Benjamin wrapped up his second semester at Georgetown, we both agreed it was time for him to return to a normal college life, one that didn't involve living with his dad. By the end of the summer, he'd be starting his second year, and after dropping Daniel off for his first year of university, I'd be back in Sausalito alone, surrounded by memories of Jackie and the moments we'd shared, with no one left to share them with. Anyone who has lost a spouse knows how disorienting that kind of loneliness can be. The truth was, I felt abandoned. Sausalito, once full of life, now felt like a place holding the past. Well-meaning questions from neighbors and friends—"How are you really doing?" or "What are you going to do now?"—only deepened my disorientation.

Before Tajikistan, it was difficult not to fixate on all I'd lost: my partner, our future plans, even the comfort of home. But after the trip, something felt different. Maybe it was the sheer unfamiliarity of the place that shifted something in my brain, or maybe it was the company of intrepid travelers.

The grief wasn't gone, but it no longer had absolute power over me. Seneca wrote long ago, "Time itself, nature's greatest remedy, quiets the most bitter grief." I read less from my collection of grieving guides, and I teared up less at seeing Jackie's emails when I was searching for something in my "family email folder" or when I heard a song we both liked. But how could I keep making progress if I lived in a house surrounded by reminders 24/7? I needed some distance from them. Travel helped. It loosened something in me, slowly easing the weight of the gaping hole Jackie had left behind.

One quote by Albert Camus from Martha Whitmore Hickman's *Healing After Loss* stuck with me:

"In the midst of winter, I discovered there is an invincible summer.... It surprises us, but we know in our gut it could be a fluke and that it might not last. But it was not just a quick flash of joy or contentment but that in some way we are going to have life after tragedy."

After a cold winter in Georgetown, Camus's words lingered: Perhaps I was finally on the verge of glimpsing my own invincible summer. So it was time to plan the next journey.

That summer, the boys and I decided to walk part of the Camino de Santiago in Spain, where Jackie had made the pilgrimage in the spring of 2017 with friends from Moscow. We had her Camino "passport" stamped with the stops along her route. Retracing her footsteps felt essential to me. The boys, as always, were supportive. I wasn't trying to recreate the past or even have fun; I wasn't there yet. But it was important to me to preserve the feeling of family that Jackie had nurtured, and a big part of this was family trips. Jackie's death shattered the family dynamics. Deep love remained between me and my boys, but something invisible and immovable kept us from truly connecting. I was very much hoping this trip could remove some of that blockage. After we lost her, I'd made a conscious effort to soften, to be more emotionally present. But no matter how hard I tried, I couldn't seem to find my way to that same lightness with the boys. And as important as being with them, no matter the dynamics, I also wanted to feel her *presence*.

In the days of Saint James, one of Jesus's twelve apostles, before the New World had been discovered, Finisterre truly was the end of the world. For over a thousand years, the Camino has drawn pilgrims tracing routes to his tomb, with some continuing even farther to the dramatic coastal cliffs of Finisterre, which in Latin means "end of the earth." For some, the Camino is a physical challenge, a chance to walk hundreds of miles and push their limits. But for most, it's a journey of personal transformation, a pilgrimage along well-worn paths in search of something deeper. I wasn't looking for anything profound. Just to walk where Jackie had walked, and to be with my boys.

The Camino, Spain

Our small group, six pilgrims plus our guide, met in Sarria. There was a woman who looked American and a couple. The man seemed familiar. "My name is Simon, and this is my wife—"

Before he could finish, I blurted out, "Simon Paterno?"

He squinted. "Barry?" Simon ran the JP Morgan office in the Philippines. We had worked together on a few deals while I was in Singapore years ago. Small world! My boys introduced themselves immediately.

That first day, twenty-five kilometers, was especially good for Benjamin. Though excelling at school, he'd seemed depressed since finishing his first year at Georgetown. On the trail, though, he was carefree, chatting nonstop. At one point, Daniel and I looked at each other, and it was clear we were thinking exactly the same thing: *It's great to see Benjamin come back to life like this, but when is he going to shut up?*

Besides spending quality time with my boys, I had one other goal: Find a four-legged friend Jackie had met on her pilgrimage. She'd texted me a photo of a little white dog and floated the idea of bringing it home.

Uh, I don't think that's the best idea, sweetie, I'd replied. Although we had only one dog at this point, down from four in the previous years, this one was probably someone else's.

There were many dogs along the Camino. But still, I searched. Then, one day, a hundred kilometers in, there she was: a little white dog sitting calmly by the trail, tail wagging.

It's her.

I pulled up the old photo on my phone of Jackie crouched in leggings and a beanie, smiling, petting that very dog. As we approached, the dog looked up at us like she'd been waiting. My chest tightened. Jackie had wanted to bring home countless dogs over the years, but somehow, this one was special. Joy, sadness, and something else, a kind of transcendence, washed over me. It felt like Jackie's happiness in meeting this dog just a year ago had passed directly to me. After taking some pictures with our new friend, I wiped the tears from my eyes, and we pushed on.

As we walked on, I kept thinking how Jackie had a way of making everyone, strangers, dogs, even difficult people, feel seen and cared for. It struck me that maybe the Camino wasn't just about walking in her footsteps but about figuring out how to carry her spirit forward. I didn't know how yet, but I felt the stirrings of a question: *How can I keep her kindness alive in the world?*

We'd often start our mornings walking with Simon and his wife and quickly move into our own pace (or rather, me trying to keep up with the boys). The rhythm of the Camino brought us into a meditative state, walking in sync with others in a global community. People from all over the world who might never have crossed paths were all headed in the same direction. With a huge diversity of languages, practically everyone we passed voiced a supportive word or simply wished us "Buon Camino," a meaningful or good journey. We'd run into the same people day after day: thirty women from Uruguay, a Spanish man carrying his dog in his windbreaker, a couple walking from France with a baby they planned to baptize at Santiago. Benjamin picked up a toy they dropped, knowing we'd see them again.

Our favorites were four middle-aged men from Puglia, Italy. When they discovered that Benjamin and I spoke Italian, they insisted on buying us a drink (and had clearly already had a few themselves). From then on, our new Italian friends would greet us with big bear hugs whenever we crossed paths.

At the end of the week, we reached Santiago de Compostela, about twenty miles from the Atlantic Ocean, or in St. James's day, the end of the world. After attending Mass at the cathedral, I did the dad thing and took our dirty clothes to a Laundromat. While folding the clean laundry, something caught my eye—a bookmark on the floor with sunflowers and a phrase in Italian, "La gioia è il segno che stiamo vicini alla luce." (Joy is a sign that we are closer to the light.)

I froze. With Jackie's sunflower tattoo firmly in my mind, surely this was a sign.

That night at dinner, I consciously avoided heavy conversations. I longed to talk about Jackie and was always somehow waiting for someone to ask me about her. Sure, with the boys, I wanted to know what was going on in their heads, to be sure they were okay. But I made a choice. I would keep things *close to the light*, letting laughter about our Camino adventures, the people we met, and our Camino stamps be the bridge. I didn't want them to feel obligated to process anything on my timeline, just to know I was there.

Back at the hotel, instead of watching *The Office*, I instinctively pulled out my journal. To my surprise, the words came out as a poem, my first ever.

> Walking on the trail in good rhythm,
> I hear three feet touch the ground in unison.
> We befriend many from Latin countries if only
> For a brief encounter,
> As we bid "Buon Camino" to all we pass.
> My love for the two boys alongside me is intensi-
>   fied by my own personal pilgrimage.
> I follow her path.
> I know the places she visited, ate, and slept.
> I find the dog she favored.

Her presence is with me.
I am comforted that she still shines her abundant
>love upon us.

Boulder, Colorado

She should be here. The thought echoed in my mind as Daniel and I wandered through Target in Boulder, shopping for sheets, a lamp, and things that could provide a sense of comfort, trying to make a sterile dorm room feel a little like home. Watching the other "complete" families buzzing with excitement stung deep. I had flown out to Colorado with Daniel to help him get settled into his freshmen dorm, not anticipating how difficult a simple trip to Target might be. Jackie had helped Benjamin settle into college. She should've been here for Daniel too.

After moving Daniel in, I spent the afternoon exploring the area with him, hoping the day would never end. But it did, and after saying our goodbyes, I went to my hotel and had one drink more than normal to coax myself to sleep. As it turned out, I wasn't the only one having a rough night. The next morning, I got a call from Daniel.

"Dad, I'm not feeling so well," he said.

Hearing his voice crack, I understood exactly how he felt. I knew from observing my boys' moods that new waves of grief, or even crippling grief, can arrive at important events or at unexpected times. Surely, not being able to say goodbye to his mom on his first night of going off to college was painful. I extended my hotel reservation and went to pick him up. After one more night with me, he seemed ready to give it another try.

When I dropped him off this time, I said, "Daniel, I will stay in Boulder as long as you need me to, until you are ready."

"I think I will be okay, Dad."

Daniel had bravely stepped into his next chapter. Would I be able to do the same? The next day, I flew back home to confront what I'd been avoiding—the truly empty nest, for the very first time.

As I arrived at the house, I felt overwhelmed by how big, quiet, and empty each room felt without the boys, *without her*. I'd left all of Jackie's things exactly where they were when Benjamin and I left for Georgetown, only six weeks after losing my wife. Her robe still hung on the bathroom door. Her conditioner, her jewelry, untouched. I wasn't ready to let go.

And the future? No kids at home. No job to ground me. Every trip ended, and then what? The only thing that seemed to help was planning the next one. So, I booked a trip to Turkmenistan, choosing Koryo again, then another to Uruguay and Paraguay. I am sure it looked like I was running away, and maybe I was. But I couldn't dwell on loss if I just kept going.

Chapter 11

The Power of Connection

October 2018
Turkmenistan

I arrived in Turkmenistan's capital. Yes, in the middle of the night. From my research, I knew there was a good bit of weirdness here: Every building and car had to be white, and dogs were banned because the "Great Leader" disliked their odor. *Jackie would've hated this place.*

As my driver started toward the hotel, I looked back in astonishment at the airport, its massive marble roof shaped like a falcon in flight. *What the . . . ?* I don't know why I was surprised. I knew Turkmenistan, the "North Korea of Central Asia," had used the earnings from its vast gas reserves to build surreal monuments to its leader's cult of personality.

Before my tour-group meeting, I had a few hours to explore Ashgabat. Using my rusty Russian, I spoke to the hotel attendant, who recommended I walk to a tree-lined area with parks and cafés. As I walked out, I noticed the city's Soviet-style architecture—orderly, subdued, with an almost sterile feel. No one was smiling. Maybe that, along with dogs, was banned?

As I walked along, I saw what looked like an army of women in bright orange vests with their heads and almost entire faces wrapped in scarves, a stark contrast against the all-white city. They were sweeping the streets along the perimeter of a park with what seemed to be brooms made of bundled twigs. They each swept in a unified counterclockwise circular motion as if putting on a show. I sat and watched for a while, and without thinking, got out my camera and snapped a photo of one of the women. She noticed. Even with her full headscarf, I could see a look of displeasure as she approached me.

I turned to walk away. She followed, so I jogged. She matched my pace. Soon I was running, *fast.* Thankfully, despite a good number of months since last running in Dushanbe, my prior half-marathon training kicked in, and after a few blocks, she gave up. *Definitely not the best for my first Turkmenistan interaction.*

Entering the hotel lobby, I ran into our local guide, Rustam. After some quick introductions, I confessed what had just happened as if I were admitting to my mom that I'd ditched school. "Oh, you have already had an encounter with the 'street ninjas,' the lowest-paid laborers in the country," he said with a dry sense of humor. "They keep the streets dust-free. We are at the frontier of the Karakum Desert, and our president wants to ensure that our city remains pristine both here in Old Ashgabat as well as in the newer part." Then Rustam half smiled as he said, "I will tell the others at our briefing later not to take pictures of them. They don't like it."

This *Twilight Zone* episode did not end there. The city holds the Guinness World Record for the highest concentration of white marble buildings. New Ashgabat was filled with marvels: the world's largest Ferris wheel, a dentistry building shaped like a tooth, the Palace of Happiness—all in marble.

But the weirdest experience was camping in the Darvaza Gas Crater, also known as the Gates of Hell. Ignited in the 1970s by Soviet engineers in the hope of burning out a gas leak from below the surface, it's still burning fifty years later, an endless inferno in the middle of the desert. Camping one night here was like pitching a tent beside the world's biggest campfire. A few days later, we found ourselves in

Awaza, billed as the "Las Vegas of Central Asia," but everywhere we turned seemed empty in this resort town filled with vacant five-star hotels, quiet streets, and unoccupied luxury housing lining artificial canals. Where were all the tourists?

Some countries you visit for the nature, some for the culture, some for the history, and some even for the food, but Turkmenistan you visit for the weirdness. With gleaming white marble buildings, street ninjas, massive burning gas craters, and five-star beach resorts devoid of visitors, Turkmenistan was like stepping onto a set of a dystopian sci-fi film. Surrounded by surreal monuments and empty resorts, I didn't feel so out of place, though. Grief had made the world strange. But here, the strangeness was external, and somehow fitting.

One evening, a few weeks after returning from Turkmenistan, I felt the need to get out of the house, and I went to a local pizzeria on Caledonia Street in Sausalito, seating myself at a communal table. It didn't take long for me to notice a young woman sitting at the end of the table. We exchanged smiles just as the owner stopped by to ask where I'd been on my latest trip.

"Turkmenistan," I said, sure I'd draw a blank stare.

"I'm going to Turkmenistan next week," the woman cut in, looking at me incredulously.

Her name was Kelly. She was heading to Turkmenistan to teach mindfulness to UN staff in Ashgabat. We became fast friends, my first real connection with a woman since losing Jackie. I'm sure neither of us was looking for anything more than connection. Just two people each carrying our own challenges, craving something real and grounded. Having a new friend in my hometown, an adventurous soul who saw me not just through my grief but beyond it, felt good.

Uruguay

I was flying out of Montevideo, Uruguay, after spending time at the understatedly chic beach town of José Ignacio, opting for its laid-back charm instead of the glitz of Punta del Este, often dubbed the Monaco of South America. Content after seeing another spectacular waterfall, Iguazú, via Asunción, the capital of Paraguay, I took out my computer to journal. This usually helped ward off unwanted conversation, but when I opened a photo of Jackie in Botswana, wearing a flower in her hair and a green tank top that revealed her sunflower tattoo, a young woman next to me took notice. It was the last photo ever taken of my wife.

"She's very beautiful."

Her words went straight into me. Seeing me trying to compose myself, the young woman touched my forearm. "Do you want to tell me about her?" I looked at her and paused for a moment. It was the question I had longed to be asked.

I told her about Jackie, our boys, our travels, our life together. It felt like unpacking a box of memories I'd stored away. She listened with care, and as the floodgates opened, an unexpected sense of warmth washed over me. When I stopped, she introduced herself as Estephany, ethnic Chinese, raised in Costa Rica, a rugby player for her country's national team, and now headed to a finance job in New York. She was driven and accomplished, yet warm and open. After we landed in Miami for our different connecting flights, we hugged and exchanged contact information at the gate.

"Can I call you Uncle Barry?" she asked.

I smiled. "It would be an honor."

On my connecting flight to San Francisco, it hit me: I was becoming more like Jackie. I hadn't consciously tried to open a channel between Estephany and me. I hadn't even wanted to have a conversation. But once it started, I was unconditionally receptive to what this fellow human being wanted to offer me. This reminded me of a quote I'd read from what had become my grief bible, *Healing After Loss*: "The true quality of our lives depends on the attention that we project on the world." That was Jackie's gift. When she focused on you, you felt seen. She offered grace without needing anything in return.

Everything I told Estephany about her was true. Jackie was smart, kind, and easygoing about almost everything. What set her apart, though, were the exceptions. She wasn't the least bit easygoing when it came to the welfare of children and animals and had a strong built-in sense of justice. Though she was small in stature, no one had more courage when it came to protecting young ones or animals. As she used to say, "All beating hearts have the same worth." The first time she said this, I knew this was the woman I wanted to be my life-long partner.

Don't get me wrong; I wasn't happy about *everything* that came with the package—messes on the kitchen floor from farm animals or the times I came home to a new rescue dog. One time, Benjamin and I were just getting home from a two-week trip in West Africa and could not even enter our house because Jackie decided to foster a Belgian Malinois that no one wanted. They are often used in military operations. Like Bob Marley is rumored to have said, "If she's amazing, she won't be easy. If she's easy, she won't be amazing." Even now, Jackie was bringing light back into my life, reminding me that love, once shared, doesn't end; it endures and keeps showing up in unexpected conversations, even in faraway places.

Somewhere between the strangeness of Turkmenistan and the warmth of Estephany's listening, I realized I was no longer traveling to transition from grief. I was traveling to reconnect with life. The ache hadn't disappeared, but it had made space for something else: a pull toward meaning, presence, and possibility.

. . .

With such positive signs taking hold and renewed purpose, I knew it was time to clear out some of Jackie's things, something I had been avoiding. As I took her robe down from the hook on the bathroom door, I remembered how she looked wearing it. Running my finger along the nap, I went a little weak, like I was about to do something I'd regret forever. Yet this was the first time the idea of packing away, or even getting rid of, some of her things didn't feel like a betrayal. I knew others who lost a spouse had cleared everything right away. I couldn't. Not until now. It was that key moment when the real separation happens. Where your loved one's existence in your physical world is no longer, but in the heart will always remain.

I took a deep breath before stepping inside a room I had been avoiding, a room, next to the kitchen, where Jackie had spent much of her time. I started with a drawer in the armoire filled with photo albums, stacks of pictures, and her notebooks. There, I saw something unexpected: a journal with a sunflower on the cover. *Oh my God, Jackie's travel diaries.* During our travels through Asia and Africa in the mid-1990s, I'd seen her writing in them daily and was always curious what was in there. Now, I didn't have to wonder anymore. Seeing the covers brought back memories of our travels. I knew I wanted to read them, even if it meant violating her privacy.

In the end, I couldn't stop myself. The promise and comfort of reliving such a special time in our lives gave me something to hold on to as I let go of many of her physical possessions. I spent the next few days reading two full notebooks filled with her daily entries from our travels. It brought forth an avalanche of memories that seemed to have no end. I felt so many emotions: awe for the experiences we got to have together, crushed by the future Jackie would never have, and gratitude for all that we shared. It hurt reading about some of our arguments. *They seem so ridiculous now.* But one of her diary entries about an argument we had made me chuckle: Men, you can't live with them sometimes, but you are not allowed to shoot them either.

That first night, I read until 2:00 a.m. After six hours of poring over our past, I finally put the diaries aside and got off the roller coaster. And to my surprise, I didn't feel guilt or even sadness. What I felt, above all, was fulfillment. Jackie and I had packed a lifetime's worth of unforgettable memories into a year and a half of travel in Asia and Africa before Benjamin came along. We'd made the absolute most of our time together, and I couldn't ask for more than that. Jackie's life had been cut short, but we'd had more adventures together than most ever experience. Between Jackie's love and our boys, I'd lived a fortunate life. Maybe this was *acceptance*.

Grief doesn't vanish; it shifts. Eventually, it no longer dominates your thoughts, creating space for something new. That shift feels like losing something, but it's not a loss of love, just the beginning of distance. And when the vast place that my grief had taken up started to recede, it gave space, both emotional and mental, for new things to enter.

Soon after finding her diaries, I decided to write a book for my boys about our adventures and share those lighter, happy memories, incorporating Jackie's voice through her diary entries. As it turned out, focusing on this writing project and revisiting these incredible adventures together was exactly what I needed. Working on "Jackie projects" gave me a new burst of energy, and now I was about to embark on another big one involving a continent where we'd shared so many happy memories.

Seeking to do something that would carry on Jackie's generous spirit, I instituted the Bourse Jackie program (*bourse* is French for "scholarship") for female high school students in Timbuktu through my foundation, Caravan to Class, a gift with the power to change the lives of young women for generations to come. This program would provide a full scholarship to a private university and was designed to send these women off into promising careers in a part of the world where scholarships and good career opportunities were male-dominant. In Mali, higher education for women can change a life, not just financially, but by opening a path toward identity, confidence, and choice. That was what I hoped Bourse Jackie would offer.

If life is measured by the attention we give the world, I wanted mine to be deliberate, an offering in Jackie's honor. And now, empowered by the launch of the Bourse Jackie program, I set off in pursuit of another dream. It was time that I returned to what I had begun in Oman before losing Jackie: studying Arabic in an Arab country. This time, I would choose Jordan.

Chapter 12

An Arabic Journey

March 2019
Jordan

I'm often asked, "Why Arabic?" As if the question were really, "What the heck would compel you to study that language?" I've spent more hours studying languages—Spanish, French, Italian, Japanese, Mandarin, Russian—than almost anything else. But to me, Arabic is the ultimate language. It's not just difficult; it's a linguistic Rubik's cube with downright unforgiving grammar. And you really need to learn two languages: Modern Standard Arabic used for news and formal speech for the twenty-two Arabic-speaking countries of the world, and in addition a major dialect like Egyptian or Levantine for real-life conversation on the Arab street. The dialects are so distinct that a Saudi might barely understand a Moroccan. Learning Arabic meant a major commitment. But eighteen months after my Oman trip, I was ready and enrolled at the Qasid Institute in Amman.

It took only a few days in Jordan for me to fall in love with the warmth of its people, the mellow cafés of Amman, the incredible food, and the deep sense of history. For a country the size of Maine, Jordan offers a stunning range of sights: the rose-red ruins of Petra, the cliffs of Wadi Rum, and the turquoise waters of the Gulf of Aqaba.

As my stay in Jordan unfolded, I felt my narrative about the Arab world changing. When I first arrived, a voice in my head whispered, *This place can't be safe; it's nearly half Palestinian.* A bias from my youth. But it quickly dissolved. Jordan was one of the most hospitable countries I'd ever visited.

At Qasid, I had four hours of private lessons each day: Modern Standard Arabic with Dana, a Palestinian teacher, and Jordanian dialect with Muna, a Syrian. There I was, an American Jew learning Arabic from two Arab women whose families had been displaced by war. We didn't discuss politics, but we shared stories. I left feeling deeply connected to Dana and Muna. If I had daughters, I'd want them to be like these two. The fact was that I felt no different about Dana and Muna than I felt about Estephany or Kelly. It was a connection that overcame all our respective grievances and narratives of the Arab-Israeli conflict.

On my last day of class, my taxi driver, Ahmed, picked me up from my hotel. I had gotten used to his energetic morning greetings, "Sabah al khir, wa salam aleikum, kefik, wa kief drastic?" (Good morning! Greetings, how are you? How are your studies?) Just then, it hit me that Ahmed was the spitting image of my uncle Sam, my mother's brother, who'd passed away recently: same short build, round face, kind bluish-green eyes, and a similar dynamic personality. I asked him in Arabic, "Can I take a video of you to send to my cousin? You remind me of her father."

"Bi altakid" (Of course), he responded. My cousin texted me immediately, "OMG, I am in tears. He looks so much like my dad."

That afternoon after class, at one of my favorite coffee places in the Jabal Amman neighborhood, I reflected on how my perspective toward this place had changed in such a short time. I found myself sharing smiles, especially with the ever-present hookah smokers lounging in the coffeehouses, and exchanging stories in my still-limited Arabic. I felt a significant shift within me toward this culture, our walls of difference crumbling to reveal a shared humanity. From my uncle Sam to my new friend Ahmed, we really are the same people. My uncle was

Jewish, Ahmed is Muslim, but both were Arabs born in the same region; they even looked alike. A roll of the dice had placed them on opposing sides of a long, tragic divide. Somewhere along the way, starting about two thousand years ago, differing beliefs in either the Jewish God or the Islamic Allah have made us think we are different.

I began to ask myself: If I was wrong about Jordan, what else had I misunderstood? What were Syria and Iraq really like?

I certainly was seeing the world differently. Passions I thought long dormant were flooding back. Eighteen months after beginning my Arabic journey in Oman, days before losing Jackie, I had come full circle. Every afternoon, as I walked back to my hotel after class, the same thought came to me: *There is no place I would rather be than where I am right now.* I felt on the right path again and was sure Jackie would have been pleased.

Sausalito

Back in Sausalito, with early-morning Arabic Zoom sessions with my Qasid tutor, a bike ride, and afternoons writing at Taste of Rome, I began building a new life with a growing sense of intention. One day, a young woman rolled up on a fully loaded bike, front and rear panniers stuffed.

"Where you going with all that?" I asked.

"To the US-Mexico border," she replied. I immediately caught her French Canadian accent.

"Where'd you start?"

"In the Yukon."

A quick search showed it was nearly three thousand miles away. She carried over one hundred pounds with gear, water, even a tent. Her name was Cat, short for Catherine. As we got to talking, she shared that she'd had some challenges in her youth in Quebec, but years ago, she had a vision of moving west and raising sled dogs, and did it. Adventure saved her. It gave her renewed purpose.

Over lunch the next day, she shared more. She couldn't live in cities, couldn't work in offices. She needed wilderness, physical challenge, and solitude to feel grounded. "I needed to do something drastic to get myself out of the painful place I was in. Through focusing on what I was passionate about, adventure, I found myself. I found belonging for the first time in my life."

I got goose bumps. Her words hit me, coming from someone who had actually rebuilt her life. We came from different worlds, but I saw myself in her.

She had cycled through India, Africa, and Latin America. Yukon to Mexico was just her latest chapter. I shared, "I dream of doing a big bike trip like that one day and have been ramping up my cycling lately after a long layoff. I was living away for a while in Georgetown with my older son. It was tough to get out there and cycle during winter."

"Why were you living away from here? It is such a beautiful place," she asked.

I told her a condensed version of losing Jackie. She gently touched my arm. Her empathy was palpable. When we said goodbye after a nice lunch and conversation, she gave me a hug, and we pledged to stay in touch. Cat added, "Somehow, I feel like we have known each other for a long time." I said half jokingly, "Perhaps we were sister and brother in another life," and waved goodbye. I knew somewhere in the cosmos that this was Jackie working her magic again. A week later, Cat sent me a picture of her in Los Angeles with the book I had written that had just come out on Amazon. As if she needed to load extra weight onto her bike.

. . .

I wrote *I Fell in Love with Your Mom on a Bus in India* as a keepsake for our sons. It wasn't for mass publication, just a tribute. But what surprised me most was how writing helped reorder my grief. Putting memories into words gave shape to what had felt like chaos. Through storytelling to my boys, I wasn't just honoring Jackie; I was reclaiming parts of myself that I thought had been lost. In telling the boys about their mother and me, I started to glimpse a path ahead.

One where love, loss, and purpose could coexist. I did do one reading at our local bookstore in Marin County, Book Passage, during the Thanksgiving holiday while my boys were home. It was our third Thanksgiving without Jackie. The place was packed despite the rain.

After some introductory remarks, I read some excerpts from the book that I thought would give clarity to why and how I came to write it. I started with a passage from the introduction that captured the moment when I realized that no matter how painful the days ahead were going to be, my gratitude for my years with Jackie was going to power me through the difficult times:

> As the flight from Madrid to DC took off, with Daniel asleep next to me, a forceful wave of emotions hit me. I can only describe it as all the memories I had of your mother and us as a family, literally thousands of dreamlike recollections. Though I was in tears, sobbing, these memories kept playing over and over in my mind as if I were watching a movie, and they buoyed me with vivid remembrances of a blessed life. I felt the most powerful sense of gratitude. It was a sacred place of exceptionally profound consciousness that I could have never known existed until that moment. I knew then that my deep love for your dear mother, that goes well beyond her being with me physically, would somehow sustain me and give me the strength to get through this horrible tragedy.

When I looked up, relieved that I'd held it together long enough to get through the paragraph, I saw lots of tissues and was reminded all over again of the love that so many had felt for Jackie.

I moved on to some passages about how we met and the course of our relationship. A question-and-answer session followed, during which I mostly answered questions about our travels and how our relationship evolved. But an old colleague and friend from JP Morgan asked me a question that caught me off guard.

"Barry, I've heard people say that after a difficult loss, through the grieving process, you come out wanting to focus on having more meaning in your life and living from your heart. In a way, you've gone to another country, taken a journey people here might not understand. Is that a source of disconnection for you, here in Marin, with people sometimes?"

It was one of those times when I truly felt understood by someone back home for choosing the path I was on. During my travels, no one knew my past. We met in the moment. No preconceptions, no expectations. Just presence. That clean slate was healing.

I took a moment to gather my thoughts. "Yes, that's right, Azita," I said. "And I think that's why my default has been travel. The more different the place, the better. The people I meet don't know my story of loss or the Barry who used to be. It helps me reconstruct myself and even reinvent parts of me that I'd like to see changed."

I thought about the question long after the reading. Even surrounded by kind people back in Marin, I still felt disconnected. They hadn't changed; I had. My values, my focus, my sense of meaning had all shifted. Bitcoin, the 49ers, political drama, none of it mattered to me anymore.

What did matter now was travel. It was no longer about escape; it had become a mirror. With each journey, I wasn't just seeing the world differently; I was seeing myself differently. The farther I went, the more I felt Jackie's spirit with me, not just to help me grieve, but to help me grow. I started to wonder: Maybe this wasn't just a season of healing, but the beginning of something larger.

As Helen Keller said, "Life is either a daring adventure or it is nothing." I was beginning to crave a community that felt the same way and had already met a few. There had to be more. And I knew that if I kept showing up on the road, I'd find them.

When I opened the world map on my laptop, my eyes went right to the continent I'd visited most recently. I'd already done the "Guays," as I'd come to think of them, and I noticed only two South American countries I hadn't been to: two countries that had quietly waited their turn, Suriname and Guyana, in the extreme northeast corner of the continent. I didn't know much about either country beyond the "Jonestown massacre" that happened in Guyana just after I started college in 1978. But it turned out that Guyana was also known for Kaieteur Falls, the longest "single-drop" waterfall in the world. Remembering how spectacular Iguazú and Victoria Falls were, I instinctively knew what my next adventure would be. Why not start 2020 by finishing the last two countries of the continent and witness another of the world's magnificent waterfalls?

Chapter 13

Finding My Place

**January 2020
Suriname**

I boarded Suriname Airways for the short flight from Port of Spain, Trinidad and Tobago, to the tiny airport in Paramaribo, Suriname. There couldn't have been more than twenty passengers, all business types. After landing, they all proceeded to immigration while I headed for the "Visa on Arrival" sign. No one was at the desk. I waited about ten minutes before showing my passport to an official and asking when someone would be available to issue visas.

"We changed our visa policy on the first of January," the officer said. "Now all US citizens must get a visa before arriving."

It was January 10. *Shit.*

But still, there's no way they're going to deport me, I thought. The officer called over a colleague, who told me to collect my belongings. In a small office, he searched my baggage.

"Sir, when I booked in November, it said a visa on arrival was available. I didn't see anything about a policy change."

"That is our policy now. You will be deported," he said with finality.

I muttered under my breath, "Well, I've never been deported before." But by his stern look, I could tell that he heard me. I'd dodged a hijacking in Morocco, tanks during an Armenian coup, and bombs in El Salvador. But this was new.

"You will be on the next flight out of Paramaribo," the officer said, "at 8:00 a.m. tomorrow to Miami."

"But I want to go to Guyana. I've booked a tour to Kaieteur Falls."

He shook his head as if to say, *Not my problem.* "Follow me."

We left the main terminal and walked across the runway to a small building, the departure lounge. It was empty, save for a woman sweeping the floors.

"This is where you'll spend the night," he said. "You'll get your passport and luggage before your flight." Then he was gone.

I got out my jacket to use as a blanket and texted the concierge at Paramaribo Marriott whom I'd been communicating with to cancel the tour I had booked the day before. Minutes later, she called me. Her name was Jennifer Sienema-Wiebers.

"I will do what I can," she said.

"Thanks," I said, not feeling hopeful as I eased onto my cold bench for the night and pulled my "blanket" over me.

· · ·

I was asleep when I felt a tap on my shoulder. It was the same immigration officer.

"Come with me."

Still foggy, I tried to prepare myself for the worst case but had no clue what that might be. My flight wasn't until the morning, yet here we were, late at night, crossing the runway. Had another policy changed while I slept? I felt like a helpless kid with no options but to be escorted to the principal's office.

"You are very lucky," he said. "Someone at your hotel contacted one of our government officials in the middle of the night. You have been granted a visa."

What?

At the immigration desk, a groggy officer stamped my passport. Jennifer had arranged for a driver to pick me up.

When I arrived, she was waiting at the front desk of the Marriott despite the fact that it was late at night and long past the end of her shift. She told me how she'd gone through her network until she reached Suriname's Minister of Foreign Affairs and convinced her to grant me a visa.

"Jennifer, I don't know what to say. Your kindness prevented me from being deported. Can I please buy you a drink to thank you?" She smiled and nodded.

As we sipped our drinks at the bar, she told me about losing her husband in the Netherlands: "About six months after my husband died, I moved home to Suriname to be closer to family and raise my children here."

She shared how she had found a way to rebuild, even to love again, eventually remarrying. "We have a nice life here," she said with sincerity. I told her about losing Jackie, about my boys, and about how travel was helping me heal my own loss.

It felt like more than chance that I had met Jennifer. I told her I hoped we could stay in touch. We hugged and said goodbye. *Was it chance that I met Jennifer who saved this trip for me, or was there something more mysterious working here?*

The next morning, I headed off for my walking tour of one of Suriname's vast virgin jungles near the capital. The guide told me that Suriname and next-door Guyana are the most forested countries in the world in terms of the percentage of their land masses, made up of 93 percent of pristine jungle with abundant animal life: tapirs, monkeys, sloths, many species of parrots, and leopards, though anyone trying to catch a glimpse of the big cats may find them elusive.

A few days later, after leaving Suriname, I found myself in Guyana at one of the world's most spectacular displays of raw power. Emerging from the small single-prop aircraft, I took only a few steps before arriving at the viewing platform of Kaieteur Falls, the world's longest single-drop waterfall. At once, I felt the thunderous sound of the falls resonating through my body, with the mist gently settling on my skin, filling me with a deep sense of awe.

The jungle in Suriname was unexpected, almost as much as my

immigration misadventure. And the falls in Guyana lived up to their billing as one of the world's most awesome and remote natural wonders. But what lingers most is my connection with Jennifer, a poignant reminder of the goodness that appears in the most unlikely places and situations. I've come to believe that if I keep putting out the kind of energy Jackie once radiated, life will keep sending me extraordinary, soul-affirming connections.

But just weeks later, the world began to shut down.

. . .

COVID-19

I had just returned from my annual trip to Mali via France, with a few unexpected days in Guinea to visit a Guinean friend from home, also in the nonprofit world. On my first night there, she introduced me to Nasser, a Lebanese restaurateur in Conakry. The next evening, he brought me to a party, full of ambassadors and dignitaries. I showed up in jeans and a T-shirt, my usual attire for the next leg of my journey to Timbuktu.

Nasser and I bonded quickly over his culture, our shared experience of losing our wives around the same time, and the fact that we both had two sons. I don't know how we find each other, but somehow, we do.

At the party, most of the conversation swirled around reports of a mysterious disease spreading in China.

Just back from my trip, on March 19, 2020, the announcement came: California had declared a state of emergency and issued a stay-at-home order. The time of COVID-19 had arrived. Benjamin was on spring break in Seattle and flew straight home, and Daniel drove home from Boulder. Suddenly, the house was full again, and while some of my friends were freaking out, I felt fortunate that the only crisis I was facing was that my travels had been grounded for a while.

While the boys studied, I kept the house running, cooking, shopping, cleaning. Benjamin was vegan, Daniel more carnivorous, and I stuck to fish, so dinners were often three meals in one. I'd never been a great cook, and my attempts to please everyone didn't always succeed. And it wasn't just a matter of bridging some pretty big dietary gaps. I'd never really learned to feed myself in style during all my years abroad. At breakfast one day, Daniel made it clear that, in his early twenties, he'd already pulled ahead of me.

"What do you guys want for dinner tonight?" I asked. "Arabian rice or meatless spaghetti Bolognese?"

Neither one looked up from the instant oatmeal I'd made. Finally, Daniel spoke up. "Dad, I think I'll just make something for myself."

Benjamin looked at him. "Daniel, can I have some too?"

I loved having the boys home, but they were busy and didn't have much time for Dad. I envied friends with spouses during lockdown. And without travel, my old grief crept back in; being grounded was a bigger crisis than I'd expected.

Then, through no conscious effort of my own, a portal seemed to open. I found myself ordering books that delved into the existential questions of our world. Kierkegaard echoed in my ear: "If you want to go deeper, select a text of spiritual and intellectual profundity and savor every word." I'd already devoured books about Buddhism and philosophy, spiritual insights, and meditation in the early stages of my grief, trying to figure out where I fit into the world without Jackie, as an individual rather than part of a couple. As I read and reflected, one question kept surfacing: What gives life meaning, across all these cultures I had visited and still wanted to see?

More than philosophical questions, I found myself asking: *What is still important for me to get done?* I was coming to grips with my own mortality and realizing that there was simply no time to waste to discover the answers to these questions.

. . .

With the pandemic lessening, it was with an immense sense of pride, and relief, that I got to see Benjamin graduate from university in May 2021. Georgetown held the socially distanced but in-person graduation at Nationals Park in DC, home of the Washington Nationals baseball team. Rather than each student walking up to receive a diploma, each one had their picture, major, and a quote displayed on the scoreboard for a few seconds. Words can't fully capture the depth of emotion I felt when suddenly a photo of Benjamin with Jackie flashed across the screen with the words *I did it for you, Mom.* No chance of holding it together for that one. He'd accomplished and endured so much, graduated magna cum laude, and was starting a job at an economic think tank at Yale University. He honored his mom in every way.

In late summer, a cyclist friend tipped me off to a travel company called Wander Expeditions. Looking on Instagram, I saw a photo of the company founder, Alvaro Rojas, in a remote, beautiful, rugged, and unspoiled place, all my favorite things. When I read the posts, I learned that the patch of paradise was Socotra, Yemen, a large island at the confluence of the Indian Ocean and the Arabian Sea. I felt that *dreamy feeling* begin to creep in again.

Wasn't Yemen off-limits? A war zone? How had I never heard of Socotra? The water seemed pristine, the sand dunes massive, and the plant life otherworldly. *I have to go there.* On the Wander Expeditions website, I discovered that Alvaro, who'd just turned thirty, had been to all 193 United Nations countries of the world.

How can that be?

How could he have pulled that off, and why didn't I know there were 193 UN member countries? It was like believing you're a master of something, only to find out you lack some pretty fundamental information and that you're actually an imposter. *We've all felt imposter syndrome at one time or another, right?*

I saw I could sign up for a thirty-minute phone consultation with Alvaro for fifty euros.

Done.

Not only had I never talked to anyone who'd been to every country in the world, but it had never occurred to me that it was humanly possible, let alone that some humans had actually *done* it. What kind of adventurer was *I*? Obviously, I needed to think bigger. Like Alvaro.

When I called him a week later, he told me the story of Wander Expeditions. In his late twenties, Alvaro yearned to travel and decided to take a sabbatical from work. *Sounded familiar.* With a longing for more travel after his sabbatical and soon after COVID hit, Alvaro found himself without a job. He took the opportunity to launch a boutique travel company for unique destinations and experiences. As the website put it, "Wander Expeditions specializes in creating travel families out of a group of strangers in some of the world's most exotic countries." In the short time it had been in operation just after the pandemic, it offered excursions to Kurdistan, Moldova, and Socotra, as not many countries had reopened yet.

As for upcoming trips, Wander planned to go to Iraq, Afghanistan, and Saudi Arabia when those countries opened post-COVID. I told him my mother was born in Baghdad and it was a dream of mine to go there. He said, "Barry, with your background and now a much easier visa policy, you absolutely have to go to Iraq. That is a no-brainer. It is your heritage." It seemed like I had been waiting forever for someone to say something like that. "But in the meantime, a Uganda expedition is going to be announced in a week. You should join us," Alvaro said.

From looking at his Instagram, I knew Alvaro's expeditions cultivated a younger group of people than I typically hung out with. I was curious how young. "What are the demographics of the people going on this trip?"

"Probably an average age of around thirty, maybe less."

"Alvaro, I'm over sixty!"

"Perfect," he said. "You'll be the senior of the group and the oldest person to have ever traveled with Wander Expeditions."

As I hung up, I was in a daze. I'd fantasized about going to all the places Alvaro mentioned, places like Iraq, Saudi Arabia, and Syria. They were destinations for the intrepid traveler: hard to reach, often labeled "no-go" zones, countries known in the world of geopolitics, but rarely understood from a human-to-human standpoint. As with Jordan, I no longer wanted to talk about countries based on something I'd read or seen on TV; I wanted to experience them. That was how I learned about the world best. Somehow, I'd never seriously explored how to reach these less-traveled places. But Alvaro said it was a no-brainer that I *should* consider widening my travel boundaries.

He told me that, like him, over two hundred and fifty people in the world had traveled to *every* country; they were called UN Masters. These were the verified ones. Alvaro estimated that there were thousands of others pursuing the same goal, "extreme travelers," and then he continued, "But the more competitive ones are sometimes disparagingly labeled 'country counters.'"

Even so, I scrambled to count. Time to consult my trusty Excel sheets: 121. *Only seventy-two to go.*

I had to laugh. *Only* seventy-two—I was already thinking like one of them, an extreme traveler counting up my countries. I had traveled a lot in my life, but until that moment, it had all felt like a series of random trips. But now, I knew. I was going to travel to every country in the world.

There had been a few moments in my life when I knew exactly what I needed to do. I needed to work in Paris. I needed to be with Jackie. I needed to create Caravan to Class. I needed to study Arabic. And now, I knew that I was incredibly lucky to be in the position to add this to my list: *I would travel to every country in the world.* I didn't just want to see new countries. I wanted to feel the pulse of the world again. Its people, its beauty, its raw edges, all of it. For the first time since Jackie's passing, I felt a real sense of direction.

Part 4

Project 193: The First Step

Starting the Quest, Carrying Her Spirit

Chapter 14

Rapids and Primates

*A journey of a thousand miles
begins with a single step.*
—Lao Tzu

**October 2021
Uganda**

Knowing what you need to do is one thing; figuring out how to begin is another. I didn't want to take just a few trips. I was stepping into something bigger that I couldn't fully name yet. But Wander Expeditions (WE) made things easy for me.

WE wasn't your typical first-come, first-served travel company: I could not just book a trip but had to apply, put myself out there, and hope I'd be chosen. To curate the best "travel family" for each trip, Alvaro asked every candidate to answer a series of somewhat awkward questions, including "When was the last time you cried?" and to send a brief introduction video and travel résumé. I was comfortable with my travel cred, but a video of myself, that was a bit outside my comfort zone.

Given that I was twice as old as most of the WE candidates, I was truly surprised when the email came through: "Congratulations! You made it and are one of the travelers selected for our Uganda Expedition."

In putting together his "travel families," Alvaro often picked solo travelers to foster an inclusive group dynamic. And dynamic the group was when we met up at our hotel in Kampala. I can't say I was feeling it as I sat among our group of energetic twenty- and early-thirty-year-olds on the long bus ride to Jinja rapids, billed as "the place for adrenaline junkies." On the way, Alvaro briefed us, describing them as world-class rapids with even a few Class Six stretches that only experts can run. Okay, *this* was not part of the plan. . . . Thankfully, a few moments later, he continued to say we were a big enough group to potentially have an "easy boat" and a "hard boat." When the briefing was over, I walked back to Alvaro's seat and kneeled beside him.

"If there's an easy boat," I said quietly, "count me in." Alvaro smiled and gave me a thumbs-up. For once, it felt okay not to pretend I had nothing to prove.

When we got to the launch site, we went over safety instructions, and Alvaro asked for a show of hands from those who wanted to be in the easy boat. I started to raise mine, but no other hands were going up. I quickly put mine back down before anyone could notice. I should have known. These were *kids*. Of course, every single one of them was game for anything. Why else would they sign up to go to Uganda with Wander Expeditions?

During the lead-up to this trip, it took me a few terse exchanges to realize that Alvaro, at that early point of launching WE, was a one-man operation and not keen on answering my many questions about the details of the trip: *Which airline should I take to Uganda? When are others arriving in Kampala? How long are some of the bus rides?* Thirty years younger, Alvaro had a more accomplished travel résumé than I. It was a reminder to let go of my need for total control. Control had been exactly what I needed these past few years. Agency over a life that had crashed and burned. Without knowing it, Alvaro had given me a wake-up call toward living again.

Once we started paddling on the water, I began to get to know some of my travel mates and found myself relaxing and thoroughly enjoying myself. That was, until I saw what was ahead.

Oh my God.

Before I knew it, we were plunging into an angry, violent cauldron of waves endlessly tumbling over each other. And then we were thrown into the water.

I'd been thrown from rafts before: on the Zambezi in Zimbabwe, the Pacuare in Costa Rica, the Rogue in Oregon, but nothing prepared me for this. One moment I was in the raft, the next I was swallowed by the torrent, disoriented and gasping. Knowing the Ugandan guides were searching for us in their kayaks offered little comfort. Trapped beneath the surface, I thrashed blindly, unsure which way was up, afraid a limb would catch on the rocks, but all I felt was water. It seemed like forever before I surfaced and grabbed the rope trailing from the raft. Manon, a young French woman, appeared beside me, clutching the same rope. Between ragged breaths, she said, "I thought I was going to die." *You read my mind.*

When we got to shore, it was clear that we all felt like we'd been through something intense together, and for me, that was the start of feeling part of this youthful group. Like I had when I ran the Dushanbe International Half-Marathon in Tajikistan, I felt truly alive. This time was different—part awe, part vulnerability, part adrenaline. I recalled a quote from Joseph Campbell, the writer and lecturer who said, "I don't believe people are looking for the meaning of life as much as they are looking for the experience of being alive." Sure, getting thrown into that furious water was terrifying, but it also shook something loose. Maybe this whole journey would require that kind of surrender.

On the long bus ride the next day, I still felt the aliveness. I also felt totally comfortable with this high-energy group of much younger people who were belting out songs that I had never heard. It was a wildly diverse group of people I never would have crossed paths with back home: Despina, a chiropractor from Cyprus; Isabelle, a techie from Poland; Rudina, working in oil in the UAE; and Brian, a New Jersey bartender with dreadlocks and tattoos covering every visible inch of skin except his face.

Queen Elizabeth National Park, Uganda

A few days later, we arrived at Queen Elizabeth National Park, renowned for its incredible biodiversity, with savannah, forests, wetlands, and lakes all in roughly 750 square miles. As we drove into the park, I began to understand why Winston Churchill said, "For magnificence, for variety of form and color, for profusion of brilliant life, bird, insect, reptile, beast, for vast scale, Uganda is truly 'the Pearl of Africa.'"

Here, we would spend the next two days checking out the big animals, the biggest being, of course, the elephants. While I'd told some of my travel mates about losing Jackie, I hadn't discussed the circumstances of her death. Up until then, I couldn't stand to talk or hear about elephants or even see pictures of them. After Jackie died, I removed the many elephant representations from the house, photos, figurines, even the pen on her desk. They were all just triggers for me. But refusing to see elephants these past years also felt like closing a door on part of who she was, her deep love for the animal, and on our shared story. Deciding to come to Uganda and see them was a decision to open up again. And now, I'd be coming face to face with the animals themselves.

When we got to Mount Elizabeth, Alvaro distributed the keys to our cabins, each with an imprinted animal image. He handed me the one with the elephant. I froze. Alvaro caught my expression. "I'll fill you in later," I said. When I did, he sympathetically offered to switch rooms for me. By then, it was too late. I was over the initial shock of staying in the Elephant Cabin.

At breakfast the next morning, I put on my game face. By then, most of the group was aware of how I'd lost Jackie. Alvaro had sensitized them to the situation. Everyone was empathetic, with more than a few gentle pats on the back. I did appreciate their concern but didn't want to dwell on my psychological state, especially not right before the possible encounter.

We got into our jeeps and started off. Surrounded by youthful energy, I could not help but be excited myself as I remembered the first time I was on safari twenty-six years earlier with Jackie. Then, only a few minutes into our ride, someone shouted from one of the jeeps, "Look at that majestic elephant!"

There it was, the "thing" that had lurked in the back of my mind for almost four years. I couldn't call it a monster. But was it majestic? It was standing just thirty feet away, chomping on leaves with its tusks pointing toward the sky. But now that I was up close, focusing on every detail, majestic was exactly what it was.

I had braced for a tidal wave of grief, but instead, I was struck by the sheer beauty of the creature. Silent. Powerful. Glorious. And then, just like that, it was gone, swallowed by the bush behind us. Our convoy pushed ahead, and the beautiful creatures just kept coming: herds of elephants, prides of lions, leaps of leopards in trees, gangs of buffaloes, and a number of other animals like hyenas and baboons. And in the afternoon, we boarded an open-air boat on a lake to see more hippos than we could count.

I barely had time to process what I was seeing, let alone feel. We were moving at breakneck speed, young-people speed. We'd only been in Uganda three days, and as far as I was concerned, we'd already done enough for a month's worth of travel. So, imagine my surprise when we got back to our camp at the end of the day and found that the excitement wasn't quite over.

I heard yelling in the direction of my cabin and could see, not more than twenty-five feet away, a massive bull elephant chewing on an acacia branch. Some of the group members were taking selfies with the elephant in the background, and suddenly, *I snapped*. After the shock of that soul-crushing day in late 2017, I was not even sure I remembered all the details. But I knew this could be a very dangerous situation, and I needed to warn the group.

"Guys, that is a very dangerous animal," I yelled. "You're way too close to it. I wouldn't be where you are and doing what you are doing." They backed away somewhat, but they continued with their selfies. I couldn't bring myself to increase the intensity of my warnings, nor could I watch. It was almost like a bad dream that I simply had to get away from. With that, I stepped into my cabin and, for the first time in a while, *broke down*. Trauma lingers, and finds its moments.

Reflecting on the Elephant Cabin incident, I realized I hadn't come to Uganda expecting healing. The experience offered a valuable lesson that maybe healing doesn't happen when you seek it; maybe it happens when you open yourself up to what the world has to offer.

A few nights later, on the last evening of the trip, we all gathered for a drink at our hotel in the capital. As I looked around the table at my fourteen travel mates, each from different backgrounds, shapes, and cultures, I realized I genuinely liked every one of them, and even planned to stay in touch with a few.

Sure, I was excited for my upcoming solo travels to South Sudan and Rwanda. But I also knew now that I couldn't separate this awe-filled journey from the people who had shared it. Right then, it hit me: Project 193 wasn't just about visiting every country, or chasing iconic sights, or even collecting unforgettable experiences. It was about something deeper.

Letting the world in, not just its wildness, but its rawness, its chaos, and most of all, its people—that's where the healing lives. In the end, Uganda, even with the elephant test, was about forging new connections with like-minded travelers and discovering an unexpected sense of belonging.

Rwanda

A forest of bamboo trees towered far above me, their trunks covered in moss and vines that created a labyrinth of green, blocking out the sun. Ahead, there was a wall of jungle, but by the time I reached it, the rangers had already cut a path with their machetes. We were trekking through Volcanoes National Park on our way to one of the great experiences on planet Earth.

There is no way of knowing when the magic moment will arrive, no way to be ready for it. One moment I was following the rangers as they cut a path through the jungle. The next, I turned a corner and there it was: a massive male silverback gorilla beating his chest and the ground shaking as he thundered past me just eight feet away. If it hadn't happened so fast, I would have jumped out of my skin. Instead, I just stood in awe. *It was the most beautiful thing I'd ever seen.*

To observe a four-hundred-pound silverback at a short distance in the jungle is something that no amount of zoo frequenting can prepare you for. The gorilla seemed aware that we were there, but he didn't try to scare us away. Surprised not to feel fear, instead, as I observed him, I felt a deep humility in the face of this animal's power and gratitude that he allowed us to be there. That is, until he got tired and rambled away. As we moved deeper into the jungle, we eventually stumbled upon the rest of the family of gorillas. In it was another, much older and less mobile silverback, some grown females, other midsized gorillas, and some babies. They ran past us and rolled down the hillside, playing games or just amusing me. And I was thoroughly amused. I could not wipe the smile off my face as I tried to keep up with them and hold my footing through a verdant and steep forest. That night, while drinking a beer in my lodge, the bartender asked me how my day with the gorillas was.

Without thinking, I responded, "My friend, *that* was a top-five life experience for me."

Gisenyi

I had one more stop to make before I could feel complete with my trip to Rwanda. During the WE Uganda expedition, I had gotten friendly with our guide named Obed, who left a profound impression on me. A Tutsi, he shared that he had lost a significant number of family members in the Rwandan genocide and had himself spent years in various refugee settlements. Rebels even kidnapped him at one point, trying to conscript him as a child soldier. His composure and ever-present smile suggested a deep resilience forged through hardship.

In 1994, Rwanda endured one of the most tragic periods of the modern era. During just one hundred days, members of the Hutu ethnic majority slaughtered close to a million Tutsi, an ethnic minority, using mostly machetes. Possibly half of the entire Tutsi population and 10 percent of Rwanda's total population were slaughtered in just over three months, as I learned at the Kigali Genocide Museum—a rate of one slaying every ten seconds. The international community did little to intervene until it was too late, a painful and tragic chapter in our shared humanity that will echo through time.

On my final day in Rwanda, I asked Obed for permission to stop by his home in Gisenyi, on the border with DRC, to give his wife, Sifa, a welcome present for their new baby girl. She'd been born while Obed was leading our group in Uganda. He had another group lined up in Uganda after our tour and wouldn't get home to meet his daughter for another week. He gave me the go-ahead, and when my guide and I arrived, I was unprepared for Sifa to invite us into their humble house for fresh fruit and drinks.

As we ate the juicy mango and watermelon she had set on the table, she brought out her new daughter and asked if I wanted to hold her. But the way she held her out to me made it clear that it wasn't really a request. It had been a while since I held a baby, but as soon as I took her in my arms, it all came back. Who does not remember holding their infant child, marveling at each tiny finger and toe? I could not contain the pure joy I felt, as holding her released a flood of memories from my first days of fatherhood. I recalled a letter I wrote to Benjamin on his twentieth birthday during his first year at Georgetown, just two months before we lost Jackie. In it, I tried to describe the feeling I had the day he was born: *It was almost like seeing life completely differently, an important reason for being alive, the overwhelming rush of unconditional love for someone that I'd never felt before.*

In the few minutes that I held Obed and Sifa's little daughter, I felt an unexpected connection to all of them, and to all those memories for which I was deeply grateful. It reminded me that no matter how many miles I traveled, the most profound journeys often take you inward.

After we left, I texted Obed a photo of me holding the daughter he hadn't met yet: Obed, my friend, what an amazing experience. Thank you. Seeing your beautiful family and holding your baby girl has been a highlight of an already amazing trip.

Obed's response came immediately, opening with emojis for tears: I am full of feelings right now. Thank you for visiting my family. So much emotion for me. More than just ticking off countries, I was gathering something else: moments of meaning, glimpses of connection I hadn't expected.

As I left Rwanda, I felt a profound respect for the country as a whole. From learning about its difficult history and speaking with people about the rehabilitation from the genocide twenty-five years earlier, it was clear that leadership had a good bit to do with its positive path. President Paul Kagame, who was the leader of the Tutsi resistance that liberated Rwanda from the Hutu rebels, took a courageous path toward reconciliation and unification after the death and destruction in the 1990s. While Kagame's administration faces increasing criticism for undemocratic practices and alleged support for M23 rebels in DRC, Rwanda has made notable progress, with universal health care, a solid infrastructure, and a strong sense of public order.

Today, many Rwandans no longer identify primarily as Hutu or Tutsi, a division once emphasized by colonial rulers. When asked, they say, "We are all Rwandan." It made me reflect on how identity can both divide and unify, and how much there is to learn from Rwanda's ongoing path toward reconciliation. If Rwanda could begin again from the unimaginable, maybe we all can find ways to begin again from whatever pain we carry.

My visit to Rwanda also reminded me that cruelty doesn't just happen *over there*. It can happen anywhere we begin to see others as less than human. And for me, now having seen this country with my own eyes, Rwanda was never again going to be "over there."

Chapter 15

Aristotle in the Desert

*Happiness is activity in
accordance with virtue.*
—Aristotle

**December 2021
Saudi Arabia**

I didn't have a plan for visiting the remaining sixty-eight countries, but apparently, I didn't need one yet. Wander Expeditions did a great job of planning for me. I had applied for the WE Saudi road trip before I left for Uganda, and on the day I got home, I had an email waiting that I had been accepted. In having to apply for a trip without being assured of being selected, I was learning that surrendering a bit of control didn't mean losing direction; it meant making room for whatever came my way.

Boasting Islam's two most important places of worship, Mecca and Medina, Saudi Arabia has the world's largest oil reserves and is going through perhaps one of the most dynamic changes of any country. The controversial crown prince is trying to open up the previously ultra-conservative country, taking power away from the hardline Islamists who have had significant control over the people's freedoms in the past. I wanted to see for myself these changes, both the old and the hopeful.

When I met my WE group at the Movenpick Hotel in Jeddah, this time I felt immediately at home. I had learned during the Uganda trip that Alvaro was an excellent judge of character, sincerely interested in the people traveling with him, but also an alpha type who could be demanding at times. We had found a good place of mutual respect and understanding. Like WE Uganda, I was the oldest of the group of nine by twenty years, with the youngest members in their thirties. Most were European, and most already knew each other from Instagram or from other WE trips. The community vibe was immediate.

Over the next eight days, I learned as much about the extreme-travel community as I did about Saudi Arabia. We had no guide this time and rented two cars. Our destination was the border areas with Yemen in the south, five hundred miles down the western coast, and then eight hundred miles inland to Riyadh. We began to get to know each other the way people do on long drives.

When we stopped to eat, it wasn't as easy as pulling into a roadside restaurant. At one place, where the chicken and meat kebabs displayed behind the counter made our mouths water, we asked for one of their many empty tables. But the man behind the counter said something in fast Arabic that seemed to amount to a no.

Hungry verging on hangry, I took him on. "Lughrati alarabia laysat jayyid jidan, wa lakin hal yumkin al'hasul ala tawila?" (My Arabic is not so good, but can we please have a table?) Sure, it was just a table and we were hungry, but asking for it felt like reclaiming a sense of fairness.

"Yumna'e ala annisae tanawul eta'am hun, wa lakin yumkin tanawul eta'am fi alkharij." His response, which I translated to the group, shut my idea of fairness down pretty quickly: "Women are forbidden to eat food inside here, but you can order food for takeout." It didn't matter that the women in our group were dressed in full-length burqas. I guess rules are rules in Saudi.

We discovered a McDonald's only a half-hour drive away. We hadn't planned on McDonald's, but at this point, any food would do. But it wasn't the familiar environment we'd been counting on. There were two front entrances, and once inside, a wall stood where the other half of the restaurant should have been. It didn't take long to figure out we were on the "wrong" side. The restaurant manager came right over and told us in English that this side was for men only, and since our group included women, we were supposed to be on the *family side*. Finally, having found our way to the end of the cultural maze, we got to eat our Big Macs and french fries.

By the time we checked into our hotel in the coastal city of Jizan, we were catching on to how things worked here. Near the Yemen border, women couldn't stay alone, so I was paired in a two-room suite with Elena from Spain and Kristina from Serbia, my new roomies. As it turned out, the arrangement offered me a fascinating window on the extreme-travel community.

In talking with Elena, I learned that she'd grown up in a conservative household in Spain, where travel wasn't an option, but while studying in France during her youth, she caught the travel bug anyway. She pursued teaching to travel summers and eventually joined the global circuit, teaching at international schools in China, Malaysia, Kazakhstan, and beyond. Every third year, she took a full year off just to travel. Elena had racked up travel experiences from a ton of countries, each one to reclaim the lack of opportunity to travel in her youth. Both of us seemed to be chasing something unfinished, Elena, her youth, and I, my future.

As we walked around the town, people were overjoyed to see tourists. I say "people"; I really mean "men." There was not one woman on the street. While we were walking around town, men would stop their cars in the middle of the street and motion with their phones, asking to take a selfie with us, and sometimes even saying "selfie." The word "selfie" had only just become part of my vocabulary, yet somehow it was well known even in the southernmost province of Saudi Arabia. *Go figure.* But my most prized selfie, while in Saudi, didn't start with good intentions.

We were on a remote road in the high desert, heading from Jizan to Najran, just ten miles from the Yemeni border. That stretch of Yemen was Houthi-controlled and at war with Saudi Arabia, an active security zone.

Without warning, two Saudi police vehicles pulled up behind us, swerving to force us to stop. What were the chances this would end well?

Two officers approached. Alvaro, our driver, rolled down his window. We had no Saudi guide, and I was the only one with any Arabic—but just enough to understand trouble, not talk us out of it.

"Jawazikum, min fudlik," one officer said gruffly. (Passports, please.) We passed them up to Alvaro.

As the officers walked away, we quietly debated our fate: a fine, a long delay, maybe even a trip to the station, despite having proper authorization.

But five minutes later, one officer returned, his serious expression gone. The others were now laughing and chatting by their cars. I leaned forward from the back seat to catch his words.

"Kul shey taman. Intum har fi althahab." (Everything's okay. You're free to go.)

"Shokran Luk, nahnu sa'id jidan an yakun hun fi al Saudia," I responded. And with my words, "Thank you very much, we are happy to be here in Saudi Arabia," I could see a smile on his face.

After all the random selfies we'd taken with strangers, why not one with the Saudi police? With that, I held up my phone to him with the word, "Selfie?" I knew it was a long shot. But surprisingly, he nodded his head and pointed to the side of the road, indicating yes. So our whole group got out of both cars, and the four police officers wove their way in between us as we snapped a few selfies, with smiles all around. When we first got stopped, I'd expected suspicion, even hostility. But what I found instead was an encounter of curiosity, friendliness, and a reminder that fear often has more to do with stories we're told than the people we meet.

Not long after, we arrived at a place very few tourists go, Najran, west of the country's Empty Quarter, and the southernmost town in Saudi Arabia. We stopped for lunch at the only open place, a Yemeni restaurant, and ate on the floor. We were quickly brought all kinds of dishes to be eaten communally: Arabic bread (pita) as big as a doormat, vegetables, kabobs, rice, and pickles. The place was packed, of course with men only. Toward the end of the meal, a man walked over to us, dressed traditionally in a thawb, to introduce himself in broken English. "I welcome you to my country. I like America." He didn't know that the group was basically all European. When we got up to leave to pay, the person at the register said that our bill had already been paid. It was a gesture I hadn't expected. A free lunch, from a stranger in the desert. Even in the harshest landscapes, kindness can still find its way.

We checked in for the last night before starting the long drive back to Riyadh. At the hotel, I saw a woman in full burqa managing the front desk. She seemed to have a longer conversation with Alvaro than I thought was normal for just check-in stuff. Alvaro noticed me listening to their conversation, and that night at dinner, he said, "She actually looked me up on Instagram, followed me, and then sent me a private message welcoming us to her town." Then, with a sheepish grin, he said, "I think she was hitting on me."

It was the first meaningful interaction we'd had with a woman the entire trip. I had read a lot of press recently about Saudi Arabia opening things up for women, like driving and unchaperoned trips. Maybe that kind of change was still mostly confined to Riyadh or Jeddah. Out here, it felt like a different Saudi Arabia.

After five days in South Saudi, we started the long drive to Riyadh, from where we'd all be departing. We spent the night in our first real city, Taif, since leaving Jeddah after the first day. Not super hungry, I skipped the group dinner and walked to the nearby mall. I saw a Starbucks sign, a beacon of familiarity, and, *of course*, I walked right up to the counter to order my usual double espresso. After paying, I turned around to discover that I was the only foreigner in the place but also the only male customer, the opposite of what we saw in Southern Saudi. There must have been fifteen or so women at different tables, all in full black burqas as if that were the required uniform of Starbucks Saudi. I tried not to stare, but it was difficult not to. I thought, *What I would give to be able to have a normal conversation with them.*

Watching them lift their veils to sip their coffee, I felt unexpectedly disconnected. I tried to be respectful, but something felt missing, like I was seeing people but not truly seeing them. It left me questioning my own assumptions and the limits of cross-cultural understanding.

The next day, we set out for Riyadh in the afternoon. After a few hours in the van, we reached a point where we were all talked out. Even with the best travel family, you run out of things to say. So, we just turned up the music. Some of the group sang, while Elena danced in her seat. It was some kind of Euro music I was unfamiliar with. Content to listen, I watched as our van neared the end of the high desert stretch, the outskirts of a large town coming into view. A quiet peace settled over me. The adventure itself—the clash of cultures, the shifting landscapes, the company—was enough to fill me with joy. But most of all, I felt a sense of belonging I hadn't known since losing Jackie. It wasn't that deep sense of "place" you have with a spouse of many years, but it was an emerging sense that I had sort of found "a traveler's home."

As dusk fell, with the sun setting in an orange hue in the distance, somebody's playlist segued from Euro-pop to a salsa number, and Alvaro impulsively pulled to the side of the road. Within seconds, everyone was out of the car, including me. Yitzhak the Aruban and Elena took the lead cutting up a rug on the side of the road in bumfuck Saudi Arabia, cars slowing down to look, some yelling encouragement in Arabic out the window.

Alvaro had been giving me some space all week about not participating in the late-night shisha sessions or having my quiet moments in the car. But somehow, I knew I wasn't getting out of this one. So I danced. And while I could not compete with my mostly Latino friends, I gave it my best shot. As I did, my face lit up with a smile I couldn't suppress. This was living, what Aristotle called *eudaimonia*: somewhere between happiness and fulfillment. For him, happiness was "an activity in accordance with virtue." *Was this what he meant, that fulfillment isn't found, but danced into?*

I hadn't just stepped out of the van; I'd stepped out of the shadows of grief. The dancing was a joyful affirmation that kindred spirits, extreme travelers, had found one another in the far reaches of Earth. Feet on the ground, heart open, I was saying yes not just to places, but to people, experiences, and reflection.

Chapter 16

Where Time Stands Still

*A great and mysterious wasteland,
a sun-punished place . . . a mystery,
something concealed and waiting.*
—John Steinbeck, *Travels with
Charley in Search of America*

**January 2022
Mauritania**

After a few Wander Expeditions trips, I realized I was sliding, almost unintentionally, into the world of extreme travel. I hadn't planned for this to become an identity, but maybe that's how purpose finds you, not with a bang, but with clues along the trail. Yes, I had set out to travel to every country in the world but thought it would be more of a solo journey. I had been unaware of the vibrancy of the community of those with the same goal. On my Wander Expeditions Saudi group trip, I discovered from Alvaro, Elena, and my travel mates that there were entire clubs and communities for people like me: Travelers Century Club (TCC), Most Traveled People (MTP), and NomadMania. How had I not known about this?

I downloaded apps like Been and Mark O'Travel to track my countries (finally embracing tech, like when Jackie and the boys pried the flip phone from my hands). Over the holidays, while the kids were home, I went down the rabbit hole: Facebook groups, Instagram feeds, even a podcast called *Counting Countries*. These weren't just travelers; they were mission-driven adventurers tracking every border crossing. For someone who still thought TripAdvisor was cutting edge, it was humbling and exhilarating at the same time.

By the time I surfaced from my deep dive into the unique world of travel addicts, I was a member of all three travel clubs and regularly using the other non-club resources, ready to take my travel game to the next level. My days were filled with researching countries, trip logistics, and listening to travel podcasts. Who doesn't remember the training they went through trying to get up to speed on a new job? Like my buddy Neil from LA said, "You have a lot of work to do. Traveling is now your full-time employment."

I decided to pick up where I left off before COVID, when I ended my Caribbean travels in Trinidad and Tobago after wrapping up South America with Suriname and Guyana. With only five Caribbean countries left, it made sense to start working through the remaining islands, especially since Saint Lucia, Saint Kitts and Nevis, and Antigua and Barbuda were all conveniently linked by the regional airline Liat. That would mean finishing not just North America, but the entire Western Hemisphere.

To keep up momentum, I realized I needed to plan further ahead, booking trips six months out instead of one at a time. The highlight of this new phase would be a five-week journey through the Middle East, including six Arab countries (five of them new to me) and a long-awaited visit to my mother's birthplace, Baghdad. I could still hear Alvaro's voice urging me, *You must go to Iraq.*

Satisfied that the first half of my 2022 travel plan looked like an extreme traveler's calendar, I turned my attention to providing the boys with some semblance of a holiday tradition. Growing up in an environment where true family feeling rarely happened on holidays, I never saw that as something missing in my life until Jackie came along, family being so central to her core. And it became my foundation as well. But since she died, I'd never re-created the holidays like Jackie did. I knew this wasn't my strength. But the boys needed it, and I owed it to them and Jackie to try. We invited a close circle of longtime friends over, and I made latkes, which even earned a few compliments. As for presents for Benjamin and Daniel, I made it a Gabby Hanukkah. Gabby, our sweet cat, was the last of the brood of pets we'd had before Jackie died. I gave the boys pajamas, puzzles, coffee mugs, and socks, all with Gabby's image. I even put up some Christmas lights and a small tree in Jackie's office. In their glow, I felt her presence in every flicker of light. She had always been the heart of our celebrations; now I was just trying to do the best I could.

The previous New Year's Day, January 1, 2021, I was unsure of what I would be doing once the boys went back to school. But this year, I was genuinely looking forward to expanding my horizons and realizing some memorable travel dreams. As a glorious Sausalito sunrise spread across the bay and the day came to life, I took it as a sign: 2022 would be a year of meaningful progress on my journey. There was no doubt that the adventures, connections, and experiences I'd gathered over the past few months, since launching Project 193, were helping to heal the loss of Jackie. It wasn't a distraction or a way to forget, or even a detour from grief, but a road back to myself.

Mauritania

Chinguetti was a crossing point for the ancient Saharan camel caravan trade dating back a thousand years. Located in the Adrar region of the northwest part of Mauritania, it's known for its well-preserved medieval architecture, including mosques and libraries with an ancient trove of manuscripts, just like Timbuktu. One evening at sunset, my guide, Med, took me by 4X4 to the top of a hill overlooking the town's serene, earth-colored maze of brick structures. It was hard to tell where the desert stopped and the town began, with sand threatening to bury many buildings and carpeting the maze of alleyways. Clearly, the sand was winning the battle, and time was closing in.

We were about to head to our bungalow when we saw something

on a dune far ahead in the distance: strange shapes moving slowly, almost undulating above the sand in single file. *Was this a mirage?* Soon, a large caravan of about twenty camels came into view, with one man leading the herd. Their golden humps swayed rhythmically as their long legs moved through the sand with striking ease, gracefully crossing our path as the sun began to disappear.

Everything about the ancient city of Chinguetti seemed to be frozen in time. I had the same feeling being there as I have each time I go to Timbuktu. What was it about these caravan towns that fascinated me? Maybe it was in my DNA, with my mother being from Baghdad. But more likely, it was the timeless intersection of solitude, survival, and human connection that drew me in. These were places where the vast emptiness of the Sahara gave rise to centers of knowledge, culture, and resilience. Places that still whisper their stories across the sands.

At dawn the next day, I stepped outside the inn with a cup of instant Starbucks and saw a shepherd milking some of his camels. I couldn't resist. I'd seen lattes made with oat, almond, and goat milk, so why not camel?

I tried out my Arabic. "Marhaba, sabah al khir, mumkin al hasul shwe halib min aljimal li qahuati?" (Good morning, can I get a little camel milk for my coffee?)

He looked at me like I had two heads. So I thought I must have mangled the Arabic. But then he gave me a big smile, as if he suddenly realized what this crazy foreigner wanted, and motioned me over. Grabbing the handle of the tin can he was using to catch the milk, he poured a splash into my cup. His smile widened as I sipped my now extra-creamy, salty latte. Not terrible, but I wouldn't recommend Starbucks add it to the menu.

"Ashukr Lak Kathir," I said (I greatly thank you), and walked to the edge of town to take in an unobstructed view of the sunrise over the desert. Here, there was no cell service, no distractions. Just me, the desert, and a shepherd who offered his hospitality. Reflecting on this interaction, I realized that it had collapsed all cultural divides. I didn't need to master Arabic to earn a smile. I just had to try. Maybe life works like that more often than we think.

Over the last few months, I had faced a steep learning curve with the world of extreme travel, and though my style was still evolving, I knew I wanted more of *these* kinds of experiences. And it was becoming clear that the right guides would factor heavily into making that possible. I'd found Med, my Mauritanian guide, on NomadMania's website. He was young and had an infectious love for his homeland. As we drove through the western Sahara Desert, where the sand swept across the highway, he said, "I love showing tourists the bright side of my country, sharing the beauty of our culture and the religion of Islam in the hope that they will come to love and respect us."

One thing I kept seeing in my travels: The need for respect is universal. Even in the humblest circumstances, people carried an innate dignity that demanded recognition. And almost everywhere I went, there was something to learn, often deep wisdom, especially from my guides.

Moments like that unexpected connection over a splash of camel milk reminded me that curiosity and kindness usually open doors. And I resolved to meet each experience with presence and intention: Energy flows where intention goes.

And more immediately, though Arabic in culture and language, the mystique of Mauritania was worlds away from my next stop: oil-rich Kuwait.

Kuwait

Sitting down at the gate for my flight from Dubai to Kuwait City, I noticed *the café*. A few years earlier, I had spent hours sitting at one of their small tables, head down in shock and anguish about the prospect of telling Daniel he had just lost his beloved mom.

To my surprise, this moment now felt distant, almost like a bad dream the day after. There was still rarely a waking hour that I did not think about Jackie, but something had shifted. Even just one year ago, the sight of this café would have broken me down. Now, I felt grateful. Not consumed by grief, but living a life of purpose and adventure while still honoring the outsized role that Jackie had played in my life.

The next adventure awaited me that night, as I was invited to dinner with two Kuwaiti princes. As fate would have it, my cousin Josh had roomed with a Kuwaiti prince named Khalifa while at San Diego State University. *That's right, the Valley Jew and the Muslim prince bunking together.* Tonight, I was the guest of Khalifa's father, Faisal, also a prince from the Al Sabah ruling family. It was his turn to host a *diwaniya*, a centuries-old social custom where men welcome other men into their homes to discuss business, politics, or anything at all. There is a get-together practically every night.

Faisal's home was relaxed, with guests lounging on cushions in a beautifully decorated room. "I appreciate how welcoming everyone is here and the luck I have to be part of this custom on my first night in your country," I said to the group of about seven, including Faisal and Khalifa, his son. I felt honored that they were all willing to keep the conversation going in English, because my Arabic was in no way up to the challenge.

One of Faisal's friends chimed in, "The regular evening get-together is a key part of our culture. It's a space for discussing important matters and building communal ties." Faisal said everybody in his diwaniya circle took turns hosting the gatherings, and he could go to a different one every night.

"I feel, in my country, or at least where I live, people are so busy that the idea of getting together this often to connect might not work. Though I love the idea," I said.

"We do, too, but we're not sure it will last into the next generation. We see our youth using technology and social media so much more than we do. That is their way of connecting," Faisal said. "But we hope they will keep our traditions alive."

For the next hour, we sampled Arabic dishes, mutabbal (a creamy eggplant dish), hummus, tabbouleh, and machboos, the national dish of Kuwait (rice with chicken cooked with fragrant spices) while discussing the political situation in the Middle East, the US, the price of oil, and more. As I was leaving, I looked around the room at the men, some dressed more casually but others in traditional attire in a white thawb and sandals, some in white checked headscarves. Somewhere in the back of my mind, I realized I was the only Jew in a room of mostly devout Muslims. But it didn't matter. We were just people, talking and eating and laughing. Sometimes being welcomed is enough to make you rethink the borders we assume exist between us.

The United States helped prevent Kuwait from being absorbed into Iraq by Saddam Hussein in the early 1990s. That could have played some role in the hospitality I felt. But would people be as welcoming in other Muslim countries on my itinerary? *Would Iraq treat me with the same kindness?* So much of my hopes for this long, five-week trip in the Middle East revolved around this question.

Qatar

My time in Doha was short, but I covered a lot of ground. The city's skyline is one of the most impressive I've seen, a blend of ultramodern architecture with contemporary Islamic design, set against the backdrop of the Arabian Gulf. Strolling the Souq Waqif, the local open-air marketplace, I stumbled onto the Falcon Souq where falcons are sold to locals, a pastime in Qatar since their nomadic existence, when they employed the raptors to hunt for food. The best-trained falcons can sell for as much as $200,000.

As my driver negotiated the maze of construction sites of stadiums being erected for the forthcoming World Cup, we stopped in a coastal area where groupings of tents, camels, and 4X4s were visible in the distance. It was a strange sight in such a modern country. My driver told me that this was a Qatari practice of *al sadu*, where families, even extremely wealthy ones, live in the desert for a month every year to honor their nomadic Bedouin lineage, bringing their falcons and camels with them.

There is so much tradition and community in the remote villages I visited near Timbuktu for Caravan to Class, and life is all about observing cultural heritage. But they also lack so much materially, seemingly stuck on the bottom of Maslow's hierarchy of needs for food, water, and shelter. But in Qatar, a country so wealthy and advanced, I wondered how cultural belonging is balanced with material progress. From what I saw, Qatar's wealth coexisted with deep tradition in ways I hadn't expected. Back in the US, affluence often seemed to isolate people. Here, it felt more rooted, tied to something enduring.

· · ·

My next stop was the place that started me down the path to extreme travel, the place I knew I had to go to the day I first opened Wander

Expeditions' Instagram and saw waves of sand dunes that floated down to the most pristine blue water: the Yemeni island of Socotra.

The one Air Arabia flight per week from Abu Dhabi to Socotra was for mostly locals. The island is the size of Maui in Hawaii, but with only about one hundred tourists at any one time. With no internet access or cell phone coverage, I'd be camping for the entire week with an unknown travel company, Welcome to Socotra (WTS). It was a leap of faith, but I was learning those were essential on this path.

As I waited for the flight at the Abu Dhabi airport, I spoke with a young Yemeni woman living in Bahrain who was traveling with WTS too. Speaking American English without any trace of an accent, Lina told me she'd lived abroad in her youth because of her dad's work. I was already fascinated with all things related to the Arab world and was technically heading to Yemen. So, I just had to find out more about her.

"Surely you lived in the US at some point, judging by how well you speak American English," I probed.

"I have actually never been to the US," she said. "Mostly, I picked up English from watching American movies."

"Mabruk," I said, congratulating her in Arabic. "If I could speak Arabic half as well as you speak English, it would be a life's dream for me."

I'd spent years studying Arabic, and she'd learned English from movies. What kind of genius was this? Whatever the case, I was certain she'd make a fascinating travel mate.

Socotra

Our first morning, we woke at five o'clock to climb the dunes behind our tents and witness a captivating sunrise. We then plunged down five hundred vertical feet of deep sand, running and screaming like kids the whole way. I hadn't even been on Socotra for twenty-four hours, and all my worries about technically being in war-torn Yemen had evaporated. And my disappointment that Lina wasn't in my group didn't last long. There wasn't time for it, as we explored the island nonstop, moving camping sites from one spot more spectacular than the next on a daily basis.

"You know, it's not a great idea to start the trip with the best place," I had teasingly mentioned to our guide, Elena, an anthropologist from Venice.

She smiled. "You should probably wait until you see where we're going in the next few days before saying that."

And so it went, one day more incredible than the next. At Dihamri, a marine reserve, we swam in crystal clear waters among more dolphins than I'd ever seen. We hiked up to the high desert to see massive rocks that formed freshwater swimming holes at their base and visited majestic, isolated villages inhabited by Yemeni family clans. We looked out over an entire valley of dragon blood trees with umbrella-shaped canopies, the trees named for their bloodred sap, once used by Roman gladiators to treat wounds.

It wasn't easy to get to this island, nor was it easy for me to sleep in a tent every night without running water or personal space and endure temperatures of ninety degrees or more. But none of it compared to the stunning beauty and the warmth of the people. We were greeted by every local we met and even welcomed into very modest homes to drink tea. *Who knows, maybe I will travel to mainland Yemen someday when the war stops.* Socotra reminded me of my travels to Africa with Jackie; sometimes the harder the journey, the deeper the memory. It was a connection to an ancient land that had confirmed my yearning to travel here when I first saw Alvaro's Instagram posts, a time when I was really searching for something.

・・・

As luck would have it, I was seated next to Lina on the flight back from Socotra to Abu Dhabi. As we traded stories from our separate adventures, I realized just how much had shifted in the week since I'd last seen her. Something in me had changed, subtly but meaningfully. With no internet or phone service, my senses sharpened, taking in a flood of visual impressions: flora found nowhere else on earth, pristine beaches, mountain lakes, vibrant underwater life, and the remarkably hospitable Yemeni culture. On that remote island, I let go of some lingering trauma I hadn't known I was carrying. What remained was a craving for more of these kinds of adventures but also a sense of expansive calm. If peace could be felt in a place like this, maybe it could be carried back with me too.

After a while, Lina pulled out a book to read, which I could see was written in Arabic. I caught a glimpse of the cover: the Koran. I thought back to all the questions I had neglected to ask Benjamin the year before, when he was deeply engaged in a course on Islam at Georgetown that included reading the Koran.

I had questions but didn't know her well enough to ask. Seeing that I was looking at the book, she preempted me. "I am not a big fan of flying, and it gives me comfort reading it." I knew this was someone I would like to stay in contact with.

Before landing, we exchanged Instagram handles. "Where are you headed next?" she asked.

"Baghdad. My mother was born there."

Lina smiled. "Ah, then we are cousins, ma shaa Allah." (God has willed it.)

Something about the way she said that, full of warmth and sincerity, made me feel as if we really could have been cousins. The world was not smaller than I thought, but simply more familiar than I had allowed.

Chapter 17

A Homecoming of Sorts

For a long time, I sat between two worlds. I had grown up in the West, but my roots were in Africa... Kenya was where I came to understand that I could belong to more than one place.
—Barack Obama (on visiting Kenya)

April 2022
Iraq

One of my favorite quotes from Paul Coelho's *The Alchemist* is "When you want something bad enough, all the universe conspires to help you achieve it." My cousin Ezra and I used to say to each other, "One day we'll go to Baghdad," but as we got older and raised our families, it began to feel as likely as going to the moon. There was a time when I felt the same way about learning Arabic; that, too, seemed as unlikely as going to the moon. During my youth and most of my adulthood, no

American tourists went to Baghdad. But here I was. *A dream deferred was still a dream. All it ever needed was a yes.*

My mom's family left Baghdad in the 1920s, part of the first wave of Jews who sensed the ground shifting beneath them. As old empires, like the Ottomans, fell and new nationalisms rose, the delicate coexistence they had known began to fray. Like so many others, my mom's family chose exile over uncertainty. Today, only faded Stars of David and scattered memories remain of a once-vibrant Jewish life in Baghdad. But it was a dream of mine to get here.

When I tell people, "My mom was born in Baghdad," I say it with pride. Yet despite how proudly I share her origins, so much of her past, like the place she once called home, was pretty much a blur to me. Now over one hundred years old and with a fading memory, my mom didn't remember the exact location of where she had lived. On the drive to my hotel from Baghdad International Airport, we passed by one of my favorite sights in the world: a Starbucks sign. Wait, Starbucks had infiltrated Baghdad? *No way.*

I knew what my first stop was going to be.

I ordered coffee and took a seat near the window. Somehow, this unfamiliar place felt more like home than anticipated. I wasn't sure exactly what to expect of my first moments in Baghdad, unease, maybe some tension. But I certainly didn't expect this, and it didn't take long to realize this wasn't a real Starbucks. Amin Makhsusi, unable to secure a franchise license, had spent years building a perfect imitation logo, menu, even the imported beans and furniture. Finding comfort in a hint of home during those first hours in Iraq might seem odd, even with it being a fake Starbucks. But the comfort? That part was real, a tiny bridge between worlds, between past and present, between me and my mother's birthplace. But from here on, I was ready to leave that bridge behind and experience something unmistakably Baghdad.

After stopping by a falafel stand on the street, I met up with my guide, Haidar, who led me through Al-Rasheed and Al-Mutanabbi Streets. It felt like stepping into a living history book, lined with dazzling Islamic architecture. A few buildings still bore Stars of David from when Jewish life thrived here, ending in the mid-1900s, like in the Al-Bataween neighborhood where my mom had lived, located along the Tigris River. Back then, Baghdad had as many or more Jews than any European city in the world. It even had a Jewish Iraqi finance minister when my mom was a child here. But now only ghosts of my people's past remained.

As we strolled along the cobblestone pathways, sellers offered tastes from their nearby market stalls, but I was tempted only by the aroma of freshly brewed Arabic coffee. That evening, Haidar and I sat at one of the many outdoor coffee shops, packed with mostly men sipping strong coffee and engaged in spirited debate, smoking shisha, playing backgammon and other board games. Those who noticed me, the only foreigner around, gave me welcoming smiles. I leaned back in my chair and took it all in. *I am in Baghdad.* I thought about the many conversations I had shared with Jackie about my dream of traveling to my mom's birthplace before my time was up. *If only she could see me now.*

Traveling in the deep South of Iraq, where the Euphrates coils through the reed-filled marshes, we glided by boat through a landscape that felt suspended in time. Nearby stood the Ziggurat of Ur, rising from the desert like a forgotten monument to one of humanity's first cities, its bricks still holding the heat of four thousand years. Among the broken walls of ancient Babylon, echoes of grandeur lingered. Scholars still debate the existence of the Hanging Gardens, but the reconstructed Ishtar Gate, deep blue with striding lions, offered a vivid glimpse into a civilization that shaped law, myth, and empire.

And amid all the antiquity, we fit in a stop at one of Saddam Hussein's many palaces around Iraq, this one on a hilltop with a commanding view of old Babylon. The interior had only faint bits remaining of frescoes that plundering looters had stripped from the walls. The rooms echoed with the ghost of Saddam, with graffiti everywhere, one reading in Arabic, "Saddam alrahid inteha" (Saddam, the Terrible, is finished).

After two days in the South, we were on our way back north. Our driver stopped at a parking garage and took us to the top floor, where he led us to the railing to take in a striking view. With structures as far as the eye could see in every direction, it looked like a large, very closely packed city.

"Is this Najaf?" I asked Haidar.

"It is the *cemetery* of Najaf," he said.

My God.

The structures were the tombs and mausoleums that made up the biggest Muslim cemetery in the world, Wadi-us-Salaam, known as the "Valley of Peace" in Arabic. It spanned six square kilometers, took up almost 15 percent of the entire city of Najaf, and contained as many as eight million graves. Shia Muslims from around the world aspired to be buried here, near the shrine of Imam Ali, the cousin and son-in-law of the Prophet Mohammed. It was hard to process that more people than the populations of some of the largest cities in America found their final resting place here. Taking one last look across this city of the dead, my breath sharply changed. I felt a strange connection to all those lives, and especially to Jackie, her memory woven into the fabric of loss and love that binds us all. So many stories ended here, and yet somehow, their presence and memory still lingered.

Arriving at a mosque with a golden dome and sparkling minarets, Haidar and I removed our shoes as we stepped into the burial shrine of Ali, one of Shia Islam's most important holy places. The rooms were packed with men sitting on the floor praying, reading the Koran, and rolling their strings of prayer beads one bead at a time. The crypt where Ali is said to be buried was filled with men performing prostrations and reading aloud from the Koran. In a corner of the room, a quiet space opened up to simply observe. The display of humility was deeply moving. I didn't believe in a higher power charting life's course, yet something about being surrounded by such yearning brought an unexpected calm. And in that calm, I found myself closing my eyes and whispering a prayer for Jackie, grateful for the journey, the love we shared, and for the road ahead.

. . .

After a few days, I'd gotten used to passing through many military checkpoints. I'd been nervous at first. But my passport was always returned to me without incident and without the kind of shakedown for money I regularly experienced while traveling in West Africa. About a half hour into this day's drive, though, we encountered something new.

"Wa salam aleikum," I said, wishing "Peace be upon you" to the soldier working the checkpoint with a rifle slung over his shoulder as I handed him my passport.

"Inta ameriki." (You are American.) He took my passport to a small office fifty feet away. A minute later, he returned and motioned for me to follow him.

Haidar gave me a concerned look and got out of the car with me, but the officer put his hand up, indicating that only I was to follow. After a discussion that was too fast for me to understand, Haidar looked at me, clearly worried. "He asked if you speak some Arabic. I told him you do."

"Don't worry, my friend," I said, and walked to the office with the soldier. But I can't say I was entirely comfortable with what could happen here.

Inside, a large man in military dress and a Saddam-like mustache sat behind a desk, smoking a cigarette. He offered me a seat and a cigarette. I accepted the first while he inspected my passport, and I calculated the possibilities.

"Lish inta betzur Al Iraq?" (Why are you visiting Iraq?) and "Wa lish inta tihki arabi?" (Why do you speak Arabic?) he asked.

When I first arrived in Baghdad, I wouldn't have told an Iraqi officer that my mom was born in Baghdad because the following question would likely be, "Are you Muslim, and if not, what religion are you?" But my interactions over the last few days had begun to make me less concerned. "Bahhki shway arabi, Immi inwaladit fi Baghdad munthu waqt tawil." (I only speak a little Arabic, and my mom was born in Baghdad a long time ago.)

Then came the question I'd figured was next. "Inta musalmin?" (Are you Muslim?)

Should I lie and play it 100 percent safe, or should I tell the truth and trust my fate to humanity? "Ana yahud," I said. (I am Jewish.) "Immi intaqalat ila New York eindema kanat sghrira." (My mom moved to New York when she was young.) In this moment, I chose trust, and it answered back.

The officer smiled and said in Arabic, "I welcome you to our country. It is your mother's birthplace; therefore, it is your country as well." I had heard this exact response a few times over the past few days in Iraq when I told people my mom was born in Baghdad. With that, he got up from behind his desk, towering over me, and led me back to the car. After shaking my hand, he touched his hand to his heart, a gesture I'd grown to love seeing in the Arab world; a simple, powerful way of expressing sincerity, respect, and warmth. In that small room with that soldier, I found acceptance. The hand over his heart said more than words ever could.

My mom often spoke of a time when Jews and Arabs in Baghdad lived side by side, with mostly good relations, though undercurrents of tension would sometimes surface. She used to recall once losing coins meant for bread and, fearing punishment by her dad, blaming "some Arab kids," a small story hinting at the complex ties of the time. Nearly a hundred years later, I walked those streets as a welcome stranger, carrying her memories, but the impressions of Baghdad were now mine, shaped by my own journey.

. . .

On the day of my departure, Haidar said he had a surprise for me on the way to the airport. We stopped at what looked like a bakery. Inside were counters packed with Arabic sweets: baklava, qatayef, pancakes with cheese and nuts. Haidar picked out a box and said, "Share this with your mom, a gift from her homeland."

I gave Haidar and our driver a bro-hug goodbye, and they both touched their hands to their heart and said, "Be safe in Beirut, and happy birthday."

I returned the gesture of touching my hand to my heart and then added, "I will never forget this trip or you both as long as I live."

Iraq turned out to be a beautiful surprise. It wasn't the war zone I'd imagined. I never felt threatened, even after telling Iraqis I was Jewish. Long off the tourism map, Iraq was just beginning to open up, yet already knew how to welcome the intrepid traveler. If I was serious about visiting every country, I'd need to get used to going where the world warned me not to. My time here reminded me why: to replace secondhand narratives with firsthand understanding. We all have stories handed down to us. Some we keep; others we outgrow. But the best ones, we write ourselves. As the plane took off from Baghdad, I looked out the window one last time and felt grateful for the opportunity: my time with Haidar, the cups of delicious coffee, my welcoming interaction with the officer, all tethered to the land where my mom was born.

I still had one country left on this Middle East trip, another place most of the world considered dangerous.

Lebanon

A lot had happened in Lebanon the year before my visit; namely, it had hit rock bottom. In 2020, more than two hundred people were killed during a massive blast at the Port of Beirut. The devastating explosion had been triggered by 2,750 metric tons of illegally stored ammonium nitrate, thought to be destined for Syria to be used for bombs. Windows and doors were blown out of buildings as far as a few kilometers away, among them the Grand Meshmosh Hotel where I was staying. That and COVID were the final straws after years of political and economic challenges in the country, causing an almost complete financial collapse, including a 95 percent devaluation of the Lebanese pound.

It was in this even more difficult economic and political environment that Pierre, my guide, a talkative, chain-smoking Christian Lebanese, picked me up for our first day trip. As happy as he was to have some work, he was even happier to have some company with whom to share his bleak outlook.

"Barry, Beirut has caught a cancer and has aged all of a sudden," he said before we'd even been together for an hour. "Its heart will give out soon. My best days are the ones when I meet interesting people like you and can add some value opening a window to my country. But I assure you that does not happen often."

Dude, I just got here. Of course, I wanted to understand the country, but couldn't we get in a little sightseeing before we explored Lebanon's dark side?

Pierre drove me up the steep highway climb out of Beirut, and we stopped for a while to appreciate the commanding view of the Bekaa Valley and the snow-capped mountains in the distance. There aren't many places in the world where you can hit the ski slopes in the morning, tan at the beach in the afternoon, and drink a good glass of local wine in the early evening, but that's Lebanon in mid-April.

This diversity and the cosmopolitan nature of Beirut made it the cultural and business capital of the Middle East. But since the 1970s, when civil war erupted between Christians and Muslims, not only have visitors stayed away, but millions of Lebanese have left the country. Their diaspora spread across the globe, along with their cuisine. I often find myself eating at Lebanese restaurants during visits to Mali and other places in West Africa, like my friend Nasser's place in Conakry, Guinea.

The main event of today's tour was Baalbek, whose history goes back three thousand years. It is thought that it began as a place of pilgrimage and religious worship for the Phoenicians and then became a Hellenistic city under Alexander the Great, finally reaching its peak during the Roman era four hundred years later. Walking through Baalbek, I felt the weight of centuries, Phoenician stones beneath my feet, towering Roman columns above, whispers of pilgrimage and conquest embedded in the dust. It was the feeling of first walking through the Old City of Jerusalem in 1982. Each step up a massive staircase to the Temple of Jupiter revealed the impeccable precision and craftsmanship of a civilization that once ruled the known world.

On the drive here, we'd passed fields of tent-like structures, and Pierre had explained that Lebanon still hosts over a million Syrian refugees, many of whom live in makeshift shelters on farms where they work for low wages in exchange for a roof over their heads. On the way back to the hotel, Pierre asked if we could stop by the tent encampment of a refugee family he knew.

"I usually buy Syrian bread from them when I am in the area."

"By all means," I said. "I'd love to meet them."

Pierre called ahead to let them know we were coming, and I could understand some of the conversation, something about it being Ramadan, and we wouldn't stay long. We pulled up about thirty minutes later alongside some farmland. There was a series of makeshift wooden structures stamped with "UNHCR" (UN High Commissioner for Refugees) and sidewalls stapled to thin wooden posts. There seemed to be three similar contiguous structures. We were greeted by a woman named Aisha Al Ismael and her eldest daughter, Amal, who invited us into one of the dwellings. Inside, there appeared to be a few rooms separated by plywood but no doors, and with corrugated metal roofing that rattled in the breeze. Beneath our feet, a thin plastic tarp, tacked to the dirt below, served as both floor and insulation.

Aisha had prepared some food and asked us to sit down at the makeshift table that overlooked the agricultural fields. We were joined by two very young children who were Aisha's grandchildren, Aisha's younger daughter, and her husband, Ahmed. I soon realized that Pierre and I were the only ones eating any of the small pizza-like food with cheese and za'atar, a Middle Eastern spice blend, and drinking the mint tea. It felt strange to be invited to eat in the middle of the day during Ramadan, when Muslims fast from dawn to sundown, but Aisha had gone out of her way to prepare this for us.

As we exchanged small talk, I caught bits and pieces of what they said, and Pierre helped fill in with some translation. With my choppy Arabic, I told them a little about myself. All the while, I was overcome by this beautiful family who seemed open and happy to have me in their humble abode. Aisha was engaged in conversation with Pierre that was too fast for me to follow. So, I started speaking with Amal. She was wearing a set of pink Minnie Mouse sweats with a black hijab covering her hair. She had a kind face and appeared to be in her early thirties, volunteering an Arabic word here and there when I struggled to complete a thought.

When we were done eating, Aisha went into the kitchen for a while, and Pierre told me that only six months before, Ahmed and his wife, who were still sitting with us, had lost their six-year-old son and Ahmed's brother, killed by a land mine in a field where they were harvesting potatoes. Before he could finish, I began to tear up and had to walk outside, telling Pierre I needed some fresh air. Losing Jackie was the hardest thing I've ever gone through, but she had been killed by a wild animal. The idea that a child could die in a field from a hidden land mine shattered me.

Soon after, they joined me outside, and it was time to say our goodbyes. As I walked to the car, I wanted to give them some gesture of support. But it was such a special feeling meeting Aisha, Amal, and their family, I did not want it to seem like it was being reduced to a transactional experience. But this time, I couldn't help it. I gave Pierre $200 to pass along, hoping that the gesture helped, even a little. It seemed to be the least I could do after such generosity and effort.

Back in the car, I watched the tent homes pass by and imagined all the families like Aisha and Amal's, living such precarious lives as refugees. As we pulled away, I just shook my head thinking about them and Jackie. *Pain knows no borders.*

"They didn't want to accept your money, but I gave them no choice. Maybe Amal could help you with your Arabic as a return gesture," Pierre said. "She is on WhatsApp."

I laughed. "I'd love that. You can see how much help I need."

The next few days, we traveled up and down the Lebanese coastline to see other Phoenician marvels like the cities of Byblos and Tyre. In Sidon, we could hear the call for prayer from the Eyn Al Hilweh refugee camp, the largest Palestinian camp in Lebanon, established in 1948. I wondered what the people inside would think of me, a Jew, *the other*, walking right along the perimeter.

That night, I celebrated my sixty-second birthday at a restaurant in Beirut by myself. I was in a reflective mood after just visiting my mom's homeland and the experience with Aisha, Amal, and their family. I thought, *In the end, maybe we don't return home to find where we belong. Maybe we return with the knowledge that* home *can be more a feeling than a physical place.*

As I waited for my baked eggplant dish with pomegranate and sipped a glass of bright Cinsault that few people outside Lebanon would ever taste, I remembered Jackie asking me years ago what I wanted to do for my birthday. "I want to celebrate in Damascus," I told her jokingly.

But here I was in Beirut, just two hours away. Close enough. *One dream at a time, Barry.*

Chapter 18

Roman Antiquity in Africa

*It is extraordinary how one travels
thousands of miles, to stumble across
traces of a civilization that once
was the center of the world.*
—Agatha Christie

**August 2022
Algeria**

For years, I've sent early Friday "Shabbat Shalom" texts to a few friends. I'm not religious, but I've always liked the idea of welcoming the weekend. Jackie, though not Jewish herself, often hosted Shabbat dinners and knew the blessings as well as I did. It was our way of creating ritual and community, a kind of sanctuary that held the family together. With the heart of our home now missing, I realized how much it challenged me to keep the threads of our family intact. But in trying, I was learning that rituals, big or small, are how we cope with loss.

Every Friday morning, a playful tradition emerged with my friend Neil, racing to see who could send the first GSM (Good Shabbos, matey) text. And it was usually me from my local Starbucks at around 5:00 a.m. while I was drinking that double shot of espresso. Now, after my trip to the Middle East, I had new friends in the Arab world to wish a "Juma'a Mubarak" (Blessed Friday). That first Friday back, I smiled at the messages already waiting for me, emoji greetings from Faisal in Kuwait, warm notes in Arabic from Amal in Lebanon and Lina in Bahrain. I might never see them again, but these small connections kept me tethered to a region I wanted to know more about and hoped to return to soon. And even emojis, from a different culture in a faraway land, felt somehow meaningful.

Project 193 was in full swing. It wasn't a hobby anymore. The quest had become my life's central mission.

And more immediately, there were happy family matters to tend to: Daniel was graduating from the University of Colorado. Had it really been four years since that Target run, shopping for stuff for his dorm, just the two of us, without Jackie and feeling so lost? Four years since I'd extended my stay in Boulder because he, or rather we, weren't quite ready to face the world alone? Daniel had not only persevered; he had thrived, graduating Phi Beta Kappa. It was bittersweet without Jackie, whose deep love had helped shape the man he'd become. Sometimes I wondered whether she somehow knew.

My belief system is generally grounded in science and what I can observe firsthand. But I've traveled the world enough, and seen how different cultures grapple with death and the afterlife, to stay open to the possibility that some form of existence continues beyond this life. Maybe Jackie's love still existed in some spiritual realm beyond separation. Or maybe I just needed to believe it to have a thread to hold on to.

As Daniel began university, our therapist warned, "Be ready for anything, especially with boys who struggle to express grief. You never know how they'll deal with losing a parent." Still unsettled from my own loss, I kept a close watch on my sons, unsure of their inner feelings but alert for troubling signs. With Daniel, I didn't see any. A few months before graduation, Daniel called. "Dad, I was thinking of taking some time off, postgraduation, and going back to Spain to finish the Spanish-immersion program I started before we lost Mom." I told him it was a great idea. We planned a few days in Portugal together before he continued on to Spain, and I would resume my travels. His success at Boulder and willingness to return to a place marked by loss told me he was doing okay.

We arrived in Lisbon and drove south to Tavira to hang out with some family friends. That first night, Daniel mentioned a stomachache, something that had happened occasionally on family trips since he was young. But this time it got worse. By day three, he was barely eating, looked pale, and didn't want to go out.

That evening, I gently said, "Daniel, this feels like more than just illness. Maybe it's the idea of going back to Spain, the place tied to losing Mom." He paused, then admitted, "That could be it. I just don't want to feel like this."

I told him he didn't have to go through with the program if it didn't feel right. The next morning, he seemed lighter. "I thought about it, Dad. I'd rather go home, but please continue with your travels. I will be okay." I booked his flight, and a friend connected us with a therapist. Unlike his brother, Daniel hadn't sought counseling before, but everyone has different needs for support after loss. University life had helped him stay grounded. Without it, the loss crept back in. And I realized grief isn't something we leave behind for good; it simply changes shape and sometimes returns to teach us more.

The day after he got home, I received a voicemail. "Hi, Dad. I'm feeling much better. I'll start therapy this week. Thanks for everything. I love you. Safe travels."

With Daniel on steadier ground, I turned back to Project 193. Next up: Portuguese-speaking Cape Verde, an island archipelago in West Africa, and an easy flight from Lisbon. Cape Verde felt more Caribbean than African. In fact, it was closer to the Caribbean than East Africa. Now, I was heading to my 138th country, known for having some of the most stunning and well-preserved Roman ruins, and it wasn't Italy.

Algeria

North Africa didn't feel African, especially Algeria. Blown away by the ancient Roman cities in Lebanon, I was eager to explore the country. Through NomadMania, I connected with Wasim Allache of Algeria

16 Tours, who personally picked me up. A passionate traveler, Wasim spoke five languages and had visited 86 countries despite holding an Algerian passport that granted visa-free access to just 26 nations whereas my passport got me into 160 countries without a visa. The travel community called him a Low Passport Index (LPI) traveler due to the difficulties in gaining access to countries many of us take for granted.

With the guide whom Wasim had dedicated to me, Billel, we first hit Timgad, a remarkably preserved Roman city from the Trajan era. Its grid of temples, baths, markets, and intact mosaics took me by surprise, *and I had it all to myself*, as if walking through the Forum in Rome with no one around. Billel was deeply passionate about Algeria's Roman cultural heritage.

We made our way through an arch, as magnificent as you will find in Rome, that was the entrance to the main part of the ancient city. Not long after, lightning flashed, and we beelined for the overhang of an amphitheater as the sky opened up with a huge deluge. While waiting out the rainstorm, I got to know Billel.

"I was inspired by my parents, both highly educated, to prioritize learning about my country's rich culture," he said. "Algeria does not promote our history and tourism much because the leaders focus on the country's underground wealth of oil and gas instead of our aboveground wealth of antiquity.

"Much of my childhood coincided with a harsh civil war that we call the 'Black Decade' where it was unsafe to be outside much. But this also gave me a lot of time to learn about the culture that lived right here two centuries ago."

Billel had weathered war and found meaning in the ruins. I was doing the same, in a different way, piecing together a new life from the fragments of the old.

Billel knew the answer to every question I asked about Timgad and Roman history, and his dedication moved me. As the skies cleared, he said, "I appreciate your sincere interest in this place; the last group of young people that came through seemed disinterested."

"Where were they from?" His response made me chuckle.

"A travel company called Wander Expeditions."

Later that evening over dinner, as I firmed up plans to head to

Tunisia, another place steeped in Roman history, it hit me that people travel for all kinds of reasons: to relax, to seek adventure, to escape. I no longer had the same goals I did when traveling with Jackie, when adventure was everything. Nor did I still share the exuberant energy of the younger Wander Expeditions crowd. My priorities had shifted. Yes, I still craved some adventure, but now I valued immersion, moments of connection and learning that lingered long after the trip ended. Traveling solo with local guides brought richer experiences: holding Obed's baby, meeting Aisha's family, hearing the passion in Billel's voice. Yes, there were lonely stretches, but the quiet, the reflection, the local human interactions, all of it made the solitude feel intentional, even necessary. As one of my travel friends, Silvia, posted on her IG, "Traveling solo is a metaphor for life: Go with yourself, without knowing, without rushing." There's a power in choosing your own company, one that teaches you to listen to your own life.

However, there were still times when it was simply too far out of my comfort zone to travel solo with a guide, where I needed some "strength in numbers." Then came an email with a subject line that made me pause and ask how far I was really willing to go to travel to every country in the world. The email headline was *"Afghanistan"*:

> Hi Wander Fam,
> I'm sending out this email directly to inform you, repeat travelers, of our upcoming Expedition to Afghanistan from September 25 to October 2.
> I want to take advantage of this window of stability that exists currently in the country. Group size will still be small, of max ten people, and women are welcome but must cover with burqa. For those of my travel family interested in visiting Afghanistan under the Taliban, feel free to reply to this email.
> Love, Alvaro

On one hand, traveling to Afghanistan under the Taliban was way out of my comfort zone, no matter how much that "zone" had expanded over the past twelve months with my trips to Iraq and Lebanon. On the other hand, how could I say no to this once-in-a-lifetime experience? WE's motto was *Just Say Yes.*

I broached the idea with Daniel that night over margaritas at our local Mexican restaurant. "Would you be comfortable with me going? It could be my one opportunity to go, you never know."

"Well, Dad, you let me get a motorcycle even though you were not entirely comfortable with the idea, so I guess I should be okay with your going to Afghanistan." And when the next email arrived from Alvaro, I had already said yes.

> Men:
> 1. Leave your beard for the next month. Don't shave it. It's the single most important thing (aside from the local clothes) that will make you blend in and, hence, keep you safe.
> 2. Dye your hair if you are blond. Go for a dark brown.
> 3. Don't be very well groomed. Keep your beards scruffy for an A+.
> 4. We will be wearing local clothes at all times to blend in.

I hate facial hair and wearing anything but my comfortable Unbound Merino clothes when traveling, but if that was the price of entry into this mysterious land, I was willing to pay it.

In heading to Afghanistan, I had no illusions about the risks. But after everything I'd been through, the idea of turning down a journey because it frightened me a bit didn't sit right. Somewhere between the salt rim of my margarita and the final click of "confirm," I knew: I wasn't just saying yes to Afghanistan; *I was saying yes to life.* I also knew that each time I stepped into a new country, I left behind an old fear. I wasn't the same man who once feared elephants. Or solitude. Or uncertainty. And then Silvia again texted me, "Pushing beyond our travel boundaries is where the soul expands and the magic hides." And if I could travel to Afghanistan only a year after the Taliban took over, what other fears could I overcome? Sometimes, the bravest thing isn't choosing safety; it's choosing possibility.

Part 5

Becoming Bolder: Beyond the Comfort Zone

Finding Grace in the World's Challenging Places

Chapter 19

Taliban Tourism

*Only those who will risk going too far can
possibly find out how far one can go.*
—T. S. Eliot

**October 2022
Afghanistan**

Some countries make headlines for violence, but countries live in their people and places, in shades of resilience and wonder that few outsiders ever witness. But first, in order to gain access to Afghanistan, I would have to secure a not-always-easy-to-get visa. I'd never had to interview for a visa before, let alone with an Afghan ambassador, but Alvaro had coached us about what to say and *not* to say: "Keep answers short. Don't mention anything about being on social media. Talk about always having wanted to visit Afghanistan."

Sitting in the waiting room of Afghanistan's consulate in Dubai, I leafed through a magazine with the headline "Invest in Afghanistan

Today." *Yeah, not likely.* Across from me hung a portrait of President Ashraf Ghani, the last Afghan president to serve before the Taliban took over about a year earlier. The Afghan embassies are a holdover from the pre-Taliban era, permitted to continue operating because no countries had formally acknowledged the Taliban government. With no formal funding, the embassies sustained themselves by charging $350 for visas, about three times what I'd normally pay. Eager to show the world they were "open for business," the Taliban honored these visas. While waiting, I sensed the road ahead, into a turbulent country, might not be a straight line but have lots of curves.

Somehow, after many questions, I came away from the interview with my golden ticket. As an American, I'm often amazed that things get done in parts of the world that appear to be in the grip of chaos, and now I was starting to wonder if some countries actually *thrive* on chaos. Vividly remembering the US military's humiliating departure from the Kabul airport a year ago, I also wondered what chaos awaited me there.

As my plane picked up speed and lifted off the Dubai tarmac, a voice in the back of my head spoke up: *You know, maybe you're taking this extreme travel thing a little too far.*

Afghanistan

On the flight over from Dubai, I got to know the small tour group of ten, including José from my Saudi trip. Alvaro had made him our WE tour leader. But the most intriguing members of the group were three digital nomads: Haley from Texas, Sibu from Costa Rica, and Dorotea from Greece, all disguised in black burqas. Typically traveling alone and with no home base, they symbolized a new breed of extreme travelers, working while traveling to finance their dreams of seeing the world.

Walking outside the Kabul airport, I was surprised to see a neon billboard that read, "I ♥ Afghanistan." The last time I saw an image of this place on the day of my country's final departure from Afghanistan, it looked like mayhem. But now, to my surprise, there was no chaos in sight.

As our guide, Mahdi, led our group around Kabul and beyond

in the week that followed, my brain had to work overtime to process what I was seeing. There was an appearance of normalcy, with people shopping at the fresh-fruit stands, meat vendors displaying goat carcasses, and shops offering tempting sweets. But beneath it all was a surreal layer: Taliban checkpoints, Toyota truck beds filled with soldiers carrying AK-47s, and strung-out people sleeping in parks. Mahdi explained, "Despite opium production falling under the Taliban, heroin addiction is still a serious problem." I later learned that historically, around 90 percent of the world's opium, which is processed into heroin, used to come from Afghanistan.

While the sights and people along the way were endlessly fascinating, and in normal circumstances I'd have been snapping photos continuously, we had to be extremely cautious to ensure no Taliban were around when we took out our cameras. Tourism was new to them. The only foreigners they had seen in the past two decades were their enemies. Our first up-close experience with the Taliban came when we were stopped at a checkpoint outside Kabul. Holding cigarettes in one hand and AK-47s in the other, the soldiers looked every bit the terrifying radicals the world had heard so much about. Just twelve months ago, these were the people the American military had been trying to kill, and who were trying to kill us. Surrounded by men with guns, I knew that if anything were to go wrong, my ability to control the situation was zero. But Zaki, the driver of my 4X4, gave them his million-dollar sheepish smile, and we were on our way.

I had a conflict going on in my mind. Everything I'd heard, read, and seen over two decades of war told me I should be shit-scared of the Taliban. But looking back at them in the rearview mirror, I wasn't scared. Our surroundings were too foreign, too fascinating, too surreal for me to feel anything but exhilarated. I realized I wasn't just surviving this kind of travel. I was doing it with clarity, curiosity, and a strange sense of calm. Was I becoming bolder or simply more attuned to the truth that danger and wonder can coexist?

Over the coming days, we were stopped over and over, but never once harassed. I've been harassed more by UK immigration authorities. In addition to Kabul, we visited the ancient Silk Road city of Herat, the country's cultural capital, where we were obliged to serve as an audience for tourism director Wahidullah Soltani at the Herat Department of Information and Culture. After we gathered in his office, his translator announced that we would be watching a video about his department's plans to develop tourism in the city. I was seated right next to this man, a senior Taliban official, who would surely have wished me harm a year ago and was now hosting us in his office.

Before starting the video, he said, "I welcome you to the Islamic Emirate of Afghanistan and the beautiful city of Herat. You may be some of the first tourists to visit our country since its *liberation*, but we will have many more in the future." His face held an odd, almost mischievous grin, and, when he glanced at me, his eyes bored straight into mine. Either way, I felt a laugh forming, but *he* wasn't laughing, so I nipped it in the bud. The whole time the video played, I thought, *Maybe this visit is feeding his delusion of real tourism in Afghanistan?* War with the Taliban and the horrific treatment of women were still at the forefront of the minds of Western tour agencies, and not many were promoting tourism in this country. I wrestled with my role here. Was showing up in Afghanistan, and this office, encouraging propaganda, or combating it by witnessing it firsthand?

And yet, despite the political theater and uncomfortable contradictions, Afghanistan's natural and cultural beauty still had the power to awe. To close our eight-day trip, we visited Bamyan, a lush valley framed by the Hindu Kush mountains, whose stunning rocky hillsides were home to a pair of sixth-century, two-hundred-feet-tall Buddhist statues until the Taliban blew them up in 2001. *So much for respecting a country's cultural heritage.* We climbed to the top, where the heads of the Buddhist statues used to be, to enjoy a view of the countryside, the river flowing through the town, and the mountains beyond. *Afghanistan has nonstop beautiful landscapes.*

Driving farther into the Hindu Kush, we turned onto a dirt road. Our guide mentioned that we were headed to a lake. We had been confined to staying close together with no walking around outside by ourselves, so we all welcomed a bit of space. As we climbed a hill, we came upon Band-e-Amir, a stunning lake carved out of the rugged terrain of the Hindu Kush. The mountains were rugged and majestic, and the lake shimmered with the most beautiful blue imaginable. "It's the minerality of the mountains," Mahdi explained, "that gives the water its color." Jackie's spirit seemed present in this beauty, reminding me that healing isn't forgetting but learning to see the world, and ourselves, with new eyes.

We made our way down to the dock to find, of all things, colorful two-person Rubber Ducky foot-paddle boats for rent. We could have been in a children's theme park in the US, but this was Taliban-controlled Afghanistan. Of course, we had to give it a go. José and I paddled out to the farthest distance of the lake and came upon a boat with two Afghan men. As we looked closer, we could see they were inhaling smoke from a plastic water bottle while screaming and laughing hysterically.

"You want?" one of them yelled to us animatedly, and waving one hand, held out their homemade pipe in the other.

"No, thank you," we said, turning around and furiously paddling away.

• • •

In Bamyan, with minimal Taliban presence, we had an authentic small-town experience as we wandered amid the market stalls, which offered a colorful array of textiles, spices, fruits, and bread. And then my travel mate, José, and I spotted a barbershop. We'd be leaving Afghanistan in less than twenty-four hours; it was time for our beards to come off.

I made the "just take a little off the top" symbol with my thumb and forefinger to the barber. He seemed to understand, but my confidence was not high. After a week of hanging with the Taliban, a *bad hair day* felt like a small gamble. When the barber was done, I looked in the mirror and saw that my risk assessment was reasonable. I gave him a few hundred Afghanis, the equivalent of about three US dollars, but his raised eyebrows and turned-up palms told me I'd paid him either way too little or way too much. Guessing it was too much, I gave him a thumbs-up, and his smile told me I'd guessed right. However much I overpaid him, it was well worth it to feel like my smooth-shaven self again. And I wouldn't be sorry to strip off the kurta either.

Democratic Republic of the Congo and Burundi

While still processing my Afghanistan trip, I was en route to a country where violence and chaos were still deeply woven into daily life. In the Democratic Republic of the Congo, the DRC, my 142nd country, I reunited with my guide-friend Obed. I'd hired him to help me climb the active Mount Nyiragongo volcano near the Rwanda border and visit a few other places in this massive country. But Obed said the park was closed because the M23 rebel group was ramping up its activities in the area. Since 1996, the DRC, due to ethnic conflict, has been one of the world's deadliest places with a reported six million deaths, many of which were in this eastern part of the country. Instead, we spent time around Goma, the border city, and then a night glamping on an island on Lake Kivu.

Now, we were reaching Port de Goma, to make our way to Bukavu, farther south and one of the most densely populated places in DRC due to a massive influx of refugees. We entered a scene that felt less like a market and more like a crisis. Hundreds of canoes jammed the water, crammed with people trying to survive another day. The port had turned into a desperate, unmoving sea of human struggle, men yelling over each other to move their goods, women clutching feverish children, families slumped over sacks of produce, too tired to speak. The stench of sweat, lake water, and despair hung heavy in the air.

We were trapped in a gridlock of boats, five or six deep between us and the dock, with our only option to crawl into one canoe and out to the next, like refugees fleeing something unseen. I glanced at Obed, palms upturned, wordlessly asking if we'd make it through. But he stayed steady. Life had thrown worse at him, and this was just another small test.

If Kabul and the Taliban had stirred my senses, this place overwhelmed them. The chaos wasn't organized. It was raw. When you realize you've gone someplace where no one knows who you are, and no one would know where to look if you disappeared, it really sinks in that you've truly stepped off the edge of your world.

· · ·

Obed and I spent several days in Bukavu. The main event had been another trek to see gorillas, this time, the eastern lowland gorillas, distinct from the mountain gorillas of Rwanda, with broader chests and larger hands. Seeing gorillas never loses its magic; it's one of nature's rarest and most humbling gifts.

From Bukavu, we crossed back into Rwanda, and the driver let us off at the Nemba crossing between Rwanda and Burundi. We walked the rest of the way through the five-hundred-foot-wide no-man's land between the countries into a small immigration building. I suddenly noticed a striking and very tall young woman approaching us from across the road at the border outpost.

"Is that someone you know?"

"That is your guide," Obed said. "You will like her. She is very ambitious, like me, and I like to support her work."

As I said goodbye to Obed, I reached into my backpack and pulled out a packet of coffee beans I'd purchased for him from the US. It was Rwandan coffee from, *you guessed it*, Starbucks. Obed thanked me, adding, "I didn't even know that Rwandan coffee is branded in the US, and I will keep the present for my wife and will offer it when I am back home in remembrance of your visit."

On the road, I was immediately impressed by my new guide. The former Miss Burundi, Dative, is the owner of Ikaze Ventures, a tourism company she started in 2021 at the age of only twenty-two. She was fluent in French, English, and her local dialect. Her excitement to show me her country was obvious. As she told me, "I am fulfilling my goal to tell the Burundian story from a Burundian perspective. The first place we will visit is a Pygmy village."

The ethnic Pygmy Twa population had migrated to Burundi centuries ago and had a hunter-gatherer existence, foraging for food and cultivating land deep in the forest. That is until the government forcibly moved them to a more urbanized area well above the jungle floor. Their new home, the Pygmy village I was visiting, turned out to be more of a resettlement where the land was marginal. Dative explained, "They have turned to tourism as a source of income and perform traditional dances for some groups I have brought here. I like to support them because they are very poor." At least six feet tall, she towered over the elders who came to greet us as we stepped out of the car.

Straw-hut dwellings and a few brick structures surrounded us. The dusty, harsh parcel of land on which this town was built was completely devoid of moisture and must have offered little sustenance for crops. What seemed like the group leader, a diminutive man wearing a worn matching jean jacket and pants, spoke to Dative, and she translated for me: "They will now perform their traditional dance." Soon, a group of women wearing vibrant bandannas on their heads and weathered but colorful *kangas* (a fabric widely used as a skirt in Africa) appeared. Watching their resigned faces, I felt uneasy. This felt like obligation, not cultural pride. I leaned over to Dative and whispered, "Please give them some extra money, and I will reimburse you later." We said our goodbyes after Dative handed the man in the blue jeans some money.

Back in the car, I tried to shake the image of their blank expressions. I wasn't sure what I'd just witnessed but registered it as a defeated look. Dative caught me lost in thought and said, "I think you'll like the next cultural activity better."

After a few hours' drive, we arrived at a field marked by a modest sign: "UNESCO List of Intangible Cultural Heritage—Royal Drummers of Burundi." As the only visitors, we were led to simple seats facing an open clearing. Before us stood fifteen drummers, resplendent in bright tunics of white, green, and red, with knee-length hides cinched around their waists. Then the drums began, deep, thunderous, and alive. They struck not just with their hands, but with their whole bodies, each movement precise, synchronized, and electric. The rhythms were layered and hypnotic, part heartbeat, part storm, while the massive drums, at times, balanced effortlessly on their heads. The earth seemed to vibrate beneath us. I was transfixed, awed by the sheer force and ritual beauty of it all, and struck by how different this was from the performance I had seen before. Yes, they were performing for me, and I'm sure Dative was paying them, but they weren't just performers; they were masters. And their joy was unmistakable.

When the drumming ended, I thanked the drummers and asked, "Would it be possible to try the drum?" One drummer looked at me uncertainly but nodded. Bending down to pick one up, I was surprised to find I couldn't budge it. *At all.* Trying to save face, I squatted like a powerlifter, wrapping my arms around the drum and using the full force of my quads. I got it about a foot off the ground before realizing that was my max and put it back down as smoothly as I could.

What can I say? Sometimes travel is a humbling experience.

Chapter 20

Stateless People

*Wherever men and women are
persecuted because of their race, religion,
or political views, that place must
become the center of the universe.*
—Elie Wiesel, Holocaust survivor and
Nobel Peace Prize laureate

**December 2022
Bangladesh**

After just a short ten days at home following a long trip to both Afghanistan and Central Africa, I was looking forward to less grueling travel to some small South Pacific countries near Fiji. The first stop was Kiribati. I hadn't been in this part of the world since 1996, when Jackie and I stopped over in Fiji on our way back from our African adventure. Flying over the capital city of Tarawa, I looked out the window of my plane to see dazzling turquoise waters, pristine coral reefs, and islands dotted with lagoons of every hue from green to blue. But as my driver pulled out of the airport, what I saw outside the car window didn't quite match my thousand-foot view.

I usually found something to appreciate in every capital, but I struggled to connect with Tarawa, apart from discovering that this place was ground zero for climate change. The highest point here was just ten feet above sea level. Trash and abandoned cars were everywhere, and after just a day of touring the island, I'd seen enough. But I still had a few days left, and there were only two flights from Fiji and back each week.

I was stuck.

But wait, there had to be a way to explore one of the smaller islands, right? I had seen a number of them on the flight in. When I asked around, I found out that I could catch a three-hour boat ride to Abaiang, a coral atoll, which turned out to be pure paradise—sun-drenched, no tourists, coconut palms everywhere, crystal clear blue water. A breath of fresh air. *This was more like it.*

I'd booked a stay at a "rustic but idyllic" beach bungalow I'd read about on the Every Passport Stamp (EPS) Facebook page. When I arrived, the owner, Tinaii, welcomed me with her adorable little daughters and directed me to a bamboo-and-palm-frond hut on stilts hanging over the sea. No electricity, no bathroom, none of the complications of modern life—*perfect*. On Tarawa, I felt trapped. But here, on Abaiang, I felt claimed.

Tinaii told me I was the only tourist on the island and lent me her husband's motorcycle so I could explore. As I rode the bike along the one dirt road on the atoll, with the lagoon to the west and the Pacific to the east, I'd sometimes encounter groups of teenage kids hanging out close to the road. Stopping to ask if I could take their photo, they always responded the same way, by assembling in the frame with huge grins.

That evening, Tinaii made a dinner of fresh fish and vegetables, and as we ate, she told me about life in this slice of paradise. She and her husband, a government minister who was spending most of the week in the capital, made their home on Abaiang because of the communal bliss to be found here. "It's like I feel the love every day," she said, "a feeling of togetherness with my neighbors. It is so easy to communicate with people here. We laugh and chat; I feel like we are laughing all the time. I know we may lack so many things here that you have where you are from, but I don't really *feel* like I lack anything." Hearing this made me realize that I was kind of craving the same, belonging and laughter.

On the three-hour boat ride back to Tarawa the next day, I felt grateful that I hadn't had the opportunity to catch a fast plane out of there. Although I would have been able to "count" Kiribati and check it off my list, I would have left no wiser about its beauty or its people. In Abaiang, I also saw the strong family ties Tinaii had described, something I was missing in my own life after losing Jackie. As I was still turning over thoughts of home and absence, the universe threw me a small surprise in the lobby of my hotel in Tarawa, one of only two in the capital.

"Renée? I can't believe it!"

"Barry!" Renée Bruns is part of the online community of extreme travelers I'd connected with since starting Project 193. There's rarely a day when I don't reach out to another traveler via Instagram, whether for travel advice or just to keep in touch, and I'd recently written Renée to commiserate after reading a story she posted on her Instagram feed. The airline had lost her wheelchair on a flight to Micronesia. It ended up in a completely different South Pacific country, Marshall Islands, and she ended up hotel-bound for two days until they could get it back to her. I also noticed she was traveling in other parts of Oceania and told her I was likely following close behind, and that I hoped our paths would cross. *And now, here we were.*

We spent part of the day together and had dinner at a seaside restaurant. While we washed down our local tuna with a beer, Renée told me about the remarkable life she was leading. "I've always been a searcher, trying to understand the world," she said. "Its inequities *and* its beauty. It's like getting an education—once you have it, you can't go back, you know?"

She'd lost the use of her legs when she was seven, and her mother wouldn't let her be a victim of her disability. In fact, her mom did not like the word "disability," telling Renée, "Everyone has challenges in life; yours is physical." Traveling around the US with her parents, she saw all fifty states by the time she was sixteen. Then, wanting more, she started traveling abroad with travel groups. One day, just after the end of the COVID pandemic and in the middle of her career in corporate America, she decided she'd had enough and devoted herself to fulfilling her dreams of wanderlust. And she was doing it mostly on her own. Spending time with Renée reminded me that despite how lost I'd felt since Jackie's death, I was part of something special now, this shared quest to see and understand the world.

The next day, we went to the airport together for our return flight to Fiji. After we crossed the tarmac to the boarding stairs, Renée worked her way out of her wheelchair and crawled up the fifteen steps on her hands and knees to her seat. As I settled into my seat, all I could think about was the many blessings that had come my way, including running into Renée in person. She'd taken her first step alone, as I had done in Tajikistan. But now I could see that we weren't on this journey alone anymore.

. . .

With just another ten-day stay at home after visiting Kiribati, Vanuatu, Tonga, and Samoa, it felt like a layover with barely enough time to get into anything resembling a routine. But it was long enough for me to realize that things had changed. Before starting Project 193, I was never entirely comfortable at home after Jackie died. But now that I'd thrown myself into this quest, I was surprised to find that I took pleasure in sleeping in my own bed again.

I also got some unexpected news that reinforced the idea that I really did belong to a new community of like-minded people. I had earned a nomination for one of NomadMania's annual travel awards, for "Most Purposeful Traveler." As the organization's website said, this award was "given to someone whose efforts to create community, help local groups, and in general travel with a purpose in the past year render them much more than just a traveler." I was nominated in recognition of my work with Caravan to Class, but as worthy as the cause was, I was still surprised to be included among so many other accomplished travelers.

I didn't win, but others I knew and respected did, like Anna

Harris from my own hometown for "Best Digital Nomad" for her off-the-charts photography. And Jacquelyn Kunz, who won for "Most Intrepid Traveler." Jacquelyn and I had connected over our mutual interest in Arabic and humanitarian work in the Muslim world. She often traveled solo to places where few young women ventured, such as Afghanistan, Iraq, and off-the-beaten-path locations in Africa. Women like Jacquelyn, Anna, and Renée were boldly traveling solo to places few others dared, pushing their own boundaries and setting an example.

Some of my most meaningful trips—Baghdad, Afghanistan, Lebanon—were the ones that pushed my limits even when some fear was initially there. And I don't think it's a coincidence that they were also some of my most profound experiences. Another of Silvia's posts resonated with me: "Go without fear, or take fear with you, but go either way." It might be difficult to travel without any fear, but traveling with it does take courage. As I set out on my final trip of 2022 to Sri Lanka and Bangladesh, I reflected on the inspiring community that surrounded me, giving me courage that I was on the right path.

Bangladesh

The country I was excited about visiting on this three-country Asia trip was Sri Lanka. It is one of those can't-miss countries like Costa Rica, Italy, and Bhutan that no traveler ever has a bad word about. And yes, it was *amazing*. Sri Lanka is a vibrant tapestry of Buddhist temples, Hindu shrines, bustling markets, and tranquil tea plantations. Amid lush jungles, golden beaches, and misty highlands, its warm, resilient people embody a rich cultural and spiritual heritage.

It even has something like twenty varieties each of bananas and mangoes. For a guy whose favorite fruits are bananas and mangoes, that's like hitting a tropical-fruit candy store.

Leaving behind the warmth and beauty of Sri Lanka, I headed to Bangladesh with curiosity, and a bit of uncertainty. Everything I'd read about Bangladesh described Dhaka as one of the world's most densely populated and unlivable cities, with traffic jams that are the stuff of legend. My first morning in Dhaka proved this: wall-to-wall people and wall-to-wall traffic everywhere. Without a doubt, it would be a challenge to live here. Yet I had to admit that I absolutely loved the place.

Dhaka is one of the most vibrant, energetic, *alive* cities I've ever visited. It's not for everybody, but if you want the authentic experience of an overcrowded, underdeveloped Eastern metropolis, then you can take a rickshaw through the streets of Old Dhaka, visit the Korail slum, or go for a taxi boat ride on one of six rivers that run through the city. With so many people packed together, I couldn't help but get a feel for the daily life of the Bengalis. I was fascinated by the place as I made my way through the packed indoor markets, where Bengalis were applying themselves to their crafts, whether forging metal into cooking items, sewing clothes, mixing teas, creating print art, or selling fish. And they were all eager to greet me.

"Bengalis are some of the most engaging people I've ever met," I said to my guide, Najib. "And I'm surprised how willing people are to be photographed."

"Bangladesh is a poor country, but it is not the only thing that defines it," he said. "You see today the friendly character of the Bengali."

After a few days in Dhaka, I flew to Cox's Bazar on the Bay of Bengal. After the exciting craziness of Dhaka, I was looking forward to relaxing on one of the longest unbroken, undeveloped stretches of beach in the entire world, at close to eighty miles. On the flight, I struck up a conversation with the guy next to me, who was doing some work on behalf of the UN High Commission for Refugees at the Rohingya refugee camp in Kutupalong, about an hour's drive from Cox's Bazar.

I knew that the Rohingya, a Muslim minority from next-door Myanmar, were severely persecuted by the military government of the Buddhist country, with upward of twenty-five thousand killed and well over a million displaced, according to UN estimates. What I didn't know was that most of these displaced million Rohingya were trying to make a life for themselves at the Kutupalong camp, the largest refugee camp in the world. After learning about this, I knew I would not be hitting the beach that week.

The next day, Najib and I went to the UNHCR's administrative office for the camp. I showed my NGO ID for Caravan to Class and asked about visiting the camp to learn more about the Rohingya's plight. "Authorization through our headquarters in Geneva takes a few weeks," the person at the front desk said. "Without that, there is no way I can let you in."

As we walked out of the office, I turned to Najib. "We're getting in there."

Circling the long perimeter, we found a gap in the fence and slipped inside. At a makeshift outdoor school, we spoke with students and their teacher, who explained that the camp had started informally a few decades earlier when a military junta seized power in Myanmar. In 2017, the population surged after the army launched a brutal campaign to drive them out. "We are not only refugees," the teacher said. "Myanmar, where our people have lived for centuries, refuses to recognize us as citizens." I stared at the students, some barely in their teens, whose only home was a camp surrounded by fences. What future could they possibly imagine? And how many other places like this exist?

Why had it felt so important to sneak into this camp? It couldn't have been just for the challenge. I knew about the Rohingya, but how had I never read about this camp in the news? I was stunned by how little I knew. Maybe I saw myself in these refugees, not stateless, but still unmoored. What does it mean to belong when your anchor is gone?

Kutupalong isn't just the world's largest refugee camp; it's a city of nearly a million stateless people. Had I followed the rules, I would have stayed ignorant. But being here, speaking with the Rohingya, gave human form to a crisis I barely knew existed. It made me wonder what else I had missed.

Chapter 21

Dancing with AK-47s

To travel is worth any sacrifice. I know the person I was when I left is not the person I am now.
—Elizabeth Gilbert, *Eat, Pray, Love*

February 2023
Yemen

I had embarked on this path as a way of searching, not for stamps on a passport, but for a way to rebuild my life shattered by loss. And finding a community of travelers helped to guide that search. As I became immersed in the extreme-travel community, I also became increasingly curious about the pioneers of this ambitious human endeavor: Who was the first person to travel to every country in the world? How many extreme travelers were out there?

I learned that the first person known to reach the goal was Rauli

Virtanen of Finland, who did it before NomadMania, MTP, and EPS even existed. At the age of twenty-four, Rauli became a war correspondent, covering the Vietnam War, as well as the Tiananmen Square protests, the siege of Sarajevo, and the famine in Ethiopia, among other international stories. Throughout his career, he requested assignments that allowed him to tell the stories of largely unknown places. By 1988, he'd visited all the countries in the world (159 at the time) and has since completed the remaining thirty-four countries, as new ones emerged. With Rauli being the first person recognized by NomadMania and the extreme-travel community as the first person to have traveled to every country in the world, it wasn't long before we met.

We shared a similar view of our travels. Rauli admired travelers driven by more than just country-collecting as the goal in itself. "We should encourage people who love to travel out of curiosity and learning, like you and me, to make efforts to produce ideas for a better world with sustainable development goals."

For many reasons, including completely closed countries, a lack of information, the impossibility of obtaining certain visas, and logistical challenges, traveling to every country in the world was a challenging endeavor before Rauli did it, and still is. By the year 2000, from the stats produced by NomadMania's verification system, only a total of about sixteen people had seen every country; however, the decade that followed brought a significant change. In 2010 alone, there were ten new UN Masters, and in 2023 alone, there were fifty additional ones.

The composition of extreme travelers also underwent significant changes. Around 2000, about 90 percent of UN Masters were Caucasian men, mostly old white guys like me. By 2023, approximately one-third were women, many of whom were young. And it's not always a solo journey, with thirteen partner pairs or spouses having achieved UN Master status, like my friends Hudson and Emily, with whom I had bonded over our mutual quests to travel the world to heal loss: me from the loss of Jackie, and Hudson (and Emily) from the loss of his dad.

And there were others in our travel community for whom travel was about something much deeper than lists or milestones; it was about healing for them as well. I realized just how real this was when

NomadMania asked me to write a short memoir, *Healing Through Travel*, and I began receiving messages from people who deeply resonated with the idea. One mom wrote to me on Instagram:

> Looking forward to your book! Found out about you from Unbound Merino. . . . We wear them too! I'm a mom of a special needs son, Wade. He's eighteen, and travel is like therapy for him. He's so easygoing, and I wouldn't want to travel the world with anyone else! It truly is healing and connecting in so many ways.

That message stayed with me. It reminded me that the modern traveler's map isn't just about borders; it's about personal journeys, transformations, and connections.

Of the roughly four hundred people who have visited every country as of the writing of this book, a third are from the US. Still, it's the Nordic countries that earn the title of most-traveled region on a per-capita basis. And right now, there are probably a few thousand pursuing their own Project 193.

Feeling part of a tribe that included people like Rauli, and having already made it to places like Afghanistan, I stayed motivated to push forward. With forty-five countries left, I realized I could possibly finish by the end of 2024. But I had to get strategic: apply early for visas, juggle both my US passports (allowed for frequent travelers), and manage the complex logistics of global travel.

Three countries were currently off-limits. Syria and Libya were closed to Americans, though I stayed in touch with fixers there. North Korea remained locked down from COVID, and US citizens were banned from traveling there. Realistically, I'd need another passport to get into the "Hermit Kingdom." That could wait. For now, I was focused on 2023 and the toughest leg of the journey, Africa, where I still had twenty-five mostly hard-to-reach countries, especially in West Africa, with its notoriously rough roads and hard-to-cross land borders. I'd use my annual Mali trip as a launchpad.

My goal was all 193 countries, but the real reward ran deeper. Even in places like Afghanistan, Iraq, and Lebanon, I found connection and beauty. What once sparked caution now fueled boldness. Visiting these countries didn't just make me a more confident traveler; it restored my trust in the world.

Mali

The French had been ousted the previous year in Mali, and now it seemed that the military leaders were also pushing for the UN mandate for peacekeeping to end. Mali has had one of the largest UN peacekeeping forces in history, along with the Central African Republic, South Sudan, and DRC, all practically failed states. *Not the best company to be in nor the easiest place to do humanitarian work.* But thanks to our Bourse Jackie recipients, I'd come to see a different, more hopeful side of this country.

With the Bourse Jackie program, we launched a monthly Female Leadership and Empowerment seminar in Bamako, where our young scholarship recipients learn nonacademic skills to enhance their lives and careers. I attended the January session, which featured four successful female Malian entrepreneurs in their early thirties and was humbled as they shared their journeys, marked by perseverance to overcome corruption, intimidation, and misogyny. It reminded me how much untapped potential exists in West Africa, especially among women, who often get just a fraction of the support that women get in my country.

This scholarship has been an essential way for me to keep Jackie's name alive. One of our scholarship recipients told me, "Your wife, Jackie, is the one who gives me the courage to dare to shine." Seeing the ubiquitous sunflowers on the women's shirts, the event posters, and hearing them talk about Bourse Jackie was incredibly moving. Another of the scholarship recipients, Fatouma Toure, struck a powerful chord when she shared, "As a woman, I am strong, ambitious, and determined." She continued, "I am sure that no field, including my field of science, is complete without the contributions of women. Women have a vital role wherever decisions are made." Even more than funding university educations, I realized this scholarship was helping pave the way for future female change-makers in this troubled country.

The next day, I arrived in Timbuktu, which I hadn't been able to visit in two years. While security was still a challenge in the wake of more frequent jihadist attacks, this year we were under Governor Bakoun Kante's personal protection. He gave us his own security detail for the inauguration of our seventeenth school, in the village of Bokyatte, and to boot, he ordered all his senior staff to attend.

Considering that the previous, democratically elected governor had never acknowledged Caravan to Class, I was impressed that the new one, a military man chosen by the new military government, had taken such a personal interest. I met with him twice in his office during my short three-day stay. Don't get me wrong; I'm not a fan of military takeovers, but I couldn't ignore the irony.

The drawback of the governor's interest was that I had to sit there in the hot sun, listening to a bunch of boring speeches by heads of departments in the governor's office. I could have been spending that time in the classrooms with the kids, but that was a small price to pay. Beyond the joy of finally getting to visit with the kids for the first time in a few years, I had the opportunity to stay at the UN military base, known as the Supercamp. A heavily fortified compound surrounded by bunkers, it wasn't the Ritz, but I'd seen worse.

During my stay, I posted about my trip on Instagram and was surprised to receive a DM from Ric Gazarian, of *Counting Countries* podcast fame. He wanted to set up a call.

"It was great hearing your story about your work in Timbuktu on IG, particularly while you're there live," he said while I sipped a beer in the mess hall after dinner. "I hope to get there someday, as do many in the extreme-travel community. I'd love to have you on the podcast sometime to talk about your work." Speaking with Ric, I realized how rare it was to find meaning and adrenaline on the same road. And I was thrilled that my post had caught the attention of someone who could spread the word about our humanitarian work to a large audience.

Counting Countries ranks among the top global travel podcasts. Ric has interviewed many, if not all, of the world's most accomplished travelers. I had recently listened to the podcast of Thor Pedersen, a Dane for whom it was not enough to travel to all the countries in the world; he had to do it without ever getting on an airplane. In total, it took him nine years of continuous travel via bus, train, and ship, but he finally made it. Or Toni Giles, who had visited 130 countries as a completely blind traveler, many of his trips solo.

Senegal, Gambia, Guinea-Bissau

Most of the time, guide recommendations work out; sometimes they don't. Either way, it's always an adventure. In Senegal, the adventure began the morning I arrived when my guide, Lamine, was late in picking me up at the Radisson Dakar. After half an hour, he texted: "There is a problem, another driver will pick you up." *Ugh.* Hours later, two Senegalese men arrived in a small, beat-up Toyota with trash scattered all over the back, informing me that they were taking me to the border between Senegal and Gambia. When I asked them who they were and why Lamine didn't show up, they had no answer.

Oh boy.

It's days like these that remind me just how wrong things can go. Sitting in the back seat, watching early-morning Dakar pass by as we left the city, I thought, *I am in a foreign country, riding in an old Toyota with two strange guys, and more hundred-dollar bills in my backpack than they probably make in a year.* Perfect *conditions for what Alvaro calls "maximum fuckery."*

About two hours later, we stopped in the city of Mbour, and another young man got in. For all I knew, this was the guy who was going to put a sack over my head and . . .

"I am so sorry," the new stranger said, interrupting my thoughts of impending death. "My bus got delayed."

Lamine, thank God. I felt my body relax.

"Okay, but where's our car?"

"At the Senegal-Gambia border with the driver," he said. Still a few more hours away.

After a very long day, we arrived at the border. But before we could switch cars, Lamine and the driver began arguing with the two Senegalese guys over price. Lamine didn't have the amount they were demanding. When loud yelling started, I was sure this was going to get physical, so I lent Lamine the equivalent of $200 in CFA, the West African currency. Given that I'd paid for the whole trip up front, I wasn't amused.

To cap it all off, when we arrived at my beautiful beachfront hotel near the capital, Banjul, there was no reservation in my name. Trying to keep cool, I gave Lamine the same look I used to give my boys when my patience had run out.

"Seriously, Lamine?"

Overall, I've been lucky with my guides and trips, but sometimes shit happens. In this case, most of it really was beyond Lamine's control. Bottom line: We found another reasonable hotel, and he apologized profusely. I learned it was his first gig as a guide, at the age of only nineteen. His boss hadn't communicated the requirements of the job or given him money to pay for things and had generally hung him out to dry. *Some first day on the job.*

After a few days of exploring Gambia, mostly watching the fishermen haul in their daily catch and walking through the local markets, we drove to the border with Guinea-Bissau, where I met my next guide, Innocencio. My travels in Guinea-Bissau proved to be better organized, if mostly uneventful other than hanging out a bit at a distant Pygmy village. The head of the village there offered to put a curse on my enemies, as my guide translated to me. I said, "But, Innocencio, I don't think I have any enemies."

The only other exception came during a stroll through downtown Bissau, the capital, when a convoy of jeeps and a group of armed soldiers on foot appeared in the street, heading toward us. A man in a white fedora, a cane, and a fancy bright white suit walked in the middle of the group. Suddenly, the soldiers pushed us off the street and into a fruit stall behind us. As the group passed by, Innocencio told me, "That guy in the suit is our president, Umaro Sissoco Embaló." I guess in his country, *nobody* walks on the street when he does.

I'd never been shoved off the street to make way for a president before, and for me, it just confirmed that there's a unique experience to be had in almost any country.

At least my next country would be a better-organized group trip by Alvaro; we were going to the mainland of Yemen. As I made my way across Africa to Cairo, my excitement began to build. I had been so taken by my experience in Socotra, almost a year earlier, of the beauty, culture, and history of Yemen and its people. Four hours after our Cairo International Airport meet-up, we were in Seiyun, Yemen, making a beeline for a men's clothing shop. We outfitted ourselves with button-down shirts in blue, white, or brown, turbans, sandals, and our *ma'awaz*, a traditional wraparound skirt worn by men.

If it is a Wander Expeditions trip in some perceived dangerous country, you know it's dress-up time again.

Yemen

Located at the crossroads of civilizations, Yemen is a complex and fascinating land. One wave of Homo sapiens leaving Africa around one hundred thousand years ago likely crossed the Bab-el-Mandeb Strait here, spreading across the world. And most importantly, at least to some of us, Yemen, along with Ethiopia, was the birthplace of coffee.

As for modern times, Yemen has been fractured by civil war, divided mainly between the North and South. The Houthis, supported by Iran, controlled the North, including the ancient capital Sana'a. This was an active war zone and off-limits to us. We were traveling in southern Yemen, which was under the influence of Saudi Arabia and the United Arab Emirates.

Early in the morning, our Wander Expeditions group headed for Shibam, *the Manhattan of the Desert*, by way of the Hadhramaut Valley, with its stunning blend of arid desert and lush oases. Set against a backdrop of rugged and low-elevation mountains, a skyline of tall buildings came into view and loomed above us. But these were not made of steel like the ones in Manhattan; rather they were made of mud brick. But the architecture was stately nonetheless, not something I expected to see in one of the world's poorest countries.

As we explored the areas around Shibam over the next few days, we got used to our AK-47-toting security guards, who traveled in their own SUV behind our convoy. A very spirited bunch, they tried to get me to share qat with them, a plant widely chewed by men in Yemen that is retained in the cheek and produces a stimulant-like effect. I gave in, whether out of pressure or curiosity, and stuffed a big wad of it into my mouth.

Soon after, our jeep convoy pulled to the side of the road at a winding mountain pass, overlooking the jaw-dropping Hadhramaut Valley. I peered down into a deep canyon to see a thin sliver of greenery on either side of a river and a small village of beautifully built, colorful mud structures. Suddenly, I heard some loud Yemeni folk music playing. As I turned around, I saw our Yemeni security guards dancing on the side of the road. Could this be the effects of the qat they were chewing? *I mean, I was feeling a buzz myself.* Our guide, Kais, grabbed my hand and pulled me toward the guards, who were dancing to the music. With my travel mates at the edge of the highway, gawking at the breathtaking scenery below, my legs started to move involuntarily. Soon I found myself dancing arm in arm with them, me with a wide grin and suspect dance steps, them with their AK-47s slung over their shoulders. Travel was teaching me to see beyond fear, to trust in the kindness beneath the surface, and to embrace life's contradictions, *like dancing with dudes with AK-47s.* And somehow roads in Arabia brought out my best effort at dancing.

During the week, I got to know one of my fellow travelers, Cameron Mofid. We had connected on Instagram about a year earlier, swapping recommendations for local guides in Africa, and coincidentally ended up on this WE Yemen trip together. Cameron, younger than my sons, asked nonstop questions about my foundation work. Despite our age difference, our views of the world were aligned. Especially, when one day he said, "We are taught from a young age that 'poor' means 'unsafe' and that exercising extreme caution should be an automatic default. I have learned that this is simply not true."

"Cameron, through your travels, at such a young age you have learned what it took me decades to learn." When he told me about Makoko, a village in Nigeria that he'd visited and his hope to help the children he'd met there, I encouraged him to pursue it.

"Just take the first step," I said, words that have enriched my life in so many ways.

On our last day in the Hadhramaut Valley, we visited some small villages where we got a taste of Yemeni life. In one, a large group had gathered to play some kind of board game. They seemed very curious about who we were and why we were there. Finally, they invited Claire from our group, burqa and all, to sit down and play with them. Most of the men had rifles slung around their shoulders, but there was no menace in the air, *even* when she won the first game. Instead, these men with their thobes and turbans on their heads wore a look of amazement that a woman, a foreign woman, had beaten them.

Yemen defied every expectation I had. Clearly, dangers existed here. We saw this when we visited a Sufi cemetery (Sufi is a mystical sect within Islam), that had been destroyed by ISIS a few years earlier. The same day, we walked past what had been the Bin Laden family compound before they moved to Saudi Arabia, but yet, I felt none of the supposed dangers.

I thought back to Iraq, Afghanistan, and now Yemen, places I once thought were no-go countries. Traveling there didn't just challenge my assumptions; it dismantled them. Each experience taught me that the most uncomfortable places often brought some of the deepest insights. The headlines never told the whole story.

Back in Cairo a few days later, I was thinking about this community I had become a part of, a community, as I said to Cameron, "where a hip twenty-four-year-old can make friends with an old guy like me."

After this compelling but exhausting trip to Yemen, I was doing my usual morning Arabic routine while taking a short break for a few days before heading to Ethiopia. That was when I saw a text from Cameron in our WE Yemen WhatsApp group chat, with the caption "Education, Love, and Care in Nigeria" and a link to a GoFundMe page trying to raise $1,500 for books, uniforms, and backpacks for the school he'd visited in Makoko.

Cameron had taken the first step. Remembering how motivating it was for me to receive support from friends and family for Caravan to Class in the early days, I became one of Cameron's first donors. In him, I saw not just youth but possibility. His boldness reminded me of what I still had to give.

A few mornings later, Cameron woke up to see that his GoFundMe account had raised $65,000! At first, he thought it was a mistake, but then learned that the famous NBA basketball player Kyrie Irving had somehow found Cameron's GoFundMe page (he often supports worthy but random causes through GoFundMe) and had made a whopping $45,000 donation. That encouraged other follow-on donors. With that, Cameron, at the age of twenty-four, had launched his own foundation, the Humanity Effect, asking me to join his board of directors. Like my first steps with Caravan to Class, Cameron's simple act of starting something led to something far bigger. Countless opportunities will present themselves to us over the course of our lives. And no two journeys are the same. But by simply choosing to act when something presents itself, we can find ourselves engaging with the world in a way that turns abstract ideas into concrete realities.

Chapter 22

Never Too Old

Travel isn't always pretty. It isn't always comfortable. Sometimes it hurts. . . . But that's okay. The journey changes you.
—Anthony Bourdain

March 2023
Ethiopia

Just four months had passed since Ethiopia's brutal civil war, a conflict that left hundreds of thousands dead through violence, famine, and the collapse of medical care. Though the guns had fallen silent in most parts of the country, the atmosphere in certain areas was still tense, and it didn't take long for my group to feel it firsthand.

After a forty-eight-hour jaunt to Somaliland to see some of the world's best-preserved ancient cave art at Laas Geel, our Spiekermann Travel tour group was on the way back into Ethiopia when we came across a random military checkpoint. We were instructed to disembark from the bus and form two lines, one for men and one for women, and then submit to a search. I had probably been through over fifty military checkpoints across Afghanistan and Yemen over the last couple of months but had never once been ordered out of the vehicle to be searched. As we walked to our respective lines, I noticed tension on the faces of those in my group. As for me, maybe I am a bit too optimistic, but I just assumed it was something routine. The soldiers in the background looked at us and exchanged words. One of them approached our guide and said something in a harsh and authoritative tone.

"Please open up your bags; they will be searched," our guide told us.

While I waited in the men's line, a large commotion broke out in the women's line. I looked over to see Josh, a New Yorker from our group, about thirty years younger than most of our crew, face to face with a rifle-packing Ethiopian soldier locked in a tense stare down. The soldier had grabbed a bunch of money out of the purse of one of our travel mates, eighty-three-year-old Helga, who stood all of about four-and-a-half feet tall.

As I made my way over, Josh shouted in his face, "You give me that money right now." With each passing second, the tension escalated. But Josh, now with me standing next to him moving Helga behind us, was not backing down.

The soldier seemed stunned, and Josh took the opportunity to grab the money back. It was one of those situations, like I had with the attempted hijacking in Morocco years ago, where you just react without thinking. Josh's reaction could have gotten us in trouble, but it worked. His loud voice and the commotion attracted the attention of a soldier who had been sitting in his vehicle nearby, likely the head of the unit. He came over and confronted the soldier who had taken Helga's money. Then, after a brief discussion with our guide, we were told we could get back on the bus. Helga was shaken, as were a few of the other elderly people on the bus. I looked at Josh and gave him a reassuring pat on the back.

Afterward, Josh and I got in the grill of our guide (who shall remain nameless) for not sticking his neck out to stop the harassment of our group, particularly Helga. His defense was that if he were as aggressive with the soldiers as we were, he would have been thrown in jail or worse, but being foreigners, we had more leverage.

There's nothing like getting through something together to unite people, and three days into our Spiekermann Travel tour, we were well on our way to solidarity as a group. Aside from Josh and me, there were seven travelers in their late seventies or eighties, far from a Wander Expeditions demographic, but almost all of them were working their way to 193. For me, it was a clear realization that this quest wasn't just for young people or even solo-travel junkies like myself. These travelers were doing it their own way, through organized groups, maybe with a bit more comfort and ease. But that didn't mean it was a low-energy group. Helga, whom I'd already nicknamed "the Energizer Bunny," captured their fortitude best. Always downstairs first in the morning, she had a love of wandering, and was about twenty countries ahead of me at 175. She didn't just show me what was possible at age eighty-three; she reminded me that I still had a couple decades of travel left in me. Traveling with Spiekermann was such a different vibe than with Wander. A bit slower, quieter, and maybe less adrenaline-filled, but the fact was they were going to the same countries—Afghanistan, Yemen, Iraq, etc.—and having the same enriching experiences.

Born in 1940 in East Berlin and orphaned young, Helga grew up in foster homes before taking the biggest risk of her life, climbing over the Berlin Wall at night. "I was scared to be on my own," she said, "but that independence was the best thing that could've happened. It was the only way out." After escaping, she built a life in the US, retiring from banking and becoming president of her local Couchsurfing chapter. She hosted travelers from around the world. "Now I have people on all continents who call me their sister." Couchsurfing was popular with younger travelers, yet Helga was the one leading the charge. I had to laugh; I barely knew what it was.

Helga's story moved me, not just for her escape over the Berlin Wall alone, but for showing that true journeys defy age. This eighty-three-year-old's courage came from a lifetime of resilience. She reminded me: It's never too late to start again, connect, and live fully.

Farther along the road to Harar, we stopped for a call-of-nature break. As I looked out at the sunbaked earth with wind-shaped trees,

I noticed a large group of people about one hundred feet ahead of our bus. Curious, I wandered toward them. They were mostly women, beautifully dressed in beaded headdresses and veils of white shrouds that partially concealed their fine complexions and lively smiles. This was a wedding party that, for some reason, had also stopped on the side of the road.

About fifteen feet away, I raised my phone as a gesturing to ask if I could take their photo. As I arrived closer and before I knew it, a group of about twenty people began to surround me. I took a selfie with a handsome little boy next to me. *What a beautiful smile!* And then one of the women thrust her gorgeous little baby daughter into my hands, and two other women stood alongside me and took a selfie for themselves. The girl had a matching beaded white headdress and was as cute as could be. And then suddenly I was taking pictures with everyone else in the group, capped off by a shot with the bride and groom. We hadn't exchanged a word, yet in those few minutes with strangers whose language I didn't speak, I felt a genuine bond, a wordless kinship. True connection lives in openness and presence.

Back on the bus, I realized that in just fifteen minutes, I'd had an unforgettable experience. These moments can happen anywhere, but I keep finding them on the road. The farther I get from home, from routine and familiarity, the closer I get to peak connections I never knew were possible.

As the driver took us the rest of the way to Harar, I wondered how different the world might be if people from opposite lives could meet, even for ten minutes, like I had with the wedding party. Travel opens the door to our shared humanity.

Eritrea

However, Harar was not only about my chance meeting with the wedding party, but also about—that's right—*hyenas*. About five hundred years ago in Harar, locals supposedly started feeding hyenas raw meat nightly to stop them from attacking livestock. Whether true or not, this tradition continued when Yusuf, known as "Hyena Man," began feeding wild hyenas and passed the role to his son before he died in 2004. Josh was beyond excited to feed the hyenas; I was skeptical. But that evening, as Yusuf called the hyenas with a bucket of raw meat, the crowd's anticipation was electric. Watching them approach, especially one moving rhythmically with an eerie, laughter-like call, was mesmerizing. Feeding the hyenas was okay, but witnessing the ritual up close was one of the most unusual experiences I've had in any city.

From Harar, we drove to Djibouti, and then an onward flight to our last stop on the Horn of Africa tour, the mysterious Eritrea. For anyone who isn't lucky enough to get a visa to travel here, it's hard to know what's really going on. The Committee to Protect Journalists, a watchdog nonprofit, ranks it as the most censored country in the world, even ahead of North Korea. *That's pretty bad.* On the flip side, when you're in Eritrea, it's hard to know what's going on *anywhere else.* Even in Asmara, the capital, there's no internet, a true rarity. Nouakchott, Kabul, and Baghdad all have internet, but not Asmara.

Called "Little Rome" by Mussolini, the city is a UNESCO World Heritage site, with Italian and art deco buildings that seemingly haven't aged since the Italians were there in the 1930s. Our guide told us that because the country has been so closed and is so poor, no modern construction has taken place since. Women roamed the streets in their white shrouds, worn over their heads and down to their waists. These shrouds reflected modesty, piety, and a deep connection to their ancient Christian traditions. The past lived comfortably here in Asmara, unbothered by modernity. I wondered if I was learning to do the same.

For a guy whose favorite country in the world is Italy, Asmara was the next best thing to being in la bella Italia. And the fresh-made pasta was not bad here, either.

The next day brought a completely distinct kind of foreignness when we traveled to Keren. There, we visited the monthly camel market, where Arabic-speaking men in white robes, with keffiyehs covering their heads, offered hundreds of camels for sale.

"Bikem had eljamal?" (How much is this camel?) I asked one of them.

"Lik-inta habibi, elf dollart," he answered (For you, my friend, one thousand dollars).

"I'll think about it," I said as I wandered away, as if I'd stepped onto a street in ancient Babylon.

In a faraway village in Arabia, the journey of Islam to Africa began in the seventh century at our next stop. After visiting Keren, we descended to the Red Sea port of Massawa, where legend holds that Africa's first mosque was built by early Muslims who crossed the Bab al-Mandab Strait. Much of Massawa is made of coral stone, its bombed-out buildings a stark reminder of Eritrea's brutal war with Ethiopia. As we returned to Asmara at day's end, the bus climbed from sea level to the capital's lofty 7,600 feet. Along the way, we passed a peloton of Eritrean cyclists in matching kits grinding up the steep incline, fitting for Africa's top cycling nation. In the opposite direction, a caravan of camels ambled down, hauling baskets of guavas. It was a moment so surreal that it felt plucked from two different centuries.

You don't see that every day.

I found myself lost in reflection about war-torn Eritrea and Ethiopia, the bombed-out buildings in Massawa, the soldiers who tried to steal Helga's money, but also the joy of my encounter with the wedding party and Josh geeking out over the hyenas. Pain and beauty, fear and hope, oppression and resilience all coexisted. As I'd learned in meditation, we can't really separate them. They're all part of the human experience, and what makes us whole.

. . .

While I was still processing all the layers of what I had seen in Eritrea, my focus now turned to Syria and Iran. Although Syria had been closed to Americans for years, *and* the Damascus airport had been rendered unusable by Israeli bombing, I was determined to get there. The first challenge was getting a visa. I was in constant touch with Fadi at Golden Team, one of Syria's most respected tour companies.

Ever patient with my persistence, Fadi called me one day to say, "I think I found a way for you to get a visa. Please find attached the business card of the Syrian ambassador to Cuba. Call the Syrian embassy in Havana, ask to speak with the ambassador or his number two, mentioning my name, and they can guide you through the process. It is not a sure thing, but let's try." *The Syrian embassy in Cuba, really?*

I wasn't optimistic. An ambassador representing a country with terrible relations with the US? And living in *another* country that also had terrible relations with the US? Why would he help a guy in Sausalito get a visa to visit war-torn Syria? I sighed.

But I guess stranger things have happened.

Remembering the saying from *The Alchemist*, I made the call, awkwardly asking in Spanish to speak with the ambassador. After a brief hold, a man answered, "Can I help you?" in Spanish.

After I explained the situation, he gave me an email address to request the application, and said to return it with an invitation letter and a copy of my passport. As soon as we hung up, I emailed the request, and just two hours later, I received the application.

Wow. Proof that a bureaucracy *can* be efficient.

Then I noticed the catch: The application was in Arabic. For all those people who couldn't understand why I was studying Arabic, I suddenly had an answer: *To apply for a Syrian visa in Cuba, of course.* With my mid-level fluency and some help from my tutor, it took a good two hours to complete it. I sent it with a sliver of hope that I'd finally make it to Damascus, and could not believe my luck when I saw the official visa approval come through.

Now, in the next few weeks, I'd be going to both Syria and Iran—the latter, a place that Jackie had dreamed of going to ever since making friends with a group of Persians also studying biology at UC Irvine. She often spoke about the homemade meals they cooked for her while they pulled all-nighters studying for exams. We'd even applied once for visas when I was doing some consulting work in neighboring Armenia and when Jackie was a few months pregnant with Benjamin, only to be denied. Iran and Syria, back-to-back, were a dream itinerary, one that I had the honor of carrying out for us both.

Iran

I had some concerns about traveling to Iran. The previous September, twenty-two-year-old Mahsa Amini died in a hospital in Iran under suspicious circumstances after being picked up by the morality police (officially termed the Guidance Patrol) in Tehran for not wearing the hijab. Her death, in police custody, sparked unprecedented demonstrations against the regime. And my friends and family thought I was crazy to consider traveling there, home to the Iranian Revolution and subsequent takeover of the US embassy in 1978. Since then, the country has been seen as one of America's greatest adversaries.

In preparation for Iran, I had to ensure that I didn't have any negative articles about the country in easily accessible folders on my laptop, as per my fixer Ahmad's instructions. I also had to download a virtual private network (VPN) to access internet sites blocked in Iran, and have all the necessary papers in hand for immigration.

There were not many licensed guides in Iran specifically authorized to tour Americans and Brits, and Babak was one of them. I took this to mean that he might be closely watched, and *that* meant *I* might be closely watched too.

It was dusk by the time I checked into my hotel in Tehran, and Babak wanted to take me to Ab-o-Atash Park for the evening. In early April, there's a backdrop of snow-covered mountains looking north from Tehran. A throng of people was strolling the park, with its colorful bridge lighting up parts of the city. Babak and I sat down for dinner at one of the lively open-air restaurants as I looked around in wonder at this city that was infamous in my country for holding fifty-two US diplomats and citizens hostage for 444 days. For all appearances, we could have been in a city with a history of nothing but peace as boys skateboarded and elderly people sat on benches, chatting nearby.

Most women wore hijab, but some didn't, especially the younger ones. You wouldn't guess, at first glance, that this was a place where women faced serious restrictions. Maybe they were undercover, but I saw none of the infamous Islamic religious police. It reminded me how little you really know a place from the outside.

The next day, I encountered another surprise. As we walked around the bustling city, with its mosques, traditional Persian homes, old palaces, and Grand Bazaar, there was no sign that Iran was still reeling from the financial shock of massive sanctions imposed by a US-led group of nations, a 50 percent currency collapse, and rampant inflation. Judging by the lively atmosphere at the cafés and restaurants, I could hardly believe I was in the same place reflected in the images of mayhem in the press back home. What was really going on here?

My mind was trying to process all the negative things I had heard about the country, some of which were undoubtedly true, against the ease with which people were going about their daily lives. Maybe it is just the incredible resilience of the people?

Soon we arrived in Isfahan, known as "Half the World," with its history dating back to the thirteenth century when Marco Polo traveled the Silk Road. Walking through the tree-lined parks of Isfahan is like stepping into an oasis of tranquility and historical charm. It was April, and the vibrant colors of the greenery, along with seasonal flowers, added a bright contrast to the historic architecture visible in the distance. It could have been a scene from any nice European city in the world with people out enjoying a nice evening. At the beautifully lit Khaju Bridge, two young lovers were hiding behind a column, kissing outdoors and in public view. Both the public display of intimacy and the woman without hijab were, I believed, illegal.

Nowhere have I seen a wider gap between perception and reality than in Iran. In places like Persepolis, history doesn't just sit in stone; it breathes through the people, woven into their identity. As Babak explained, "We transitioned from Zoroastrianism, which still shapes our heritage, to Cyrus the Great, to Alexander and the Greeks, and then to Islam." What remained unsaid, perhaps couldn't be said, was how that faith has been politicized since 1979.

Since the fall of Saddam in neighboring Iraq, Iran's ayatollahs have increasingly projected their power across the Middle East, often with destabilizing consequences. And yet, despite the iron grip of ideology, modernity is making quiet inroads. You see it in the eyes of Iran's youth, like the couple kissing under the bridge, in their hunger for connection, self-expression, and a future less confined by clerical authority.

In a nation that has absorbed wave after wave of civilization, the current tension between closed and open, past and future, feels like a battle for the soul of the country. History shows that those in power have often twisted religion to tighten their grip, betraying the spirit of the faiths they claim to uphold. But my bet is on the people, and their longing for freedom, dignity, and change.

Traveling to Iran was something I'd waited nearly thirty years for, and it was every bit as layered and illuminating as I'd imagined. I hadn't come just to admire beauty but was searching for the gap between what you're told and what you see. My travels had taught me that truly living means seeking direct experience, questioning narratives, and opening ourselves to new understandings.

Even as I tried to take in everything this trip offered, I kept thinking about how much Jackie would have wanted to travel to Iran. No doubt, it was bittersweet, filled with both joy but also an ache that she was not physically here with me. But somehow, I felt her presence beside me, sharing the journey in spirit.

And yet, even in that moment of reflection, my thoughts began to drift toward the next destination that Jackie surely would have wanted to make with me.

Chapter 23

A Birthday to Remember

*You go away for a long time and
return a different person—you
never come all the way back.*
—Paul Theroux

**April 2023
Syria**

On the morning of my sixty-third birthday, I woke up in Beirut only to realize that it was my second year in a row in Lebanon on April 16, and in a few hours, I would be *in Damascus.*

Heading out of Beirut, it was like déjà-vu when my driver, Ahmed, stopped at the same exact place Pierre had stopped one year earlier to admire the view of the Bekaa Valley below. "Eid Milad," he said, wishing me a happy birthday. "I am buying you a coffee today." As we crossed the Lebanese border, Ahmed dropped me off at what he called no-man's-land, the border crossing between Syria and Lebanon. We stopped at a large building with few cars, where he handed me off to a man with a long beard and ponytail. This had to be Fadi.

"Happy birthday and welcome to Syria," Fadi said with a grin.

As we began to drive, anxiety crept in at the sight of the countless posters with Assad's face, undercutting the excitement of finally making this long-held dream a reality. "We have a big day and evening planned for your birthday," Fadi said. "I hope you are not tired."

"No way, I want to make the most of the only sixty-third birthday I'll ever have."

When we arrived in Damascus, Fadi handed me over to Tilka, a guide who worked for his tour agency, Golden Team. Walking through the old city of Damascus together, I remember how I'd longed to see this ancient place ever since Jackie took me to see *Lawrence of Arabia* on the big screen in London. It was the scene of T. E. Lawrence's triumphant entrance after galvanizing groups of Arab tribes to help Britain defeat the Turks, who'd ruled this part of the world for the previous four hundred years. He called it "the city of jasmine" and wrote of it: "I loved you, so I drew these tides of men into my hands and wrote my will across the sky in stars to earn you Freedom, the seven-pillared worthy house, that your eyes might be shining for me when we came." Lawrence had long been enchanted by Damascus, seeing it not just as a strategic prize but as the symbolic heart of Arab identity and aspiration.

I fell in love with it too. Navigating the crowded maze of narrow cobblestone streets and alleyways, with their mix of Ottoman, Roman, and Islamic architectural styles, I felt like I had when I walked the Old City of Jerusalem the first time forty years earlier. The coda to our walk through the old city was the sprawling Umayyad Mosque, known as the Great Mosque of Damascus. Built in the eighth century, it's one of Islam's most historically significant places of worship, centered on a vast courtyard featuring beautiful marble pillars and intricate mosaics. As we explored the majestic edifice, the peace and serenity of the place were palpable. In the mosque's courtyard, I found a welcome calm. The previous week's travel had been hectic: Tehran—Beirut—Damascus.

On the walk back to the hotel, I was in awe; my physical surroundings felt too magnificent to be real. And maybe it made perfect sense. According to the Bible, while Paul was on the road to Damascus, "a light from heaven flashed around him." It *felt* like I'd spent the day at least a few steps above the earth myself.

Around sunset, Fadi drove us to his home in the suburbs for dinner, passing Syrian soldiers at multiple checkpoints, each calmly holding a rifle with one hand and inhaling a cigarette with the other. Arriving at Fadi's apartment, I was greeted by his wife, their two daughters, his sister-in-law, mother, and his father, Nadim, as we found places around the table in their tiny kitchen. And then the food arrived, bowls and platters to no end: lentil soup, baba ghanoush, fattoush salad, kibbeh, labneh, muhammara, and some small pizza-like dish with herbs and cheese on top, a true Syrian feast.

Just before starting to eat, Fadi toasted, "Happy birthday, Barry. We are so happy to have you in our home to celebrate, and I am looking forward to showing you my beautiful country over the next week." Raising my beer for a "Cheers," I thought of Jackie and the many times I said I'd someday celebrate my birthday in Damascus, wondering if, somehow, she could see me now. After less than twelve hours in Damascus, I'd already had an incredibly memorable birthday.

Afterward, Fadi pulled up to my hotel and said he wanted to show me a beautifully renovated building a few doors down. As we walked, he explained that it had been owned by a very old, wealthy Jewish family from Damascus, who left during the large migration that followed the founding of Israel in the late 1940s. It now housed a bookshop on the first floor. Inside, I followed Fadi down to the basement. When I took the last step into a dark room, the lights suddenly flickered on.

Surprise!

I was in a room of a few dozen strangers, mostly young, smiling Syrians in jeans and T-shirts, blasting rock music and drinking beer. I blinked back a wave of emotion. Was this really Damascus?

Fadi had assembled his employees, some of their friends, and the hotel staff to surprise me with a party complete with rock music, beer, a cake that read "Happy Birthday, Barry," and women who weren't wearing the hijab. I could've been at a party in San Francisco.

For the next hour, I had countless conversations that all began with "Eid Milad" (Happy birthday). At one point, the hotel manager told me that I was the first American to stay at her hotel in over ten years and that she was happy to see me in Syria, a sign that her country was coming back from the dark ages. It clashed with the Syria I'd heard about on the news—Assad's bombs, ISIS executions, refugees on foot toward Europe, and perhaps hundreds of thousands dead. Amid laughter and music, I wondered how joy thrived here despite the destruction and pain. Maybe resilience is not denying suffering, but choosing to celebrate life anyway.

When I was too exhausted to stand, I said my goodbyes and thanked Fadi for an unforgettable birthday. With the convergence of cultures, religions, and even universes I saw here, this would be a hard birthday to top. On this night, the world became very small, and I felt a part of it. A part of a world of people from many different cultures, all simply trying to live their lives.

. . .

Before arriving in Syria, I had only known it as a place of war, brutality, and repression, a view largely shaped by news reports and grim footage. I wanted to understand how Syrians, ordinary people, caught in the middle, have endured this complex tragedy.

During the long drive north toward Aleppo the next day, I told Fadi how surprised I was by what I'd seen of Syria so far.

"I'm sure people have been through hell here in the past decade plus," I said, "and I'm sure we'll see a different Syria along the way, but what I saw yesterday didn't correspond to my impressions of what this country would be like. Everyone was so happy to see and engage with me."

"Habibi," he said, using a term of endearment and warmth toward friends in the Arab world, "you will see that Syrian people are among the most resilient and hospitable in the world. And yes, you will see a different side of Syria shortly."

Not five miles outside of Damascus, I saw it. At first, there were a few buildings reduced to rubble or skeleton frames. Then, farther ahead, dozens of bombed-out buildings came into view.

"This is what some who were part of 'the resistance' did. They almost made it to central Damascus but thankfully were stopped by the army," Fadi said.

There is well-documented evidence that President Bashar al-Assad and his army at first, and then with the help of the Russians, had indiscriminately bombed "the resistance," killing hundreds of thousands and sending millions of refugees fleeing the war. In the vacuum, ISIS and other militant Islamist groups had reared their ugly heads. But, according to Fadi, the Western press hadn't gotten the whole story. He made it clear that the situation was far more complex than was portrayed.

"You see, Barry, while there are those in the resistance who truly want a more open Syria, it was those who want to go back to the Stone Age of orthodox Islam that were close to taking over. I am a Christian who would have no place in a Sharia-ruled Syria. That doesn't mean I support the regime, far from it. But when it came down to it, I had to choose between the survival of my family and the triumph of extremists. And yes, that meant searching for common ground with those I would not vote for in an open, democratic Syria."

Here was Fadi, a liberal Christian Syrian who was highly educated, drank alcohol, and had a ponytail, whose wife and daughters didn't wear the hijab. He was a guy whom I would be happy to grab a beer with any day of the week. For him, this wasn't theory or debate; it was survival. It's easy to question and judge from the comfort of our safe homes, but it made me think: *What would I not do or risk to save my own family?*

What Fadi told me challenged everything I thought I knew. How could some people yearning for freedom not be against a man whose bombs have killed so many? But Fadi's story reminded me that some choices are not between good and evil, but survival and annihilation. I hadn't come to Syria to exonerate Assad. He had too much blood on his hands. Assad and those around him, motivated by power at any cost, were directly responsible for hundreds of thousands of deaths, torturing many whose only wish was for a more open Syria. But in looking into the faces of people still here, ordinary Syrians, I found people making impossible choices in impossible circumstances. I wanted to meet them where they were, not where our politics placed them.

When we stopped in the village of Maaloula, high up in the hills about an hour's drive from Damascus, I saw evidence of what Fadi had been talking about. The Al-Nusra Front, a group affiliated with Al-Qaida, had taken over the predominantly Christian village with a monastery dating back to the fourth century AD. Fadi told me that some residents escaped but that many were killed. Nuns were held captive for three months until they were released, through Qatari mediation, in exchange for prisoners held by Assad. *Taking nuns hostage—how does someone with a beating heart do something like that?*

A woman chanted in Aramaic as we walked into the monastery. Maaloula is one of the few villages in the world that still speaks Aramaic, one of the world's oldest languages still spoken and from which Arabic and Hebrew are derived. The chant's cadence bore into me. This village, with its ancient language, had nearly vanished. Fortunately, government forces liberated the town.

In the days that followed, the signs of destruction intensified. In Homs, Fadi's hometown, there was a section where blocks' and blocks' worth of buildings had been reduced to rubble and steel skeletons. In Aleppo, one of the world's oldest cities, the losses were staggering. The Syrian military dropped bombs that destroyed about 40 percent of the city, forcing many to flee the country, like my Arabic tutor Zahra from years ago when I was living in Georgetown, still grieving the loss of Jackie. Back then, when traveling to Syria was only a dream, I had vowed to one day visit her city. And seven years after fighting was halted and government control was imposed, a 7.8-magnitude earthquake rocked Turkey and western Syria, dropping dozens more structures and killing more than one thousand people. As I walked through sections of downtown Aleppo, there was a Syrian flag raised on what was a bombed-out shell of a structure amidst a whole block of destroyed buildings. I struggled to process the devastation and the suffering that the people of this city had endured. I'd never felt more disoriented in my travels.

But rebuilding has started in earnest, with scaffolds and men in orange hard hats everywhere, reconstructing sections of the two-thousand-year-old Al-Madina Souk, the world's largest and oldest souk before the war. In the underground section, I met a man who has a small shop selling ceramic containers. He's had the shop for forty years, and his father had it for forty years before him. Despite losing a good part of his family due to the war and his business being shut down for almost a decade, he was one of the first to reopen the previous year. Few have followed him, though. Customers are a rarity, with the man sharing that he opened the store every morning, even so.

Why was I so captivated by this man? Maybe it was his weathered face and perseverance that struck a chord in me. It was a sign that shared grief can be a bridge rather than a wall. In that moment, though we were strangers separated by continents, I somehow felt like a companion on a similar journey. Loss does greatly extend our empathy, vulnerability, and awareness. Swept up in the moment, I asked if I could take a photo with him, and he graciously agreed.

As Fadi and I walked away, I studied the photo. The man's face was worn by the strain of challenging years, yet he indulged a privileged Westerner collecting visual mementos. I can't imagine the resilience and tenacity it must take for him to go through the motions of opening for business in this place every day. How does *anyone* in Aleppo make ends meet with all the sanctions imposed by governments such as my own? Workers earn a paltry salary of twenty-five dollars a month here, and the cost of living is ten times that. Suddenly, I wondered if it was insensitive or worse to take this tour of modern-day ruins.

I asked Fadi, "How would I treat someone walking through my bombed-out city, taking photos in the aftermath of this level of destruction?"

"They see foreigners coming to take pictures as a sign of hope," he said, "a sign of life after being disconnected and abandoned by the world for a decade." It had not crossed my mind that with all the misery these people endured, equally so, they yearned to be noticed by the world. The resilience of the human psyche stunned me, allowing people to survive even in the most extreme conditions. I realized that meeting this man and witnessing Aleppo wasn't tourism; it was testament. This place deserved to be seen, not as a headline, but as a human story.

The next day brought a whole different kind of devastation at Palmyra, farther east into the desert: the eradication of history, at least in a physical sense. It looked like about half the remaining ruins of the ancient city, built by the Romans in the second century, had been purposely destroyed by ISIS in an attempt to remove any trace of non-Islamic history. Fadi showed me a photo of the city a decade earlier. Similar in scale to the Parthenon in Greece, the Temple of Baal

Shamin had been almost completely intact, but now only one column was left standing.

The city was just now opening to tourists, though the only foreigners I saw were two Russian soldiers. We descended into some ancient tombs, and the literal writing on the wall was clear: ISIS had been here. "Brothers to cooperate and do a good deed inside by cleaning up," a likely ISIS fighter had scrawled in Arabic across the wall of one tomb. I felt a chill as I realized that ISIS militants had holed up down here in this exact spot not long ago.

At the local museum, I learned about Mr. Khaled al-Assad, the country's foremost archaeologist, who managed to bury and spirit away a significant number of Palmyra's movable artifacts, an act of heroism for which he paid his life with an ISIS beheading.

The discrepancy between what I'd expected and what I'd found in Syria was so radical that it made me wonder if I knew *anything* at all about the world. My heart and my mind were consumed with the plight of real Syrians who had no choice but to side with those who would protect their families. How could it be that life hadn't given them a better choice? When we think of a country like Syria, we think of Assad and those around him or ISIS and the crimes they have committed, or we think about the Syrian refugees in Western countries. We don't think about the average people stuck here and their lives. It's like they do not exist. The press has not reported on them or even Syria without a political lens. But politics means little to them. They are simply trying to get by. But they have been forgotten, dehumanized.

It took my trip to Syria to see that this was the real story, at least for me. It was a watershed, making it clear that I needed to see things firsthand, to be my own journalist and seek out the real story without an agenda. Through Fadi and what I saw with my own eyes, I felt that my understanding of Syria was closer to the truth. Closer than reading about it back home through the media. My heart was full. Syria wasn't just "over there." It was real, human, and unforgettable. I truly hope, someday soon, the warmhearted and long-suffering Syrian people will not have to choose between a dictator who bombs his own people and potentially something even worse.

I still can't reconcile the horror this regime has inflicted on its own people with the relief many feel that the country hasn't fallen to groups like ISIS. I don't claim to have an answer. But I do know this: Syria is not Assad. Syria is its people, the survivors, the shop owners, the families who've held on with nothing. That's who I came to see. That's who I will remember.

Haiti

I had only two countries left to visit in the Western Hemisphere: Dominica and Haiti. It had been a year of traveling to countries perceived as dangerous—Yemen, Somalia, Syria, Iran—so why not press my luck with Haiti?

I'd considered going to Haiti the previous year to see the capital, Port au Prince, but it was still a gang-related war zone made worse by the devastating earthquake in 2010 that killed roughly two hundred thousand people. Since then, however, a number of friends from the extreme-travel community had visited the other side of the island, the old capital, Cap-Haïtien, and reported that things were much safer there.

Once I got there, it didn't take long to figure out that while this part of Haiti might be a lot safer, it was no walk in the park. The scene outside the airport was chaotic, with scores of people on the streets, a few in arguments that seemed about to break into physical altercations, and others sitting on broken chairs outside their wooden shacks, wearing vacant expressions. Everywhere you looked, the roads were filled with trash, in some places piled higher than one-story buildings. Haitians were hawking items on the roadside, particularly plastic one-gallon containers of gasoline, which were selling for thirty dollars due to a severe fuel shortage plaguing the country, a shortage partly caused by companies withholding supplies to drive prices up, further bleeding the population.

The state was failing before my eyes, and as my few days here drew to a close, it was hard to escape the grim thought that maybe in places like this, democracy can't survive without order first. In stable democracies with trusted institutions, military strength matters less. But in many failed states, like Haiti, the lack of a capable security force fuels instability.

As my guide, Augusne, told me on our last day together, "Earthquakes, assassinations, and chaos in the country have left Haiti with a fraction of the tourism of nearby countries like the Dominican Republic and Jamaica. Let's hope things will change one day."

I wish I could say I see that possibility, but I don't. Here in Haiti, there were no sparks of hope in the eyes, at least that I saw, just blank stares and slumped shoulders beneath the weight of something heavier than hardship. Some places break your heart because you cannot find stories of hope. Others, like Syria, show you how much hope survives in spite of everything.

Timbuktu, Mali, 2021. The eighteenth school built by Caravan to Class.

Kampala, Uganda. Hanging with the children.

Socotra, Yemen. With my hiker-guide and a forest of Dragon Blood Trees.

Al-Baha Region, southern Saudi Arabia. Meeting some Saudi tourists from Jeddah.

Baghdad, Iraq. Drinking coffee in the city center on my first night in Baghdad.

Bekaa Valley, Lebanon. Spending time with a Syrian refugee family.

Herat, Afghanistan. A friendly connection with worshippers at the Friday Mosque.

Kandy, Sri Lanka. Visiting a girls' school.

Cox Bazaar, Bangladesh. The Kutupalong (Rohingya) refugee camp.

Hadhramout Valley, Yemen. Hanging with my security detail.

Harar, Ethiopia. Fortuitous encounter with a wedding party on the highway.

Massawa, Eritrea. Meeting with students on their way home from school.

Shiraz, Iran. A favorite traveling pastime—getting a haircut in a unique place.

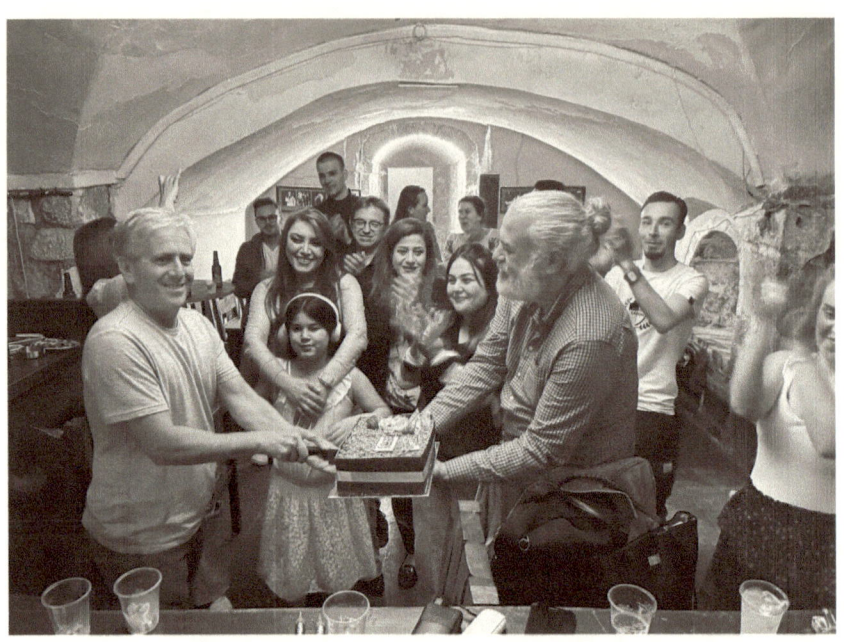
Damascus, Syria. A very special sixty-third birthday.

Liberia-Sierra Leone border. Buying fruit from some friendly children.

Hausa Villages, Niger. Visiting one of the beautiful mudbrick mosques.

Palau. A visit with the presidential office.

Hunza Valley, Pakistan. Speaking to a boys' high school class.

Bhutan. The peaceful Punakha Dzong Monastery.

Timur Leste. A special encounter with a group of nuns at the Cristo Rei statue.

Kalahari Desert, Botswana. Learning the customs of the San Bushmen.

Papua New Guinea. The sweet and curious children of the Western Highlands.

Taj Mahal, December 1994. With Jackie. The day of our first kiss.

Botswana, November 13, 2017. The last photo of Jackie.

Dominica, November 2023. With Daniel at a rum bar.

Bhutan, March 2024. With Benjamin.

Part 6

Halfway: The Farther I Go

Finding Meaning at the Edges of the World

Chapter 24

Lemurs and Rubicons

It is not the strongest of the species that survives, nor the most intelligent, but the one most responsive to change.
—Charles Darwin

**May 2023
Madagascar**

Africa is vast: fifty-four countries, the world's biggest desert, two of the nine longest rivers, and nearly three times the size of Europe. In other words, *it's a big-ass place*. I'd spent more than four months crossing most of it, north to south, with Jackie in 1996 and had returned nearly every year since 2010 for Caravan to Class. But I still had twenty-one countries to go.

My Air France redeye landed me back on the continent in Luanda, Angola, with my guide, Felicio, meeting me at the airport. We spent the day exploring the capital's modern buildings, good roads, and a waterfront corniche with a colorful "I Love Luanda" sign that signaled the country's rebound from the long civil war, from 1975 to 2002.

Stuck in traffic, I asked Felicio, "What are the best years you can remember in Angola?"

He thought hard before saying, "Honestly, I cannot remember any good year." Still, he said he felt lucky. Guiding allowed him to earn a good living and learn about the world through his clients. One of eleven siblings, he had fled his village to avoid conscription into the military, disappearing into the vast capital, now one of Africa's largest cities. Angola's oil and mineral wealth had transformed the place, creating opportunities for the lucky and connected few. But I was here to see more than just the big city of Luanda.

We flew south to Lubango, in the highlands. Beyond the towering rock-face mountains lay the Namib Desert. On the plateau, we passed a group of young men selling charcoal, the primary cooking fuel across much of Africa. I asked Felicio to stop. "Sure," he said. "I want to buy some for my family anyway. It's much cheaper here than in the city." They were six teenagers, shirtless and barefoot, with colorful cloth wraps and silver chains, standing tall. Their physical appearance was striking, and I caught myself thinking, *I wish I had abs like that.* Speaking Portuguese, Felicio mentioned I was from the United States. As they stared blankly at me, I wondered if "United States" meant anything to them.

We stopped at a market where Mumuíla women sold jewelry and textiles and approached an elderly woman selling ceramic jars. She seemed about my age, dignified and striking but a bit weathered. Her braided hair was threaded with colorful beads, and a layered necklace draped from her chin to her chest. Like many women in her culture, she was bare-chested. I focused on her eyes, though I couldn't ignore my own self-consciousness. There's a fine line between staring and truly seeing, and I was trying hard to see. "That headdress is a marker of her age; she is about my age," said Felicio. I gave him a questioning look and he added, "Around forty-five." *I was off by about twenty years.*

We drove farther south into the Namib Desert. With an average annual rainfall of just a third of an inch, it's one of the driest places on Earth. Only the Welwitschia plant grows here. I was fascinated: A single plant can live for fifteen hundred years. My mom's reaching one hundred years seemed modest by comparison. Nearby, a lone jackal watched us as we drove toward the coast—other than the Welwitschia, one of the few signs of life in this dry, windswept landscape.

The town of Tombua marked the end of the road. From there, it was only sand. Our driver, Fernando, swerved expertly across dunes and through waves crashing onto shore.

"Felicio, aren't we a little too close to the water?"

"No problem." He grinned. "Fernando is a very experienced driver."

We continued about another thirty kilometers, stopping to examine whale bones and beached ships from voyages past. The Angolan coast felt like a forgotten sibling of Namibia's Skeleton Coast, just as eerie, just as empty, but with no name to capture its desolation. It stretched like the edge of the world: harsh, wind-carved, and hauntingly barren, where the desert seemed to dissolve into the sea.

Eventually, the jeep climbed a dune and stopped at a steep drop. I got on the hood of Fernando's car and leaped, flying into the view of blue ocean and whitecaps before landing in soft sand, tumbling farther until I hit a spot not far from the water's edge.

"Barry, you are crazy!" Felicio yelled.

"Not as crazy as Fernando's driving!" I shouted back.

Seeing the vast desert meet the Atlantic Ocean awakened something childlike in me beyond a head full of sand.

I hope to return someday to explore this desert from the Namibian side. Jackie and I had once considered it in 1996, but headed south from Vic Falls to Cape Town instead to finish off our Africa trip. Saying goodbye to Felicio, I flew to Cabinda, Angola, to reunite with a friend I'd now seen in four African countries.

It had been six months since Obed had left me at the Rwanda-Burundi border. Now, as I walked into the lobby of my hotel, it felt so good to see Obed's big smile. "Great to see you again. How's the family?" I asked as I greeted him with a bro-hug.

"They're well. My son is four, and my daughter almost one and a half years. . . . Can you believe it?" he said in his usual happy, Zen-like manner. I almost couldn't believe it myself. I had held his newborn daughter in October 2021. It seemed like yesterday, and yet so much had happened since then.

The next day, our journey continued north to the Republic of

Congo, known locally as Congo-Brazzaville. Though nearly identical in name to its neighbor, the Democratic Republic of the Congo, the two are worlds apart in history and identity. *Why do they have to make it so confusing with such similar names?* The French colonized the former; the latter was infamously claimed by King Leopold of Belgium as his personal possession in the late 1800s. *And I mean not just ruled, but owned.*

Republic of Congo (Brazzaville)

After a two-hour drive north along the coast, we reached the border between Angola and Congo-Brazzaville. After easily clearing the Angolan border formalities, I stepped out of the car, close to the Congo immigration office, and was instantly surrounded.

"I can help you with your visa," one man said in French as a dozen others vied for my attention.

"I don't need any help," I replied. "I already have a visa."

A few laughed.

Uh-oh.

At the immigration window, I showed my visa to a stern officer. "Where did you get this?" he asked. "It's not valid here. This is a special border crossing."

"I got it from your embassy in my country, in Washington, DC," I said. "The application mentioned this exact crossing, Massabi."

He raised his palms, the universal gesture of indifference.

I considered holding my ground, but that could take many hours. *It was time for a more pragmatic approach.*

"Sir, maybe there is a way to speed this up," I said, handing over twenty dollars. He took the bill and stamped my passport, *country 159.* Sure, I was contributing to corruption at this place, but I didn't want to spend my day here.

Another few hours later, we arrived in Pointe-Noire where Obed had booked us at the Atlantic Palace Hotel. The manager greeted us, and from his look, I guessed he might be Lebanese. Their diaspora is prominent in West Africa, especially in the restaurant scene, like my friend Nasser, the restaurateur I spent a fun evening with in Conakry, Guinea.

"Wassalam Aleikum," I said.

"Oh, you speak Arabic," he replied. "Tahaiti kum ila fundukna."

I guessed right.

"Where can I find a good coffee and sandwich?" I asked. He walked me to the door and pointed across the street to a French boulangerie. I smiled. *I think I will like Pointe-Noire just fine.*

But as Obed and I explored the city, I realized that it was likely downhill from here. Seeing smoke looming on the horizon, Obed said, "That's the oil industry. Pointe-Noire is one of Central Africa's major oil hubs."

He added that it had also been a slave transshipment port. Over a million poor souls had passed through here. "Is there a monument?" I asked.

"We'll find it," he said. Eventually, we reached the Point of No Return, one of the last spots on Africa's West Coast where enslaved Africans stood before being forced onto ships, never to see their homeland again. Just a weathered sign, barely visible. No plaques, no names, no place to reflect.

Compared to memorials like Gorée Island in Senegal or the Cape Coast Castle in Ghana, it felt forgotten. Surely this sad history deserved more. I stood there for a moment, trying to summon the weight of what had happened here, but the silence and neglect made it harder. And maybe that was the tragedy too.

Once in Congo-Brazzaville, we then spent a few hours on the mighty Congo River. From our small boat, we glided past low-lying islets where villagers tended gardens, cast fishing nets, and slapped laundry against smooth rocks, their laughter carrying across the water. The river itself was immense, its vast, sediment-rich current the color of tea, pulsing with life and mystery. Even in stillness, the river felt alive, its slow, powerful churn a reminder that this was no ordinary waterway but a vital artery. The Congo River and its tributaries flow through a good part of Africa.

That evening, the western sky lit up in farewell colors. I knew this would likely be my last journey with Obed.

"Take care of yourself and your beautiful family. I hope our paths somehow cross again," I said, shaking his hand with a firm grip.

"They will, my friend. I will make sure of that. Safe onward travels," he replied.

Over time, Obed had become a true friend. Many guides enter my life intensely for a week and then vanish. But some of them, like Haidar, Fadi, Felicio, stay with me. Obed belongs in that category. They weren't just guides, and now friends; they were teachers and witnesses to this journey's unfolding purpose. Like a spectacular sunset that lingers in memory, Obed's role in Project 193 will remain with me always.

Gabon

If you want African wildlife without DRC-style chaos, Gabon is your place. A tenth the size of DRC with just 2 percent of its population, it's rich in biodiversity and has one of the world's largest populations of *forest elephants.*

In Uganda, about one and half years earlier, during my first encounter with elephants after Jackie's tragic death, it wasn't difficult because of the animals themselves. It was about untying them from trauma that often remains buried. When I planned this trip to Gabon, the idea of seeing elephants lingered like a much smaller dare than before. But now, as I made my way to Chez Beti, I felt no fear.

After a ninety-minute boat ride from Libreville, the capital, and a bumpy hour through the jungle, I reached a rustic lodge with no hot water and internet that did not work. Unspoiled beaches and a pod of whales greeted me on my first walk. *A good omen.*

Later, my guide and a group of elderly French tourists set off in an open-air truck. Within minutes, we encountered a herd of forest elephants, not more than about twenty feet away. Again, I surprised myself. No anxiety. No breakdown. Just awe. Previously, in Uganda, I'd wondered if my calmness was a fluke. Now, feeling like it was real, I acted like a typical tourist seeing elephants in the wild, feeling the expansiveness of being awed by them. I had no fear at all. It was just one of the many moments of rebuilding trust with life during this healing journey.

We saw more herds that afternoon. Seeing the elephants stirred a familiar awe, not quite the same jolt as seeing the gorillas in Rwanda, but still unforgettable. Back at the lodge that evening, I marveled at how far I'd come. That was until dinner, when a guest asked if elephants were dangerous. "One of our guides was killed," said the French proprietor, Bernard. We used to do walking tours. A tourist used a flash. The elephant charged as the guide stepped in the way to scare it off, paying with his life.

As much as Jackie's death devastated me, at least it wasn't caused by someone's careless mistake. That kind of loss felt even harder to bear. I'm usually good about not going to bed upset. But that night, it wasn't so easy.

Madagascar, the Seychelles, and the Comoros

After a few weeks at home, I was happy to be heading to some of Africa's Indian Ocean islands. My first stop was Madagascar, home to twelve thousand endemic plant species. Sometimes called the "eighth continent," it's one of the planet's most biodiverse places. I was especially looking forward to going to Andasibe National Park to see the lemurs.

Jackie had three favorite animals: dogs, elephants, and lemurs. She, of course, had many dogs in her life, had worked with elephants, but she never had the opportunity to see a lemur in person. For her, lemurs were the holy grail, kind of like me getting to Baghdad or Damascus. "Lemur" was even the password for most of her electronic gadgets, and Madagascar had always been high on our empty-nesting bucket list. I felt bad about the idea of seeing them without her but was still looking forward to the experience. At least, I *thought* I was looking forward to it.

It turned out that although Andasibe was less than a hundred-mile drive from my starting point, Antananarivo, the capital, usually shortened to *Tana*, it took more than six hours because the roads were so deeply rutted. *That's less than fifteen miles an hour.* Madagascar has some of the worst roads in Africa.

After bouncing around in a 4X4 for that long, I needed a rest before the tour. Bracing against all the wild, erratic movements had strained muscles that hadn't been used in years. I felt like I'd been stuck on an amusement-park ride that nobody could figure out how to shut off. *Sometimes the journey is just something to get through.*

By the time I recovered, it was pitch black. I set out for a night tour with a local area guide. We walked alongside the jungle, down another rutted road, with him shining a flashlight into the undergrowth. All of a sudden, he grabbed my arm.

"You see the tiny little sparkle in the bushes?" he said excitedly. "That is the pygmy mouse lemur, the smallest primate in the world. It's nocturnal and weighs less than thirty grams."

As I strained my eyes to look where he was shining the flashlight, I could just make out the silhouette of a creature the size of, *you guessed it*, a mouse.

Whoa.

It may not sound thrilling, but it was. Lemurs have one of the most fascinating evolutionary tales. Madagascar broke off from India and Africa over one hundred million years ago, but primates didn't arrive until sixty million years ago. So lemurs likely floated across the sea on vegetation rafts to make it here. From there, more than one hundred species evolved. Unlike on the African continent that Madagascar was previously attached to, there were few other primates here to get in the way of the massive species diversification of the lemurs. It's an evolutionary marvel that Darwin would've been obsessed with. All I could think was how much Jackie would have geeked out on this stuff.

I was also fascinated to find that, despite being one of the world's largest islands with about twenty distinct ethnic groups, approximately 90 percent of Madagascar's population speaks the Malagasy language. That seemed to be a linguistic oddity and a stark contrast to the over one hundred different ethnic languages spoken in each of the countries I had just visited—Angola, the Republic of Congo, and Gabon.

I posed this question to my main guide, Oliva. "Research shows that our language comes from faraway Indonesia; I think it is Borneo. It was brought here by people who arrived by small boats about fifteen hundred years ago. Somehow our language was flexible enough to adapt to the local influence of Arab-traders and other people who were here." Her answer raised more questions, but I'll leave that for another day. *If I were a scientist, I could lose myself here for a lifetime.*

I thought about this as we went on to see the ring-tailed lemur, the indri, the common brown, the white-headed, the bamboo, and on and on. The one that made the biggest impression on me was the aye-aye, a nocturnal lemur that looks like a cross between a bat and a monkey, with large ears and beady eyes. *Definitely not the prettiest of mammals.*

Over the last few weeks, I'd crossed a personal Rubicon with elephants again, and come through (mostly) unscathed. It was a clear sign that healing had taken place on this journey. Seeing lemurs and thinking about how much Jackie would have loved to see them, I didn't feel gutted. But rather I felt privileged to fulfill Jackie's dream of seeing them. Like the forest elephants in Gabon, the lemurs were more than wildlife; they were whispers from the past.

Now, more than halfway through Project 193, I'd crossed another Rubicon. What began as a way to remember Jackie had become something else. I wasn't chasing her memory; I was building a new life. This journey was no longer about the past; it had become about a path forward. It was about saying yes to wonder as I had always done before we lost Jackie.

With each new country, a true clarity emerged: The real finish line wasn't 193. It was how fully I chose to engage, with people, with place, with the present.

At home, I sometimes worried about what came next. But here, now, I knew what mattered was staying immersed in the road ahead. The future would meet me when it was time. For now, my immediate future meant a few days in paradise.

Chapter 25

A Coca-Cola Celebration

Not all those who wander are lost.
—J. R. R. Tolkien

**September 2023
Libya**

For the next three days, I snorkeled, biked, and rested in the Seychelles, a rare indulgence. I'd spent the past eighteen months hyperfocused on this quest, always learning, engaging, organizing, pushing. But here, I allowed myself just to be. Aldabra tortoises lumbered around like four-hundred-pound emeralds, moving at their own pace, and so did the island. No cars, just bikes. I'd forgotten that many travel just to *unwind*. My first time out cruising on my bike, I nearly crashed into a giant tortoise strolling across the road. *You don't take a selfie with one of those every day.*

As I made my way home after a stopover in Comoros for a few days, the news flashed on Reuters: "Military Coup in Niger, developing." *Got it, won't be crossing Niger off my list anytime soon.* I knew I got lucky last year getting into Syria and Iran, so now it seemed to be two steps forward, one back.

Instead of Niger, I had planned to head to Nigeria. It was Africa again, making names strikingly similar. Someone from Niger is called a Nigerien and from Nigeria, a Nigerian. *Good luck with that.* Back in 2016, I came close to visiting Nigeria. I had a visa but never made it. On a two-day trip from Accra, Ghana, through Togo and along the Gulf of Guinea with my driver, we reached the Benin-Nigeria border after paying several bribes at ubiquitous police checkpoints. My twenty-dollar bills were vanishing fast. The final straw was our car being impounded for an expired fire extinguisher. When immigration officials in Africa suspect a bribe is coming, they'll find a reason. We hadn't even reached the Nigerian side, and after bargaining the $1,000 "fine" down to $100, we turned back, my Nigerian visa unused.

This time, with a guide named Confidence, I figured things would go smoothly. *How could they not with a name like that?*

Nigeria

Confidence was waiting just outside the Lagos airport as I entered country #165, getting through immigration with only modest challenges. "Nice to finally meet you, Confidence," I said. "We're going straight to my hotel, right? I'm beat."

"It is up to you," he replied, "but today is special in Makoko. It's Sunday, and the school your friend Cameron supports is holding a celebration. I think it's something you won't want to miss."

An hour later, we reached a tiny port where young men guided canoes through canals lined with homes and shops on stilts over the water. This was Makoko, home to the seafaring Egun tribe, who migrate every few generations in search of better fishing. Skipping a post-flight nap was worth it; the canoe ride was a sensory journey. As we pushed off, the sun cast a golden glow on the water, framed by lush mangroves and clear blue skies. A young boy steered our canoe with a long pole while women in white dresses floated past us on their way to church. Despite my fatigue, Makoko stirred all my senses, a sprawling, makeshift village of thousands built on stilts above the Lagos Lagoon.

It's where life flows through a maze of canals in what locals call the "Venice of Africa."

We stopped at a large hardwood building on stilts. On the upper floor, people in their Sunday best gathered. We stepped out, and the village chief's son named—*you guessed it*—Sunday, led us to the celebration. A sea of children reached out to touch my hand, their smiles piercing deep. I felt love flowing back to them as naturally as an exhale follows an inhale. It brought back the feeling I had with the wedding party in Ethiopia, an open channel of connection. There's something about smiling children all over our world that always hits me at my core and makes me automatically smile right back. I've often wondered why. Maybe it's the contrast between their material lack and emotional abundance, a sense of hope before life's challenges arrive. I feel it every time I return from Mali, and here in Makoko, knowing the influence Cameron had on the lives of these kids, it was magnified.

Seeing the impact of Cameron's bold action in his twenties in Makoko sparked a reckoning in me. He didn't overthink it. He saw a need and had the courage to act on it. It took me longer to find my path. Maybe that's the gift of youth—not knowing what's "impossible" yet. His early steps reminded me that legacy doesn't begin at the end of a journey. Sometimes, it starts in motion, while we're still figuring things out. And maybe that's the point: We don't build a legacy to be remembered; we build it because the world needs it and we have the ability to help.

Afterward, Confidence drove me back to Lagos, where I spent the next four days visiting sites like the Nike Art Gallery, home to impressive local art. During my travels, I rarely buy anything, a habit shaped by growing up surrounded by boxes of things my mom collected. But one painting I saw mesmerized me, and I had to have it: a vibrant, expressive portrait of a strikingly beautiful woman with bold, colorful brushstrokes and intense emotion in her eyes, blending realism with abstract elements. While Nigerians are renowned across Africa for their creativity, music, and drive, who would have guessed that Nigerian immigrants are among the most successful in the US, with nearly two-thirds holding university degrees?

Although I only saw Lagos, Makoko, and the Nigerian coast up to the Benin border, stopping at Badagry, another old slaving port,

I found the country a place of extremes, bumping up against chaos and brilliance both; a place of immense scale and striking contrasts, where creativity, promise, hardship, and despair all coexist in intense concentration.

Ghana

Nearby Liberia and Sierra Leone were on this itinerary, but I decided the previous week to stop in Ghana first. Five of our Bourse Jackie recipients from Timbuktu were studying English in Accra, and I wanted to check on their progress. I also wanted to meet George, the director of the BT Institute, where our Malian scholars pursued their English-language studies. That night over dinner, with our five scholarship recipients, I suggested we speak in French for half the time, then switch to English. Just six months earlier, only two could form basic English sentences.

"I would like each of you to tell me in English about your experience here," I said.

Nana Djenne went first. "It's a new experience living on our own in a new country and culture. It's still Africa, but very different. And it's a blessing to feel what it's like to be independent." Others followed. We were having a relatively easy-to-follow conversation in English. Beaming with pride, I knew this new skill would surely open doors for them. I remembered traveling through Mali with Jackie and the boys in 2011. Meeting a young girl, like Nana Djenne, in a school in a faraway village, I could hear Jackie telling me, "A girl with confidence like that, and given some opportunity, could change her whole village."

The next day, George introduced me to the BT Institute's staff and showed me around. The classrooms were filled with students learning English, many from French-speaking countries such as Mali, Guinea, Burkina Faso, the Ivory Coast, and Niger. George clearly cared deeply about his students, knowing personal details about their lives and progress. I left thinking, *Could Caravan to Class expand this opportunity to other young women from across Francophone West Africa?* All we needed was a partner and a rigorous selection process.

By the time I landed in Liberia, I'd drafted a partnership proposal and emailed it to George. "I was impressed by your operation," I wrote.

"Visiting your school gave me the idea to extend the Bourse Jackie program to include female students from other French-speaking West African countries."

That night, George replied, "I find your idea very interesting, so helpful, very generous, one that carries hope and promises a great future for the selected females from those poor and needy communities."

After a few follow-up messages, the new Bourse Jackie program was officially launched. What began as a tribute to Jackie by funding scholarships for girls from Timbuktu had now expanded to eight West African countries.

Watching these scholars transform in real time gave me a purpose deeper than anything I'd known in my career. It hit me: This wasn't just Jackie's legacy anymore. Both the Bourse Jackie program and the journey I was on were becoming my life's work. My spirits were high leaving Ghana but quickly unraveled arriving in Liberia.

Liberia, Sierra Leone

At the airport late at night in the pouring rain, the taxi I had arranged was nowhere to be found. It took a good twenty minutes to find someone to take me on the long drive to the capital, Monrovia. But it turned into a three-hour trip after a flat tire. *Sometimes, shit happens.* Liberia turned out to be another tour of poverty rooted in leadership challenges, even more distressing, given Liberia's unique founding. Under US President James Monroe, former slaves were repatriated to Africa in the early 1800s, from where millions had been violently taken in horrific conditions for a life of misery. Monrovia was even named after the fifth president of my country. Liberia is one of only two of the fifty-four countries in Africa that was not colonized. It was a story with such promise, derailed by generations of misrule.

In Robertsport, one of Africa's surfing hotspots, pastel houses with faded colonial charm hint at its founding by repatriated American slaves, while just a few miles away, the nearby village endures grinding poverty, with mud huts and no running water, a stark contrast rooted in history and inequality.

The promise spiraled out of control during the brutal reign of Charles Taylor in the late 1990s, whose presidency plunged the country into civil war, corruption, and unspeakable violence, erasing what hope remained. And because of him, Sierra Leone unraveled as well. By the time I left these two countries, I was ready to get back home.

. . .

Having visited Syria, one of the three no-go countries when I began the year, I now turned my attention to the two remaining obstacles: Libya and North Korea. For North Korea, I realized that no travel company would take me as a US passport holder, and the Trump-era travel ban wasn't going to be lifted anytime soon. If I wanted to go, I'd need a second passport.

After researching, I found that Dominica offered one of the easiest and most affordable citizenship-by-investment programs. I'd spent my life seeing the world, and I wasn't ready to accept that only North Korea was off-limits. It might've seemed like overkill, but I called it "Trump Insurance." Soon after, I got confirmation from a woman named Nancy in Dominica, helping me with the process: "Once you notarize the documents, your new passport will be issued." With that, I planned a visit to Jungle Bay in Dominica for early November to explore my "new country" and hoped I'd get Daniel to come along.

Meanwhile, there was even more promising travel news: Ihab Zaki, owner of Spiekermann Travel, was organizing a small group to another country on my list, Libya, including Josh from my Horn of Africa trip and other extreme travelers. Ihab was confident about visas, saying that the Libyan ban on Americans was over, and the trip aligned perfectly with a visit I had planned to Chad for the Gerewol Festival, both trips via Cairo.

Three weeks out, I submitted my passport to Annette at Travel Document Express. But as time ticked down, delays threatened my plans. Five days before my flight, I called Josh.

"Josh, huge favor. I fly to Cairo in a few days. If my passport with the Libyan visa isn't ready tomorrow, could you pick it up when you take the train from NYC to DC to get yours and bring it with you to Cairo? I can use my other passport to get into Egypt."

After some pacing and nail-biting, he texted back: "Yes, I will do that for you. See you in Cairo."

I dubbed him "the Courier."

Good thing I hadn't relied on Libyan bureaucracy to move quickly. Josh picked up our passports just in time, the day I flew out. After law school and landing in NYC's legal world, Josh had started chasing 193 himself, albeit at a slower pace. He'd already proven his worth by fending off a would-be soldier-thief during our Horn of Africa trip. Now, he was saving my Libya trip.

At 5:00 a.m. the next day, Ihab led our group of eight to the EgyptAir counter at the Cairo airport for our morning flight to Tripoli. We handed over our passports, visas ready. But the attendant frowned.

"I don't see your names on this list. Where's your security clearance?"

Seriously?

Though our visas were valid, the mandatory security clearance hadn't been approved. We waited at the airport, hoping for a green light that never came. Not the next two days, either, with our group waiting at a Cairo hotel. On the third morning, in the hotel lobby, we circled up to discuss plan B. Josh leaned over and said, "You say 'inshallah' a lot. Maybe do a special one?"

I dropped to my knees in front of the group, hands raised in prayer to Allah or whoever had the power to get us in.

Maybe it was a coincidence. Maybe not. But late that day, the clearance came through. We were headed to Tripoli the next morning. *Praise be to Allah.*

Libya

Other than Saddam Hussein, no Arab leader had the global name recognition of Muammar Gaddafi. Seizing power in 1969, he played a central role in the 1973 Arab oil embargo that triggered a worldwide energy crisis, and he also sponsored terrorist acts that culminated in US airstrikes under Reagan in 1986. Remarkably, Gaddafi gave up his nuclear weapons program in the early 2000s, leading to a brief normalization of relations. But when a pro-democracy uprising referred to as the Arab Spring erupted, Obama sided with the revolutionaries. Gaddafi was captured and killed by a rebel militia in 2011.

Like in Iraq after Saddam, Ghaddafi's fall unleashed chaos. Libya fractured into civil war, the US ambassador was killed in an attack on the embassy, and the death toll climbed to fifty thousand. The country became the epicenter of a refugee crisis as hundreds of thousands of people from across Africa made the perilous journey through the desert, hoping to reach Europe by crossing the sea from Libya's shores.

"Yes, we hated Ghaddafi, but at least we knew where we stood," our guide said cautiously, eyes scanning the area. "Now it's chaos. Militias carve up Tripoli and Benghazi. We trust only our own clans."

Delays in Cairo cost us a few days, forcing us to skip the vast southern deserts I'd hoped to explore. Libya had been one of the hardest countries to enter, and after two days stranded in Cairo, we were on borrowed time. That afternoon, we explored Tripoli, a city of contradictions. On paper, Libya is oil-rich and modern. But in Tripoli, gleaming neighborhoods stood beside bullet-pocked buildings and refugee stalls in the souk all with a heavy air of instability.

I usually try to feel the pulse of a capital city, its rhythm, warmth, or rawness. But Tripoli was elusive. It wasn't threatening, just unsettled, with too much changing too quickly.

But my main reason for coming wasn't Tripoli; it was to see Leptis Magna. I've visited many of the world's great Roman ruins—Jerash, Palmyra, Timgad, Baalbek—but nothing prepared me for this place.

Entering through an arch as grand as anything in Rome, I was struck by the scale and preservation. Known as the "Rome of Africa," Leptis Magna began as a Phoenician settlement and became a jewel of the Roman Empire by the second century BC. Once home to nearly one hundred thousand people and the birthplace of two emperors, it showcased the heights of Roman engineering. The amphitheater was the star, its tiered stone seats rising above the arena floor where, centuries ago, gladiators and animals waited in the shadows, all set against the aqua-blue Mediterranean.

Libya is a dry country, so on our final night, we toasted with glasses of Coke. We'd hoped to toast with one of our local guides, but he abruptly left for Friday prayers and never returned. Things often didn't seem to go as planned in Libya, but we had much to celebrate. Three people from our group, Patrick Gilliland, Laurie Campbell, and Gary Krosin, had just visited their final country and became UN Masters. Patrick put it well. "This journey changes you. I'll keep traveling as long as I can, and I feel incredibly lucky to be doing what we do and hopefully doing some good along the way."

Later, I congratulated him. "We'll need to do this toast with a real drink someday."

He smiled. "Yeah, after you finish too."

Something in his voice gave me the impression that getting to 193 might not have felt like the triumph he'd expected. A realization that it was not a flag we plant on our final country, but something we build slowly—knowledge, connection, memories. I had twenty-five countries to go, so it would be a while before we could have that drink, and for a brief moment, it occurred to me, *Maybe I should take my time.*

Chapter 26

A Mating Dance

Go far, as far as you can. The harder it is, the farther it is, the more unknown it is, the more it will teach you.
—Tiziano Terzani, Italian journalist and mystic traveler

**October 2023
Chad**

My Leptis Magnus experience was still going through my mind when my phone lit up with horror. We had just landed in Cairo. While I'd been blissfully unplugged, war had erupted: Hamas had attacked Israel. Over a thousand dead and hundreds of hostages taken, even small children. *I sat staring at my phone, not able to process what I was reading.*

As the unthinkable details of what happened unfolded, it provoked the long-held narratives on both sides in such extreme ways. It was hard to read some of the posts from friends on Instagram, both Jewish and Muslim. I understood how tribal loyalties surfaced, particularly after events like this, but the sweeping hatred toward entire populations was too much. I am a problem solver by nature, and when something seems unsolvable, I tend to disengage. It was clear there was not going to be any solution between the Israelis and the Palestinians anytime soon.

It was Friday, and time to send my usual "Shabbat Shaloms" and "Juma'a Mubarak" to both my Jewish and Muslim friends. And after a few days of silence from Lina, my Yemeni friend in Bahrain whom I met on the way to Socotra, I began to wonder if she no longer wanted to have a virtual Jewish friend. As global anger on both sides grew, and Israel mobilized for a siege of Gaza, the possibility seemed increasingly likely. President Biden ordered two aircraft carriers to the Middle East to deter Iran and its proxy, Hezbollah, from initiating fighting on another front. Clearly, this wasn't going to be a skirmish. There was a risk of a conflagration in the Middle East like we'd never seen before.

In light of this, it was possible that some of my nascent friendships in the Islamic world could be on hold at best or over at worst. This had happened only a few years earlier when some Russian friendships, from when we lived in Moscow, abruptly became distant after Putin's invasion of Ukraine.

When I checked my list of Instagram followers, my suspicion was confirmed. Lina's name was no longer there.

My heart sank. I usually try to understand both sides of a conflict, but Hamas's attack on Israel on October 7 was a big red line for me. And yet, I knew deep down that both people, Palestinians and Israelis, carried legitimate, long-standing grievances, and tragedies like this rarely happen in a vacuum.

I had grown up in a deeply Jewish community. Although Jackie wasn't Jewish, our boys attended a Jewish day school from kindergarten through eighth grade. At the same time, Caravan to Class had built schools in Timbuktu, one of Islam's most historic centers in Africa, and I had traveled across nearly every Muslim-majority country. Those journeys had challenged and reshaped some of my assumptions. Now, all of it was colliding in my mind as I wondered what Lina was thinking.

I decided to email her.

> Dear Lina,
>
> I noticed you'd stopped following me on Instagram, and I hadn't heard back after my usual Friday greeting.
>
> That made me sad. Even though our friendship was virtual, I always looked forward to connecting. You helped me with Arabic and taught me about your culture. I will always be grateful for that. I imagine this might be about the war in Gaza, but I'm not sure. It's ironic: I've lost friends on both sides for trying to stay in the middle. And if someone like me, who sees the humanity in both peoples and wants to stop the violence, can't find common ground, what hope is there for peace?
>
> Regardless, I think you're an amazing person, a loving mom to two wonderful girls, and I wish you only peace, health, and happiness.
>
> Sincerely, and sadly,
> Barry

Her reply came within minutes:

> Oh, Barry!
>
> I haven't even finished reading your email, but I had to tell you, I didn't unfollow you! I deactivated my account. I just couldn't take the images anymore.
>
> I did remember I hadn't sent you my usual Friday greeting and thought about emailing you. . . . Yes, I've been deeply depressed. Watching those videos of children dying, families buried in rubble. It broke me. We agreed not to talk politics, but it's so hard to watch the constant suffering in Gaza and the West Bank.

I feel much better being off social media. As a mom of two little girls, I had to protect my sanity.

And, Barry, please DO NOT think for a second that I see you differently because of religion. That's not how we were raised.

We're cousins at the end of the day.

She had said the same thing about being cousins while we were deplaning after our trip to Socotra. I felt relief, then a flicker of shame. For a moment, I gave in to the fragility of the connection, thinking about how easily it could fall apart. Maybe it was a bit of legacy of "abandonment syndrome" from losing Jackie, something here one day, gone the next.

I doubted whether two openhearted people from different worlds could truly weather disagreement. Fear filled the void. But these are the times we live in—hard times marked by deep divides, but also times when two people from opposite worlds can still call each other cousins.

I thought, *Maybe peace doesn't start with negotiations. Maybe it just starts with emails like Lina's.*

Chad

The journey to find the Wodaabe and the Gerewol Festival was Africa at its most raw and beautiful, mud-brick towns with tiny mosques; nomads guiding their camels, cattle, and sheep across the horizon; women in brilliantly colored dresses that shimmered against the dusty roads. Reaching them took two full days over rough roads into remote stretches of Chad. We'd be off-grid for the week, no cell reception, no electricity, no aircon, no running water. But with the world in turmoil, especially in the Middle East, I again welcomed the disconnection.

The Gerewol Festival is both a rite of passage and a seasonal celebration marking the end of the rainy season, when fresh grass returns for the herds. The festival is particularly important to the Wodaabe, a nomadic cattle-herding subgroup of the Fulani ethnic group, found mainly in Niger and Chad. Numbering around 150,000, the Wodaabe often travel over three hundred miles a year on foot, migrating their prized cattle and goats in search of the best grazing conditions.

When we arrived, in as isolated a place as one will find in Africa, one small group of travelers had already set up camp. We pitched ours a few hundred feet beyond them. It looked like we were the only foreigners. The heat was brutal, no aircon, no fans, no trees, no shade. I could stand to lose a few pounds, but this wasn't the ideal way to do it. I wandered over to a group of Wodaabe men preparing for the evening's dance, a key part of the Gerewol. Some practiced their moves, others applied brightly colored makeup that completely covered their faces. All wore feathered headdresses and trinkets hanging from their tunics. They looked like peacocks, proud, dazzling, and spectacular, each one trying to outshine the other with their colors and flair. Many bore ritual scarification, slashes across their faces and arms, symbols of ethnic identity and perceived beauty.

Nearby, another group danced in a trance, eyes twitching and rolling. The Wodaabe believe that certain roots and barks possess magical powers, and they chew them to enter this altered state. Probably hallucinogenic, I figured.

Just as I was about to join the half circle of observers, *I froze.*

Twenty feet away stood a bald woman with a tattoo of the world map across her entire back. I knew exactly who that was.

No way.

"Haley?"

She turned. "Barry!" she said, and came over to throw her arms around me. *That's how our extreme-travel community rolls.* Like Renée in Kiribati, Haley was another kindred spirit, a mirror held up at just the right moment.

We'd only recently begun messaging on Instagram. Ten days earlier, she wrote, "Hey Barry, I was traveling with Jacquelyn Kunz in Guyana, and she told me about your humanitarian work in Timbuktu. There aren't enough people in the world like you." I thanked her and replied, "Hope we meet on the road one day. Good luck rounding out your 193."

Haley had alopecia universalis, which explained her baldness, and also macular degeneration. "I felt compelled to see the world while I still could," she told me as we eyed some Wodaabe putting on their makeup. Her first big trip was to Namibia at age seventeen. Then, after reaching her hundredth country at thirty-six, she celebrated with a full-back tattoo of the world map.

"Travel gave me the confidence to own how I looked and who I am," she said as we sat away from the dancers, digesting the scene and getting to know each other better.

I asked how it felt to travel the world as a woman with a disability. "It's not always easy," she said, "but it's made me more adventurous and resilient. And this travel community? It's the first place I've ever truly felt accepted."

Later that evening, the Gerewol began in earnest. My guide from my Socotra trip, Elena from Italy, told me, "The Wodaabe women select male dancers, those they find most attractive. After she makes her choice, the couple may spend the night together, and if both agree, it can lead to a relationship or even marriage."

In the dark, lit only by the stars, the men stood in a line, swaying rhythmically, singing in unison, clapping, beating small hand drums. Across from them, the young Wodaabe women watched, eyes scanning for the men with the most beauty, posture, and grace. I watched one woman lock eyes with a dancer. Her gaze said everything. Moments later, he stepped out of the line and walked away with her. I assumed they were no longer in the friend zone.

Back in the capital, N'Djamena, I reflected on the Wodaabe. Their lives were materially spare but rich in meaning. Everything centered on cattle and milk, and from that, they shaped purpose, through rituals like the Gerewol. With their concept of beauty and through their resilience, they had passed down their culture for generations.

From what I saw, their life was hard, very hard. But it was focused, free from the clutter of modern existence. In their simplicity, there was clarity and in their rituals, rhythm. It was a reminder: Meaning doesn't come from abundance, but from focused attention.

These days, I am looking for meaning the way some chase adrenaline, across borders, languages, deserts, and memory. Not for the thrill, but for the moments that connect me to something deeper and lasting, those flashes of insight. And hopefully, my brain holds onto those impressions when I need them most. Maybe that's what this journey has always been about: not collecting countries, but collecting moments of clarity, moments that remind me who I am, and what really matters when everything else falls away.

Moldova

While I was grateful to be back in air-conditioning and to have a working phone, it also meant returning to grim headlines. The Israeli hostages in Gaza weren't being released anytime soon, and the toll on a good number of innocent Palestinian lives was rising by the day. *So much for escaping the world's worries.*

At least I could now check off the last of the forty-four countries on the European continent. Moldova, a small nation the size of Maryland with just 2.5 million people, is a blend of hilltop monasteries, Soviet relics, and sprawling vineyards. After a stretch of traveling to dry, no-alcohol destinations with my trips to Libya and Chad, the wine history of Moldova offered a welcome change. Once responsible for producing a third of the Soviet Union's wine, the country's wineries easily stole the show.

Cricova Winery impressed with the quality of its wines, but Mileștii Mici was astonishing. It has 120 miles of underground tunnels. To put that in perspective, that's a greater distance than the drive from New York to Philadelphia, all below ground. Even more remarkable, it holds the world record for the largest wine collection on the planet, with an astounding 1.5 million bottles aging in its cool limestone corridors, earning it a Guiness World Record.

While I enjoyed visiting serene monasteries and sipping vino, I also wanted to better understand the security challenges this small country faced. The shadow of Russia loomed large here. With Russian troops supporting the breakaway republic of Transnistria and launching airstrikes just 120 miles away in Odessa, Moldova's sovereignty felt under siege. If not for Ukraine's resistance, it was likely that Moldova would have been next on Putin's list.

The most fascinating part of my trip was a visit to Transnistria, where Putin had clearly stirred up tension. "We'll pass a Russian checkpoint, then enter Transnistria's immigration office," my guide, Natalia, explained. "They'll stamp your passport even though it's technically still Moldova."

Go figure.

Crossing into Tiraspol, the largest city in Transnistria, I felt transported back to my days in Moscow with Jackie and the boys. I even got to dust off some of my Russian. Though the people were ethnically Russian and Ukrainian, Stalin merged Transnistria with Moldova to dilute Romanian influence. After a brief war post-USSR collapse, it gained de facto autonomy with its own army, government, and currency. Yet no country in the world, not even Russia, had recognized its *independence*.

On our return to Chisinau, we passed grim-faced Russian soldiers at the border. The whole experience underscored how fragile Moldova's independence really was. With one of the weakest militaries in the world, ranked 144 out of 145, it wouldn't stand a chance without outside help. Life here was already hard: a brain drain fueled by economic struggle and Russian threat, and the lowest GDP per capita on the European continent. I hadn't expected this kind of fragility so close to the heart of Europe.

"Natalia," I asked, "what percentage of Moldovans support Ukraine?"

"One hundred and ten percent," she said without hesitation. "I dream of peace for innocent people, soldiers, children. I want all wars to stop." Natalia's faith and hope in peace seemed like the best act of resistance.

That night, I tuned into the annual NomadMania Travel Awards from my hotel in Chisinau. I'd been invited to present the "Most Purposeful Traveler" award remotely.

It was a thrill to recognize fellow travelers advocating for global causes. The nominees included my friend Cameron and Ric Gazarian of *Counting Countries*, plus a very bold traveler named Charlie Christensen from Denmark, who founded *Walking for Water* after witnessing the daily struggle for clean drinking water in a Tanzanian village. He had already walked over eight thousand miles from Denmark to Tanzania to raise funds for boreholes.

As I watched the livestream, I spotted familiar faces, Lucy Tsu from the Bay Area and Mette Mikkelsen from Denmark, both on NomadMania's board of directors, cohosting in elegant gowns. Lucy, like Elena from Spain, was a teacher using her free summers to see the world. She had just reached her 193rd country, traveling through Syria with my friend Fadi; Mette was one country shy, with North Korea still closed. I was glad to see Rauli Virtanen receive a lifetime achievement award, not only for being the first human being to visit every country in the world, but for shedding light on global conflicts along the way.

When my turn came, Mette asked me to say a few words about Caravan to Class before announcing Charlie as the winner. After the applause, Lucy followed up.

"Barry, can you share your advice on how travelers can do good while exploring the world?"

"Sure," I said. "Most of us wouldn't pursue a quest like this if we didn't care about the people and places we visit. The needs can feel overwhelming, but find a cause that stretches you, one you believe in, and *take that first step*. Don't let doubt paralyze you. For me, founding Caravan to Class in Timbuktu has been the most fulfilling thing I've done, other than marrying my wife and raising my kids."

It wasn't lost on me that this year's ceremony was held in a bunker in nearby Ukraine, a symbol of solidarity from the travel world.

The final award, for best travel book, went to UN Master Boris Kester for *The Long Road to Cullaville*, a book I'd read and enjoyed. As he gave his acceptance speech, I found myself quietly wondering . . . *Maybe one day, that could be me.*

Dominica

I'd never spent a week at a resort during Project 193. But after Libya's postwar chaos, Chad's lack of basic comforts, and feeling the threat of Putin's Russia in Moldova, the idea of a relaxing week sounded more than welcome. Best of all, Daniel was on break from his firefighter training, and I was overjoyed that he'd be joining me.

When researching Dominica for a second passport, I was struck by the images of rivers, waterfalls, volcanic terrain, and Caribbean mountains. Known as the "Nature Island," it's also a year-round nesting ground for sperm whales.

Two weeks before our trip, I got a text from Nancy, the yoga instructor at the Jungle Bay Resort who worked on the side to help foreigners, like me, get Dominica citizenship: "I have a present for you upon arrival." It could only be one thing: *my new passport.*

On our flight to Roseau, I sat beside an elderly woman named Jennifer. We connected instantly. Within ten minutes, she told me she had moved back to Dominica from the US after her husband passed, to be close to family. I shared my own loss, and the fact that I had become a citizen of her country. Before we landed, she handed me a piece of paper with her name and number. "Welcome home," she said.

Sure enough, Nancy presented me with my Dominica passport when we arrived. "How about I show you around my new home?" I said to Daniel.

"It's about time, Dad," he replied, grinning.

Our first hike took us through lush rainforest to a canyon where hot volcanic water funneled into a pool. We scrambled into a cave and swam toward a crashing waterfall, horsing around like kids. I'd always been the jokester with my boys when they were young, but after Jackie died, I had become the rock-steady dad, serious and dependable. Believe me, I tried to bring back the playfulness, but it rarely surfaced. That day, it did, and it felt good. *My new home was starting to suit me just fine.*

The next day, we hiked to another waterfall with an American mother and daughter staying at our resort. The daughter, Ella, was in her twenties and had beautiful tattoos.

"I like your art," I said.

"I'm a tattoo artist," she replied. "I have a studio in Berkeley."

"My wife had a sunflower tattoo," I said as I told her about our loss of Jackie. "Recently, I met someone in Africa with a world map tattooed across her back. I thought maybe I'd get a globe with a *J* for Jackie in the center."

Ella paused. "The J might be confusing. But what if the globe were bordered with a sunflower? That way, her spirit is surrounding the world that you are exploring."

As we scrambled across boulders, I smiled. Thinking about it, I said, "That's brilliant. Would you do it for me?"

"Of course," she said.

Daniel raised an eyebrow. "Really, Dad? What will Benjamin say?"

"He'll be fine," I said. "Mom had two hummingbirds tattooed on her back in addition to the sunflower. No one objected."

"Dad, I'm fine with it," he said. "Just asking."

What a reversal, my son questioning me about a tattoo I wanted to get. I'd met countless travelers covered in ink and never imagined joining them. But by the end of that hike, I was sure. When I decide something, *I go all in.*

"Really glad I met you," I said to Ella. "See you in Berkeley."

The next morning, Daniel and I spotted sperm whales from a boat we chartered: *awe-inspiring*. That afternoon, Weefee, a Jungle Bay guide, gave us a tour of Dominica's wild fruits—mangoes, papaya, passionfruit, guava. "No one goes hungry here," he said. "There's always fresh fruit."

That evening, he invited us to his rum bar, where we sipped raisin, coffee, and chocolate punch, all local, all strong. Slightly buzzed, we walked back under the stars, marveling at Weefee's life: tour guide by day, bartender by night, and—as if this were not enough—also mayor of his village, Soufrière, one of the world's premier free-diving sites.

Traveling with family reminded me what I loved most about it: stepping out of routine, making memories, and reconnecting without distraction. The golden age of family trips may have passed, but this one with Daniel felt like a golden echo, just as meaningful, maybe even more so.

We were sad to leave. Dominica's beauty was undeniable, but it was the warmth of its people, like Weefee, Jennifer, and Nancy, that truly stayed with us. Not long after, Condé Nast named it the "friendliest country in the world." I smiled when I read that. If the world ever became too unstable, I knew I'd found a place I could return to. Not just for its natural splendor, but because of what it represented: kind people and joy for life's simple pleasures.

As we boarded the plane for the return flight home, Daniel turned to me and said, "Let's bring Benjamin next year." A simple sentence, but it landed deep and was an important intention and thread of continuity, even in the absence of Jackie. The power of saying simply, *Let's do this again.*

My time with Daniel had reenergized me for my last big swing through the African continent for 2023, including a place that had the polar opposite of Dominica's reputation as one of the friendliest.

Chapter 27

A Christmas Ride on the Tarmac

*I can't think of anything that excites
a greater sense of childlike wonder
than to be in a country where you are
ignorant of almost everything.*
—Bill Bryson, *Notes from a Small Island*

**December 2023
Tuvalu**

The roar of a waterfall echoed through the jungle as we veered off the highway in Cameroon. My guide, Mebah, said old Tarzan movies had been filmed here. Moments later, twin chutes of water came into view, plunging roughly three hundred feet into the river below. A perfect rainbow arced across the mist, framing the falls in a cascade of color. I hadn't seen anything this majestic since Kaieteur Falls in Guyana. Mebah told me this was Ekom Nkam Falls, among Africa's largest by volume in the rainy season. Even in the dry season, the force was staggering. This 2023 seventh and final trip of the year to Africa carried a different weight. It was my first end-of-year holiday season without the family, but the Ekom Nkam Falls experience was a striking way to begin the adventure.

Some in the travel community knock out parts of the continent in one long stretch, staying six months, a more environmentally responsible approach. But I returned home every few weeks to be with my centenarian mother and see Daniel and friends. To offset my footprint, I bought sixty tons of CO2e removal credits through the International Small Group and Tree Planting Program (TIST), which pays Ugandan farmers to plant trees, an environmental investment in the country where Project 193 began and still holds personal significance.

I was still dazed by the spectacular waterfall as we drove on to Bafoussam. From the window, I watched fruit sellers, cabinetmakers, and colorfully dressed women pass by like a living tapestry. Then something jolted me back to attention.

Stop!

Jumping out of the car before it even stopped, I hurried toward a hawker's table. There, sitting in a large bucket of water, its legs draped over the side, was the biggest frog I'd ever seen, nearly raccoon-sized, with webbed feet as big as my hands. It was on a rope leash, which the vendor held tightly.

I'd found the legendary Goliath frog that can weigh up to ten pounds, native only to this part of Cameroon, and it was for sale.

Mebah had caught up to me. "I need more info on this creature," I said. After a quick exchange, Mebah translated. "He searches the swamps downstream of the waterfall where a specific grass grows. If lucky, he catches one a day, selling them for ten dollars apiece, considered a delicacy."

"Is this the only place in the world they exist?" I asked, staring at the frog.

"Yes, I've actually never seen one in person," Mebah said. "You're very lucky!"

Naturally, I had to ask for a selfie. *No one's going to believe this otherwise.* The vendor agreed and handed me the leash. Mr. Goliath immediately leaped out of the bucket and toward me, with water spraying like confetti. I jumped back, with him nearly getting away.

But I managed to hold on and tightened the rope while lifting him cautiously. His mouth was the size of a small dog's, and I wasn't about to grab him barehanded.

Mebah took the picture. Back in the car, I studied the photo, my expression frozen in a mix of disbelief and wonder. In that instant, holding this prehistoric creature, I felt like a wide-eyed kid again, reminded that the world is still wild, magical, and waiting to surprise us if we're willing to leap toward the unknown.

Central African Republic and Equatorial Guinea

After a few more days exploring waterfalls and visiting villages of various ethnic groups in Cameroon, it was time to move on to the Central African Republic, CAR, and find out firsthand what made it one of the least friendly countries in the world. According to Expatsi, a service helping US expats adjust abroad, CAR ranked second from the bottom. Widespread crime, armed roadblocks, and a lack of basic services have long made it a no-go zone for most travelers despite its having an amazing jungle full of large animals.

I'd been to dangerous places: Afghanistan, Yemen, Syria, Iraq. But CAR stood out for the sheer volume of cautionary tales. I was grateful to have William, a trusted guide the travel community had thoroughly vetted, to show me around. Over three days, he led me on a tour of waterfalls, Pygmy tribes, and the capital, Bangui, where I saw not one but four different armies patrolling the roads: the CAR military, UN peacekeepers, Rwandan troops (*yes, Rwandans*), and the Russians, specifically the Wagner Group. There's even a monument in Bangui honoring Wagner soldiers. *Not exactly my idea of heroes, but it's not my country.*

All this foreign military presence is supposedly meant to stabilize the capital, but William said the biggest difference-maker wasn't any army; it was Pope Francis. Against the advice of his staff, the pope visited Bangui in 2015, not long after civil war had split the capital into Christian and Muslim zones, no-go areas for the opposite side. The UN estimated that as many as five thousand had been killed and hundreds of thousands displaced during this time. In a bold gesture, Francis visited a besieged Muslim neighborhood of fifteen thousand, prayed in a mosque, and delivered a powerful message of reconciliation. Many in Bangui credit that moment as the start of a fragile peace.

In Africa sometimes, cycles of violence and poverty can wear you down. Then, all of a sudden, one person shifts the tide. Francis gave people hope and reminded me why I still believe in the power of presence and goodwill. For him, just showing up was his own form of revolution.

One other highlight came not from tribes or waterfalls, but children. On our final evening, we stopped in a small town so William could buy vegetables for his wife at an outdoor market. Music played from a boombox across the street. I stepped out of the car and noticed a bunch of kids, girls and boys, maybe eight to ten years old, sitting on a log and gently swaying to the music.

Looking at me, they started smiling, stood up, and then started dancing, barefoot or in sandals, shirtless or wrapped in colorful prints. As I started filming them, they lit up even more, their movements growing wilder, their joy more contagious. Laughter burst into the dusty air, eyes gleaming in a moment of pure, unfiltered childhood freedom. Then an older man walked over, scolded them, and turned off the music. *Buzzkill.* The moment passed, but I'd captured it on video.

Back in the car, I replayed it over and over. These kids were radiant. Maybe CAR was unfriendly, but no one is born that way. Joy is surely a child's natural state. Something breaks along the way. But here, today, these children were simply waiting to be seen. *Aren't we all?*

Thanks to William, I made it out of CAR without a single bad incident. Just one African country remained on this Central Africa leg: Equatorial Guinea.

On paper, it intrigued me. The only Spanish-speaking country in Africa, it had gone from poverty to massive oil wealth in the 1990s. I wondered what that kind of transformation looked like.

I found out as soon as I landed in Malabo. The brand-new airport fed into a gleaming six-lane highway, something I'd never seen in Africa. As my guide, Epiphanio, drove me to the hotel, we passed mansion after mansion, eerily identical and seemingly empty.

"What are those?" I asked.

"They were built for the African Union Summit in 2022," he said.

"One for each of the fifty-four African heads of state. Used for three days. Empty ever since."

Even my hotel, the extravagant Sofitel Malabo, felt like a government-subsidized stage set, impressive but hollow. Nearby, we passed an under-construction eco-resort complex featuring beach villas, a convention center, and even a mindfulness retreat, all deserted.

Later, I asked Epiphanio to take me to where regular people lived. About twenty minutes from the city, we turned into a village of shanties, scrap wood and corrugated metal structures barely holding together. I saw an elderly woman sitting in front of one of these shacks. Her expression, tired and sad, told me more than a photo ever could.

I suddenly just *wanted out*, something I'd never felt so strongly in my travels. Thank God I'd only booked three days.

President Obiang is the second-longest-serving head of state in the world, after the sultan of Brunei. His son, the likely successor, was convicted in France for embezzling tens of millions to fund a lavish lifestyle and has had assets seized around the world for various crimes. Despite the oil wealth, little of it seems to reach the ordinary people. In the villages, and even in Malabo, people looked dispirited. According to the UN, roughly one-third of the population lacks access to clean water, and nearly 8 percent of children die before the age of five.

What was it that made me want out so badly? Maybe it was the soul of a country, smothered by greed. People living in shadows while their leaders hosted ghost summits in mansions. I felt complicit just being there, taking pictures.

When someone asks me about the most haunting place I've been, I'll have a clear answer.

After armed convoys in CAR and the hollow opulence of Equatorial Guinea, I welcomed a more tranquil close to the year: Nauru and Tuvalu, the two least-populous, least-visited countries on Earth. Neither had an army. So, there'd be no soldiers, no soulless infrastructure, just small island nations with minimal hassle, and hopefully, no heartbreak.

South Pacific

On one of the many connecting flights to Nauru, I struck up a conversation with a woman sitting near me, and she turned out to be another extreme traveler. Aruna told me she had more than 140 countries under her belt, and as usual, we found that we knew some of the same people. *There really aren't many degrees of separation in this community.*

She mentioned she was heading to Oceania to knock off a few more countries, though her plans might change. Tuvalu had just closed its airport due to rain damage.

Wait, what?

Sure enough, I Googled "Tuvalu" to find that flights were canceled indefinitely. I took a deep breath. If this journey taught me anything, it was the importance of flexibility. At the very least, I could get to Nauru, no small feat. It's one of the few countries in Oceania that requires a visa for US citizens, and the process is notoriously vague. You have to email this one Nauruan guy in Australia. Sometimes he replies. Sometimes he doesn't. It took months of follow-ups before I finally got my visa. Any delay can mean eating the cost of an expensive, nonrefundable Nauru Airlines ticket. And as fate would have it, even with visa in hand, I ended up stuck in Brisbane for two extra days due to mechanical issues with the plane, one of only two in the entire airline's fleet.

When I was finally able to fly to Nauru, it looked from the air like just another idyllic tropical island. But I knew better. On the ground, driving into the interior with my guide, Kozay, I saw trash-strewn yards, abandoned cars, and a landscape ravaged by phosphate mining. The island sat atop a calcified mound of seagull guano, *a nicer name for "shit,"* once one of the richest phosphate deposits in the world. In the 1970s, Nauru had a GDP per capita comparable to Saudi Arabia.

"I wish we'd never found phosphate," Kozay said. "The land's ruined, and the money was wasted. People used to buy Lamborghinis in a country with only ten miles of road."

Nauru was a case study in how short-term gains can undermine a nation's future, leaving it dependent on Australian payments for a refugee resettlement camp to maintain financial stability.

My only one full day on the island, because of the canceled flights, was enough to tour the ten-mile perimeter and return to the lodge for dinner. That was, until I learned the restaurant only served breakfast and lunch.

"Where can I get dinner?"

"There's one restaurant open for dinner. It's on the other side of the island."

"Can I take a taxi?"

"There are no taxis in Nauru."

"How am I supposed to get there, or to the airport tomorrow?"

"You can rent our car. Just leave it at the airport with the keys on the floor." Of course. And that's exactly what I did.

Tuvalu

By some miracle, Tuvalu International Airport reopened. On Christmas Eve, I flew to the capital, Funafuti, my vote for "best capital name." It was a thin sliver of coral atoll, flanked by turquoise seas. Like Kiribati, Tuvalu, with its nine islands, is one of the world's lowest-lying nations. With an average elevation of just six and a half feet, NASA predicts half of Funafuti will be underwater by 2050. Australia has already pledged resettlement for Tuvaluans when the time comes.

After we landed, I noticed people moving onto the runway to walk their dogs, play soccer, or simply stroll.

"What are they doing?" I asked a woman outside the airport.

"This is where people hang out when planes aren't landing," she said.

Why not? With only two flights a week, the runway doubled as a park, plaza, and promenade. *Brilliant.*

I wanted to explore further, so I asked the hotel receptionist about taking a boat to the outer islands or getting a tour. She gave me a puzzled look. "You do know it's Christmas Eve, right? Everything except church is closed until the twenty-seventh."

"Do you have any motor bikes for rent? I can explore the island myself."

"All booked," she said, "but maybe check the airport ticket desk."

No luck there, either. Then she suggested an old-school approach: "Walk the main road and knock on doors."

After about eight knocks, I found a guy willing to rent me a bike, no forms, no fuss. Just like that, I was cruising the island on Christmas Eve.

In some places, it was only ten feet wide with aquamarine water inching in on both sides. I even took a spin down a stretch of the runway. *That's not something I will likely be able to do ever again.* Like the Wodaabe's rituals or the joy of barefoot dancers in CAR, this, too, was a celebration of what mattered most: life's simplicities. Even in places at risk of vanishing, unforgettable moments aren't hard to find.

Chapter 28

A Visual Desert Treat

In an age of speed, I began to think, nothing could be more invigorating than going slow.
—Pico Iyer

January 2024
Niger

I began 2024, hopefully the final year of this quest to visit every country in the world, with a visit to Mali for Caravan to Class, followed by a trip to Niger. With Air France suspending flights to both countries due to the aftermath of coups in both places, I rerouted via Royal Air Maroc through Casablanca, a city I hadn't visited in over thirty years since I'd been caught up in the attempted hijacking in 1991. I hoped for a quieter landing this time.

Mali

Landing in Mali with a full heart but an ache of absence, I'd come to witness something beautiful—young women stepping into their power through the Bourse Jackie program. But just beyond that hope was a shadow: Timbuktu, always the soul of my journey to Mali, was still out of reach. The UN had pulled out, and violence had surged. And once again, I was kept from embracing the friends who had become family.

Fifteen years earlier, Caravan to Class began in Timbuktu with a simple mission: Build schools and bring education to forgotten communities. But over time, the mission evolved. Now, our focus is higher-education scholarships for young women in West Africa through our Bourse Jackie programs, based in Bamako and Accra. It means I spend less time in northern Mali, but Timbuktu is still in my heart. Abdoulaye, my longtime friend and partner there, made the arduous and uncertain journey south to join us in Bamako.

The seminar, held at the Onomo Hotel in Bamako, brought together Bourse Jackie scholars, as well as representatives from the US embassy and USAID. I gave the opening remarks.

"This program carries my wife's name for a reason. Your academic success matters, but it's not enough. I'm counting on you to rise, to overcome challenges, to become the leaders your communities need, and to light the path for others."

No pressure, right?

But the young women didn't shrink from the challenge. One scholar, Fatoumata Randane, stood up and said something I'll never forget. "Education is the most powerful tool we can use to change our lives and the world. This scholarship is the most beautiful thing that has ever happened to me and ever will."

That night, as I embraced Abdoulaye in the hotel lobby, I felt the full weight of our shared history, launching Caravan to Class in 2010, and seeing it survive even after the jihadist takeover of Timbuktu in 2012, grieving Jackie's death in 2017, and planting the seeds of Bourse

Jackie in her honor. He shook my hand warmly and said he would carry my love back to our friends in the North.

Later that evening, he sent me an email: You gave everything to me and my family. I only want to serve you and make you proud. If you are satisfied with my work, I thank God.

The word "gratitude" echoed in my mind. It's a word we often throw around, but I didn't truly grasp its gravity until just after the night Jackie died. Something cracked open in me, and thankfully it hasn't closed. Since then, gratitude has become a way to transform grief into purpose.

Fatoumata's words. Abdoulaye's message. These voices remind me that love and loss, hope and heartbreak, are bound together. And that this work, this mission, is not just about education. It's about honoring what remains—and building what's next. What started as a tribute was now a movement, one that demanded my full heart, not just Jackie's name.

Niger

I had been closely monitoring the situation in Niger since the July 2023 coup, wondering if the door to this long-anticipated country had closed for good. But late that fall, Yaou, the owner of Zenith Tours, gave me the green light. While tensions remained high between Niger and several West African neighbors, the airspace was open, though few tourists were willing to take the leap.

I had wanted to visit Niger for years, but it had never worked out. After the coup, I'd feared I had missed my window. Like Mali, it is a vast desert country, largely Muslim, with the Niger River running through its capital. Both places cradle ancient Tuareg cities, Timbuktu in Mali and Agadez in Niger. I had long dreamed of visiting Agadez, but like Timbuktu, it was off-limits due to extremist threats. Instead, I'd explore closer desert villages and the surrounding countryside near Niamey.

Before setting out, I had something far more personal to look forward to. We had recently selected five young women for the inaugural Bourse Jackie English-language scholarship, based in Ghana and offered to women across eight West African nations. Coincidently, one of them was from right here in Niamey. That afternoon, twenty-one-year-old Aida Mistral met me in the hotel café. Within minutes, I knew we had chosen wisely.

Calm, articulate, and clearly driven, she shared her story with me. She'd never met her father, and when she was just two, her mother remarried a man who wanted nothing to do with another child. Aida was left with her grandmother and never saw her mother again. Against all odds, she graduated at the top of her high school class and earned a scholarship to university. But she had to abandon her studies after two years. Despite perfect grades, her grandmother simply could not afford the cost of books and transport.

"I aspire to become an entrepreneur," she said in French, "to build a business where I can hire other young women who've faced struggles like mine. This scholarship, this chance to become fluent in English, brings me closer to that dream."

All I could say, with deep sincerity, was "Inshallah." Hearing her speak so openly made me realize how many voices like hers go unheard in the West, stories not of despair, but of strength and determination.

The next morning, I met Hama, one of Yaou's most trusted guides, for a four-day desert tour. With tourism nearly frozen since the coup, Hama was overjoyed to be back on the road. But there was a catch.

"Barry," he said as we shook hands in the hotel lobby, "the military government now requires that all tourists be escorted by soldiers."

I nodded. "No problem. I've had military escorts in Afghanistan and Yemen. Usually a truck or two behind us."

Hama smiled faintly. "Actually, they'll be in the car. With us."

Flexibility is the currency of travel. "The more the merrier," I joked.

Sure enough, I climbed into his Toyota sedan to find two soldiers, both named Boubakar, in full camouflage, AK-47s resting between their knees. "Enchanté," I said with a laugh, quickly nicknaming them Boubakar 1 and Boubakar 2.

It was a journey both stunning and surreal, as if I'd stepped into another era. Sitting in the front passenger seat, I felt as though I were in a movie theater watching a visual masterpiece. We passed earthen villages and roadside scenes that belonged to centuries past: women wearing brilliant multicolored abayas as they balanced goods on their heads while walking across the sand; camels grazing lazily by desert trees; men and boys pumping water for livestock beside ancient mosques. This was Africa at its best.

At one point, we encountered a group of women pounding grain with long wooden pestles. I approached with my camera, unsure how I'd be received. They burst into laughter, some covering their heads, others waving me on toward them. Their joy felt infectious and free despite the hard, physical work.

Later, Hama spotted a caravan of camels heading across the horizon and abruptly stopped the car on the side of the road. We took off running after them, scrambling over dunes. When we caught up, we were met by a father and his two young sons, all riding the same camel, who greeted us with the traditional hand-to-heart gesture I'd come to love. Watching them disappear back into the horizon, I imagined a different life, one where I was riding alongside my sons on a camel in the desert as part of life's routine.

The desert kept revealing its treasures. In a Hausa village, I admired cylindrical granaries and rows of prized purple onions, destined for markets across West Africa. Boubakar 2 turned to me and asked sheepishly in French, "Would you mind if we stop? I want to bring a sack of onions home. It's my wife's birthday."

"Bien sûr." I smiled. *Not my idea of a romantic gift, but love takes many forms.*

One of the most unforgettable scenes came atop the sunbaked minaret of a desert mosque. From the roof, I looked down to see a group of teenagers pumping water from the only village well, filling buckets for a procession of cows, camels, and goats, the rhythm of survival. At the base, a crowd of children formed, thirty joyful faces, beaming simply because a stranger had chosen to visit their village. It was a mutual exchange of friendliness.

The nonstop procession of images—the mud-brick homes, the richly hued abayas, the vast silence between villages—made me long for simplicity. I didn't have to endure the harsh realities here, desertification, food insecurity, ethnic violence. But I couldn't help noticing the sense of balance and purpose. A life stripped of excess. Back home, sometimes simplicity can seem like a performance, minimalism as the life of the loner. But here it was necessity, not choice, and what I saw was not depravation, but grace. I remembered the value of clearing my own emotional and material clutter after Jackie's passing. That openness led me to this journey. And now, as Project 193 neared its end, I asked, *What comes next?*

On the long drive back to Niamey, I realized something important. I hadn't reached Agadez. I hadn't checked off every highlight on my wish list. But I had been given something far richer—a window into Niger's soul, and a reminder that presence, not perfection, is what makes a journey complete.

Country #177. Maybe not the itinerary I had hoped for, but still a gift.

Part 7

Full Circle

The End of the Road and New Beginnings

Chapter 29

Bearing Witness

*If you are neutral in situations of injustice,
you have chosen the side of the oppressor.*
—Desmond Tutu

February 2024
Sudan

Buried farther down on CNN's online portal, though without much detail, were the following headlines: "Fighting between military rivals in Sudan erupts, dozens dead, US embassy staff evacuated from Khartoum." *Oh great.* Right around the time I was celebrating my birthday in Damascus in April 2023, Sudan erupted into a full-fledged civil war, shutting its doors to tourists. Unsurprisingly, the long-awaited Sudan tour I had booked with ITC for September 2023 was canceled. Now, as I planned my final sixteen countries for 2024, reports said the war continued to rage on, especially around Khartoum and Darfur. Still, a friend in the travel community, Anna Harris, winner of Best Digital Nomad at NomadMania's travel awards the previous year, suggested I try Port Sudan, where there was supposedly no fighting. She knew of no one who had managed to travel there recently, so the suggestion wasn't much, but it was something. After all, Syria and Libya had opened up to me with constant persistence and a bit of luck.

Carla, my contact at ITC Sudan, confirmed that no one was currently entering the country, but she could send me a letter of invitation and arrange a guide and driver if I were to obtain a visa somehow. Turning to my superstar visa agent in DC, Annette, her initial answer was "low probability," but fifteen minutes later, she called to say, "The embassy mentioned that because of your foundation's work in Africa, you can go ahead and apply."

Great news. But then a key question hit me: *If I got the visa, would I actually go?* Sudan was an active conflict zone. Port Sudan had avoided fighting thus far and had become the de facto capital. Khartoum, the actual capital, was destroyed. But when my visa was approved, I thought once again about that line from *The Alchemist* about making things happen. I'd weighed the risks in Afghanistan in 2022, and that trip turned out to be one of my most meaningful trips of this quest. The chance was worth it, and I felt the need to go.

Before long, I found myself once again at Cairo International Airport, with my boarding pass in hand for my flight to Port Sudan. When I arrived at the gate, an EgyptAir agent asked, "Can I see your visa?" and I showed it to her. But she was searching for something else. "Can I also see your Port Sudan entry permit?" *I knew my plan had gone too smoothly.*

The Sudanese embassy in DC had said nothing about an entry permit. The agent said she'd call Port Sudan to check if I could board and asked me to step aside. This felt ominously familiar, as I had been denied boarding months earlier, heading to Libya from the very same terminal at the Cairo airport.

The decision was out of my hands. *Inshallah.*

As the line of passengers boarding the plane grew shorter, I decided to jump in at the end. When my turn came, I offered my boarding pass with my hands together, as though in prayer, and said softly,

"Please let me on. I'll sort it out with the authorities in Port Sudan if needed."

She looked up and nodded.

Yes! I was going to Sudan.

Sudan

I felt nervous throughout the two-hour flight. There was no guarantee that I would be allowed entry once I arrived in Port Sudan. Yet, upon landing and deplaning, and after checking my visa, no one at immigration even mentioned the words "entry permit." Within thirty minutes, I'd found my guide, Khalid, hailed a cab, and we were on our way to the hotel. "The country is in chaos, but it's easy to find a taxi. Almost everyone with a car is trying to earn a little extra money," said Khalid. The first few moments of meeting a guide in a strange new country are always interesting. I've generally had good luck, but you never know how it will go. With Khalid, I instantly felt comfortable. It was his kind, dark face with gentle eyes, slim build, and a baseball hat covering what appeared to be a graying bald head. He looked about my age.

As we arrived at the hotel, the streets were jam-packed. Khalid explained that now that Port Sudan was the capital of the country, the city had filled with refugees from most parts of the war-torn republic. With our actual driver for the trip nowhere to be found, we left our bags at the hotel and caught a taxi to a crowded section of downtown. It appeared to be the market area, with stalls selling fruit, nuts, vegetables, and numerous street-side coffee shops. Pointing at me, a well-dressed man approached and said to Khalid in Arabic, "He is the first tourist I've seen in my country in nine months."

I'd been to places that had experienced recent coups (Niger and Mali), and places that had previously been war zones (Iraq, Syria, and Afghanistan). But this was the first time I'd visited a country that was an *active war zone*. In the past nine months, Sudan had deteriorated into one of the world's largest underreported humanitarian crises. NGO logos were everywhere: Relief International, the Red Cross, and the International Medical Corps.

I spoke with a few men at some of the ubiquitous outdoor cafés where coffee is brewed with ginger powder, a distinctly delicious Sudanese twist on java. Stretching my Arabic as much as I could with Khalid's help, I learned of the horrific stories of people who fled the original capital when fighting began, with bombs and RPGs striking buildings everywhere. This was not a war of ideology, but a struggle for power between a ruling clan and the government, fought for control over the country's gold, oil, and other mineral riches.

Khalid, a painter in addition to a guide, had to escape the capital himself after his house was ransacked and many of his paintings, his sole wealth, were stolen or destroyed. Carla had previously mentioned the possibility of getting some of his paintings out of Sudan before more were stolen and to help him earn some money. Paid work was very rare these days.

Another two coffees with ginger later, Khalid and I headed back to the hotel, where we were greeted by our driver, Ibrahim. Younger, taller, and more fit than Khalid, he was the kind of guy I welcomed as a driver in this uncertain environment. Nine months earlier, he had also fled Khartoum. "My wife was eight months pregnant, and no hospital could guarantee admission," Ibrahim told me. "I didn't know if we'd make it out alive." After he and his wife fled, RSF soldiers took over their apartment and stole everything they owned.

Despite what they had been through, in addition to a grueling bus ride of more than twenty-four hours just to guide me around the Port Sudan region, Khalid and Ibrahim gave no hint of complaint. They both escaped with their lives from Khartoum and now were simply happy to earn some money. It hit home how so many people in the world face suffering and extreme uncertainty regularly, but they simply don't have the luxury of wallowing in their difficulties. How often had I taken my own comfort and stability for granted?

Listening to Khalid's and Ibrahim's stories, I felt unsettled: How had I not heard more about Sudan in the news? No suffering anywhere in the world should go unreported, but the media decides what to tell us and what not to tell us, what suffering is "in" and what's "out." I heard Jackie's voice in my head: *One beating heart is the same as another; none is superior.* When that simple phrase sank in long ago, I knew I was lucky to have made my life with a woman like her. When I scanned the news, with the situations in Ukraine and Gaza dominating the headlines, it seemed as if the media decided that Sudan's suffering was "out."

Maybe it was simply too hard to fathom a country that had experienced sixteen coups, more than any other country in the world, since 1950. Since the civil war erupted on April 15, 2023, thousands had been killed and several million had been displaced. Along with countless schools and other structures, 90 percent of the factories in Khartoum had been destroyed.

That afternoon, after experiencing sporadic internet connectivity in Sudan, I was finally able to reconnect and check my emails. A message from Carla awaited me.

> Barry, I wanted to let you know that Khalid was able to bring some of his paintings with him to Port Sudan. It would be very good if those paintings can get out of Sudan, and you are our only chance. As you can imagine, it is indeed quite special you are actually there.

She had planned to organize an exhibition in Italy to raise awareness of the war in Sudan and sell the paintings to help Khalid and his family.

I responded without really thinking, "Of course, Carla, I'll bring them out."

This wasn't exactly the Sudan trip I had imagined when I first booked with Carla's company, before the civil war. I'd hoped to see the capital, Khartoum, and the ancient Nubian pyramids along the Nile, which are said to be more magnificent than those in Egypt. But I felt lucky just to be here. I wandered through the markets, sipped coffee, and visited the dilapidated Sudan Red Sea Resort, where we ate fish in an eerily empty outdoor dining space. The owner said she hadn't seen tourists in ages.

As the trip went on, I began to shift my focus. More than anything, I wanted to be fully present to the devastating reality that many had endured. I couldn't offer aid or solutions, but I could *bear witness*. And somehow, that felt like something. The stories I heard, harrowing accounts of violence at the hands of the RSF and the tragic fallout from the Sudanese army's efforts to reclaim control, left no doubt: Suffering had touched nearly everyone.

Just outside Port Sudan, I visited a sprawling UNHCR camp sheltering thousands of refugees, many of whom were from Darfur. A long line of women waited under the searing sun, dishes in hand, for what was likely a small ration of grain to sustain their families. As I looked closer, what I saw stopped me in my tracks. These women, despite everything, were dressed in radiant, flowing gowns and brilliantly colored headscarves, as if walking a runway rather than standing in a food line. Their elegance was defiant, almost transcendent. I couldn't reconcile the desperation of their situation with the pride and grace with which they carried themselves. It was as if, for them, dignity was not just a part of survival; it *was* survival. *It was utterly breathtaking.*

I couldn't fully grasp the scale of destruction in Sudan, nor imagine how it might end. The global community remained largely disengaged, while some nations lined up to supply more weapons to one side or the other. No one seemed to ask the obvious: Why didn't the world care? Perhaps because apathy demands nothing, and caring, especially when one is powerless, can feel overwhelming. Still, I had the chance to make my care tangible by supporting Khalid and his family. It was the only way I could quiet the guilt of knowing that, in just over a day, I'd return to comfort while they would be left to endure a nightmare without end.

On my last full day in Sudan, I sat at a weathered outdoor café in the ancient, half-ruined Red Sea port of Suakin, a city built entirely of coral. As I sipped the gingery coffee I'd come to love, I watched local men in white turbans and brown vests chatting animatedly, seemingly unfazed by my presence. I felt oddly at peace, despite knowing everything that had happened here.

Sudan was the final Arabic-speaking country on my list, my twenty-second. Before Project 193, the Arab world had felt distant, even dangerous. My only previous glimpses were fleeting: a night in Amman, a trip to Cairo in my youth, and a visit to Dubai. I was curious about my mother's Iraqi heritage, but for years, I hadn't acted on it, maybe out of fear. Now that I had seen the full range of Arab countries, my perceptions had shifted profoundly. The richness, resilience, and humanity I encountered far outweighed the warnings and stereotypes I once believed. What was once unknown and intimidating had become familiar and deeply meaningful. And here, in just four days, Sudan transformed from an abstraction into a place I had now seen with my own eyes and an open heart. It would never again be a place *over there*.

The next morning, Khalid brought his paintings with him on the drive to the airport. Carla had updated him that I was willing to get his paintings out of Sudan and into secure hands. I took a quick look through the paintings.

Wow. "Khalid, they're beautiful. I particularly love this one." It was an impressionistic watercolor of faceless people walking away from a city that appeared to be in chaos. The soft combination of colors and the vague outlines of the people and landscape made the piece a bit surreal, almost dreamlike. Everything in the painting blended seamlessly. "How much do you want for this? I would love to have this on my living room wall."

He gave me an embarrassed look. "I am not good with prices. Maybe $40?"

I look back in astonishment at how little he valued his exceptional skill. "How about $200?"

"I will humbly accept," he said with a kind smile. Before putting the painting away, I took a hard additional look at it. In the watercolor, the faceless figures weren't just fleeing a city; they were dissolving into it as if war didn't just displace people but erased them altogether.

Soon after, we said our goodbyes.

Iraq, Yemen, Syria, and now Sudan. I've never seen myself as an adrenaline junkie, but I do believe in going beyond my comfort zone, because that's where the most meaningful moments in my life seem to happen. Over time, I've come to understand that the feeling of being truly alive often arrives not in safety, but in the courage of stepping toward the unknown. Before deciding to come, after researching Port Sudan, I decided the risk was worth it. And I was right. Bearing witness wasn't just worthwhile; to me it had become a necessity.

Maybe helping Khalid get his paintings out offered him some much-needed income, and that matters. But more than that, I left with a deeper understanding of what the people here endure: the weight of war, the ache of displacement, and the strength it takes to survive both. They carry on, often overlooked by the world, yet still surviving, still hoping.

It is the essence of shared humanity, seeing not just suffering, but the spirit that persists beneath it. I didn't just add my 178th country; I left with a responsibility. Not just to remember Khalid and Ibrahim's stories, but to share them. *And with Khalid's painting on a wall in my house, I would not forget the people of Sudan.*

Chapter 30

Tranquility in a Buddhist Kingdom

*We lost the story. When you lose
a story, you lose meaning.*
—David Brooks

**March 2024
Bhutan**

As word got out that I had been to Sudan, my Instagram lit up like a pinball machine with messages from fellow extreme travelers. They all wanted to know how I managed to get a visa and enter a country in the midst of a civil war. Even Alvaro wrote, "Very well done, amigo. Hustling your way through. Proud of you." I had to laugh. When did I become the kind of guy thirty-year-olds feel proud of?

With just fifteen countries left, the clock was ticking on my reintegration into full-time life in Sausalito. But for now, after an emotional trip to Sudan, the tranquility and blue water of the South Pacific were beckoning. I was embarking on what the travel community calls

"United's Island Hopper trip," a flight itinerary that includes the former US territories of Micronesia, the Marshall Islands, and Palau, with a final stop in Guam (still a US territory).

The South Pacific, the Island Hopper

After a few days' feasting on fresh tuna in the Marshall Islands, my second stop, Micronesia, was night and day from Sudan. Though the country has a central government, many villages still follow hereditary chiefs and time-honored traditions like kava rituals and yam ceremonies. Yams! Entire rituals are built around the harvest, with the chief blessing and tasting the first yam on a ceremonial platform before the village erupts in music, dance, and a communal feast. I was both impressed and slightly amused by the reverence for a vegetable I don't even like. As for actual sights in Micronesia, what captivated me most was Nan Madol, a place I'd never heard of, yet one of Oceania's largest ancient ruins, comparable in age to Angkor Wat in Cambodia. Massive stone structures rise mysteriously from a lagoon. No one actually knows for sure how they arrived here a millennium ago. And I had this place all to myself.

Boarding the plane for the next stop on the Island Hopper, I was heading to the place I was most looking forward to on this trip. Palau is billed as the "Underwater Serengeti." And it was time to dig out my scuba certification after a long hiatus. When asked when your last dive was, how do you say, "Twenty years ago" with a straight face?

Somehow, I passed the dive shop's protocols, though a fellow diver quickly pointed out I'd attached the regulator backward. I sheepishly accepted help, and once I was underwater, it all came rushing back, with perfect visibility. Floating past coral gardens, pink and yellow sponges, and parrotfish, the real stars finally appeared: a school of thirty gray-reef sharks just ten feet in front of me, cruising over the coral. *It felt like a dream.* Why had I waited twenty years?

Despite the supernatural beauty, I discovered that the population in Palau had declined by 10 percent in the past twenty years. I got the chance to visit the office of President Surangel Whipps and meet with his chief of staff, Ms. Landisang Kotaro, who told me, "The declining population is an even greater existential challenge to Palau than climate change." Palau belongs to the Compacts of Free Association (COFA), along with the Marshall Islands and Micronesia. Through COFA, the US compensates the islands for injuries and damage caused by nuclear testing in the Marshall Islands from 1946 to 1958. As a result, citizens of these countries are permitted to reside in the US and obtain citizenship.

This has opened up opportunities for the youth of Palau who are leaving in droves in search of better careers. For the world's third least populated country, with only sixteen thousand inhabitants, it won't take long for the decline to pose a full-blown crisis. Landi told me, "We've experienced a major youth brain drain that hampers growth and innovation. This threatens our future, creating an imbalance between the elderly who stay and the youth who leave."

What she said paralleled Palau's exceptionally low fertility rate, which is well below the replacement rate needed to stabilize the population. Aside from Landi, I didn't meet any native Palauans. The hotel workers, restaurant employees, taxi drivers, and my dive guide were all Filipinos, who account for almost 40 percent of the population. I can understand the idea of paradise fading. Nothing lasts forever, but choosing to leave a genuine paradise behind? That's harder to make sense of.

. . .

After returning to San Francisco, I'd usually ease into my routine: Catch up with Daniel, see friends, plan the next leg of my journey. But this time was different. Something big was on the calendar, something I wasn't entirely chill about, but I forced myself to stick to the plan.

I drove to Ella's tattoo parlor in Berkeley, agonizing all the way. What had I been thinking? Maybe I'd just been intoxicated by the beauty of Dominica last November, and hanging out with Daniel. *Who makes good decisions when they're under the influence?*

When I walked in, I immediately felt intimidated. There was a dentist chair in the middle of the room, and the walls were lined with bottles of ink. I felt like I was in a witch's den where potions were tested on anyone crazy enough to sit in the chair.

What am I doing?

Not letting on that I was having second thoughts, I did my best to keep up a brave front. And then Ella showed me the design.

Whoa.

It was a globe with Africa in the center, bordered on top by a sunflower. There were *layers* here: the sunflower in remembrance of Jackie; the globe representing my travels; and Africa, where I lost Jackie and where I'm honoring her memory with the Bourse Jackie scholarships.

My God, it's perfect.

Ella smiled. "I felt especially inspired with this one."

The process turned out to be a little painful, but the pain was fleeting. What mattered was what it meant. It was a small price to pay to have a permanent memento of Jackie on my back, just below the shoulder.

When Ella finished two hours later, and I looked in the mirror, I felt an immediate sense of comfort. More than comfort, *awe*. With the sunflower, she had captured the essence of Jackie's beautiful soul. Sure, it was in a place that few would see unless I was at the beach, but I knew that it was a perfect tribute. Beyond a tribute, it was a declaration, something sacred to always carry with me.

Singapore

My life journey with Jackie began just off Orchard Road, the main street of Singapore. The country was the jumping-off point for visiting three of the last five Asian countries on my list: Bhutan, Timor-Leste (also known as East Timor), and Pakistan. In 1994, during my time in this island-city-country, I lived a stone's throw away, on Jalan Lada Puteh, where Jackie stayed with me when we were still in the friend zone. Soon after that, in India, we declared our love for each other at the Taj Mahal. It seemed like a lifetime ago.

Having Benjamin with me here was comforting, as it was special to have each of the boys join me on different legs of Project 193. Since those mournful months in Georgetown, only weeks after we lost Jackie, Benjamin and I had lived on different coasts. With neither of us being good on the phone, there was more than physical distance between us that I couldn't seem to bridge. *And it plagued me.* Perhaps it was some kind of blockage, the shared grief of losing Jackie, and the silence around so much we couldn't say out loud. I am sure that happens to many loved ones after traumatic loss.

I pined for the days of summer trips with all four of us together. But now, with the boys into their careers, that kind of quality time is rare. I'm proud of how my boys honor their mother by being so focused on their work life, but I miss our family. Especially our travels. Still, I felt lucky that Benjamin got the time off.

I thought about what an amazing place Singapore is, and what an incredible ride it had been since leaving here: traveling with Jackie through Asia, then living in London and Moscow with the boys, and finally settling in Sausalito. It was the opposite of my friend Roy, whom we'd had dinner with the night before, along with his wife and son.

He and I worked together at JP Morgan on Wall Street in 1986, and he came to Singapore to work with me in 1990. Roy, an American of Chinese descent, met a Singaporean woman, married, and stayed. Now, as I sipped my coffee before heading off with Benjamin on another Project 193 trip, I couldn't help but wonder: What made Roy stay put while I kept moving? Sometimes I think about what might have been had I stayed. But I knew what I would have missed if I hadn't left. Choosing one life means sacrificing another.

Why was I still drawn, at sixty-three, to roam the world, while Roy seemed perfectly content after thirty years in one place? Here I was, 181 countries into Project 193, and I still didn't have an answer to a question I'd been asking my entire adult life.

Maybe it was as simple as "the world needs some wanderers," and I'm just filling that role. Roy and his family are well traveled, but they have found a deep sense of community in their life in Singapore. But now, since losing Jackie and starting this journey, I felt that my home was not just one physical place, but rather the road itself, the mosaic of countries I'd passed through and the connections I'd made. As one travel mate said, "I have developed an unconditional love for the beauty of this world, its people, cultures, and places." For now, this tribe of open-minded people fascinated by the majesty of our world feels like home.

Bhutan

When I started planning my trip to Bhutan for Benjamin and me, I read about the requirement to pay a "Sustainable Development Fee" of one hundred dollars per day, in addition to other travel costs. I guess they don't want low-budget wanderers. Something else I had not seen was a different standard of country measurement than GNP, "Gross National Product." Bhutan is guided by and measures GNH, "Gross National Happiness." What is happiness actually? Is it the quantum of pleasure, joy, and fulfillment, or something else entirely? I learned that for Bhutan, it is prioritizing the physical, mental, and emotional well-being of its people over material development. Having been immersed in capitalism my whole life, I had a hard time imagining what this philosophy would look like on the ground. Would literally everyone be smiling? Would a serene vibe be palpable everywhere we went? Looking out into the clouds from my airplane window, I had the sensation that we were headed for Shangri-La, that fictional valley in the Kunlun Mountains where all is harmony.

As I turned back to my laptop, a face behind me lingered in my mind. "I think the guy behind us is from the travel community," I told Benjamin. "Dutch. Been to every country and wrote a book."

Benjamin listened for a moment. "Dad, he's speaking Italian."

"Good point. Probably not him."

Suddenly, the plane banked hard to clear twenty-thousand-foot Himalayan peaks, then dropped into the narrow Paro Valley. It reminded me of flying into Hong Kong's Kai Tak Airport in the 1990s, dodging mountains, banking steeply alongside apartment buildings. But Paro was next level: the world's most dangerous landing, certified for only twelve pilots.

The drive to Thimphu, the capital, was equally thrilling, narrow mountain roads hugging the cliffs. At the hotel, glad for solid ground, I opened Facebook, and at the top of my feed was a post by Boris Kester from Bhutan.

That's who it was. I messaged him. "Boris, you were sitting behind me on the flight to Paro."

He replied instantly, "I was wondering if that was you . . . cursing myself for not asking." A few more texts confirmed we were now headed in opposite directions.

"My friend," I wrote, "we *have* to share a beer somewhere in the world."

Lesson learned again: If someone looks familiar seven thousand miles from home, they probably are. The extreme-travel world is small. Running into someone in Paro is no more unlikely than at the local Starbucks.

The next day, we settled into a rhythm of seeing monasteries, trekking, and generally just enjoying this, yes, *very happy country*. Our driver, Pubh, had the most infectious smile that rarely left his face. Our guide, Ugyen, painted a picture of Bhutan as a supremely enlightened country doing its best to *spread* the enlightenment, with monasteries tucked into the mountains everywhere you looked. Most impressive among them was the Tiger's Nest, which was built in the 1600s about ten thousand feet above the Paro Valley. Clinging to sheer granite rock face, it is a sacred place for Bhutanese and the country's most iconic monastery. Normally, tourists walk up from the valley floor starting at about eight thousand feet. But for me and Benjamin, we were descending to it from glamping at thirteen thousand feet the night before. Arriving before the large influx of tourists, mainly from India and China, we had this magnificent place all to ourselves. Looking down on it was breathtaking. Was there a more beautiful structure? Maybe the Taj Mahal, where Jackie and I had our first kiss, comes close. Benjamin and I sat peacefully for a while, admiring the beauty. Knowing the spiritual importance of the Tiger Nest in the world's happiest country, a sense of reverence settled over me, and it was unmistakable.

On the descent, I asked Ugyen, "Why are there so many monasteries?"

"We have many monks who dedicate their lives to prayer. Even regular people go up for retreats."

"For how long?"

"About 10 to 15 percent of Bhutanese men will spend up to three years living in a monastery."

Though I appreciated the desire to understand the mind, especially after my own grief-fueled journey into Buddhism, I couldn't imagine three years away from "normal" life.

Still, I struggled to believe everyone was as happy as they seemed. A quick Google search showed that 94 percent of Bhutanese consider themselves happy. Really?

"Bhutan is amazing," I told Ugyen, "but surely there are challenges?"

"My country is starting to be challenged by our youth not wanting to adopt all the stringent rituals and rules that limit their freedoms," he said. "There's tension between preserving tradition, like mandatory dress, and the youth's push for Western culture. Elders see change as a threat, but we're trying to balance heritage with progress to improve the well-being of all Bhutanese."

His words still echoed in my mind a week later as Benjamin and I wandered through Singapore after our week of trekking and tranquility in Bhutan. Despite our success and virtues in the US, the idea of preserving culture at the expense of certain personal freedoms would be considered radical in my country. We often do the opposite, prioritizing individual liberties even if it means losing shared values or any sense of a unifying "national story."

Singapore looked to the future, while Bhutan looked to its past, yet both had found ways to foster unity without losing themselves. Benjamin and I stood gawking upward, beneath the towering "Supertrees" in Gardens by the Bay, manmade giants draped in lush vegetation, rising over 160 feet into the air like futuristic baobabs. I realized how powerfully this city-state had cultivated both innovation and identity, impressive for a place that had become a country only sixty years ago. Within twenty-four hours, I had been in two of the most contrasting places on Earth: the Tiger's Nest Monastery in Bhutan and the Supertree Grove in Singapore. And yet both played a similar role in shaping the soul of their respective nations.

Bhutan's story is rooted in ancient spirituality, while Singapore's story is one of futuristic ambition. Where Bhutan's monks pursued inner stillness in mountain monasteries, Singapore's citizens pursued modernity inside vertical gardens and AI labs. And yet both, in their own way, built something enduring. They both often rank among the world's happiest and most cohesive societies and have done something rare: They honor their citizens by prioritizing collective well-being, fostering pride without tipping into supremacy.

As I said goodbye to Benjamin, making his long way back to New York, I remembered again that here in Singapore was where it all began with Jackie so many years ago. Here I walked these same streets with my son, but in a different chapter of life, grateful for the circle of love that had started here, and for the chance to still pass it on—*a very grounding feeling.*

Chapter 31

A High-Elevation Highway

The unexamined life is not worth living.
—Socrates, 399 BC

April 2024
Pakistan

By the time I got to Timor-Leste, I was feeling depleted. Benjamin had flown back to New York, leaving a gaping void after our twelve days with each other. With the tranquility of Bhutan and our time together, it seemed that we had started to bridge the gap of both physical and emotional distance. But now, I was traveling alone again, still feeling hobbled from the five-thousand-foot descent the last day of our trek. On top of that, I had to route through Bali, stay in a crummy airport hotel, and catch an early-morning flight to Dili. It was a long journey for a place I might never have visited if not for Project 193, my quest to visit every country in the world. Timor-Leste had been an independent nation for only roughly two decades.

When my guide, Eddy, picked me up at the airport, I wasn't up for exploring another capital.

"Welcome to Timor-Leste, Barry," he said. "Are you ready for your city tour of Dili?"

"Honestly, I'm exhausted. I need to take a day off. Can you take me to my hotel?"

"Of course. How about I pick you up later around 6:00 p.m. and we climb to Cristo Rei to watch the sunset?"

As much as I didn't want to go, he was so eager that I couldn't turn him down. "Perfect."

That evening, with my leg muscles screaming all the way, we climbed up the roughly six hundred steps toward the statue of Cristo Rei (Christ the King). The air was thick with humidity, cicadas chirping in the distance, as we ascended the worn stairs, the statue looming larger with each step. As we climbed, Eddy told me of the difficult years of his youth. His people had voted to separate from Indonesia in 1999, and massacres at the hands of the Indonesian military swiftly followed. He was eight years old when his family fled into the mountains. Some of his cousins and uncles sadly did not escape the violence.

"I'm so sorry to hear that," I said. "What about now? Are you married? Do you have children?"

He hesitated. "I have one son, age nine. My wife died two years ago, giving birth to my second child, a daughter. I lost them both."

My God. His wife *and* a child. I felt closer to him instantly, just as I had with Jennifer in Suriname and Nasser in Guinea, when they shared their personal losses.

"Eddy, I am so sorry. I can't imagine how tough that must have been on you."

Wanting him to know I truly understood, I told him about Jackie, her spirit, her light. As my words faded, we arrived at the statue, where sunflowers lay scattered at its base, their bright yellow petals stark against the weathered stone. Without a second thought, I slipped off my shirt, revealing the sunflower tattoo etched across my back, Jackie's symbol, forever inked on me. His face softened, and a smile spread slowly across his lips. "I love that," he said, as if he could feel her presence through the ink.

Just then, a group of nuns appeared in navy habits and white veils.

"They're from a nearby convent that takes in orphans," Eddy explained. "They rarely leave the convent grounds. You are lucky to find them here."

I quickly pulled my shirt back on, not just out of modesty, but because of being self-conscious that I carried the few extra pounds I'd gained during this travel quest. Eddy spoke softly to the group in Portuguese, then turned back to me.

"I told them your story. That you're traveling the world to heal a loss."

Their faces shifted; some seemed very touched, with a few nuns wiping tears from their cheeks. Moments later, they gathered around me, warmth radiating from their smiles as we posed for a photo with Cristo Rei standing tall behind us, as if offering a silent blessing.

After heartfelt goodbyes, I stepped to the edge of the platform, the cool breeze brushing my skin, and drank in the breathtaking panorama of Dili. The green hills below gently sloped toward the horizon, where a few islands sat offshore, and the vast sea beyond.

As we descended the steps, I tried to process what had just happened. I hadn't even wanted to come out, but here I was at sunset, embraced by strangers and this sacred place. And I wasn't exhausted anymore, nor did my legs still ache. It reminded me again: Often, the best moments come when you're least looking for them. Leaving Timor-Leste behind, I soon found myself thinking about another adventure, this time in the towering mountains of northern Pakistan.

Pakistan

My college buddy, whom I had known for forty-five years, Lee, had been following my journey to visit every country in the world and kept wanting to join one of my trips. To my surprise, when I sent him my 2024 itinerary, he chose Pakistan.

That prompted a call. "Are you sure you want to go to Pakistan with me? I mean, there are better, easier travel choices—Palau, the Marshall Islands, even São Tomé. Chill beach places."

He replied, "No, I'd like to go to Pakistan. It's something totally different for me."

In the months that followed, he peppered me with questions about our trip. *What should I pack? Do I bring snacks? How much cash?* I held back sarcastic replies, remembering how I'd done the same thing with Alvaro before my Uganda trip when I started Project 193. Still, I was a bit worried. I was used to solo travel or companions familiar with rough conditions. This would be ten days of uncertain lodging, food, and terrain.

Now, on our flight to Skardu in the far north of Pakistan, my thoughts drifted to the country's complex image, Taliban ties, and the US raid that killed Osama Bin Laden in 2011. But those thoughts disappeared as majestic waves of snow-capped peaks, including Nanga Parbat, Pakistan's second-highest mountain at over twenty-six thousand feet, dotted the landscape outside my window. It was like the breathtaking scenes of a mountaineering documentary unfolding before my eyes.

We were on the edge of two of the world's most beautiful mountain ranges, the Karakoram and the Himalayas. A few days later, our guide, Manzoor, drove us along the Karakoram Highway from Skardu to Gilgit to Hunza. Sometimes called "the eighth wonder of the world," it's one of the highest roads on Earth, climbing from thirteen hundred feet in the distant south to sixteen thousand feet in the far north toward the Chinese border. It winds through tunnels and around towering cliffs, with villages carved into the rock face. For context: the US has one peak above twenty thousand feet, Denali, while Pakistan has over four thousand. The scale was staggering.

Amid our sightseeing, Manzoor arranged a visit to a private K-12 school where tuition was just ten dollars a month. That was still a stretch in a place where I'd just paid eighty cents for a haircut, shave included. When the principal learned this was my 184th country, he asked if I'd speak to a tenth-grade class. I gladly accepted.

After fifteen minutes sharing my travel story, I opened the floor for questions, and hands shot up as if I'd asked, *Who likes ice cream?*

"What do you think of Pakistan?"

"What does your country think of ours?"

"Are there any leaders you admire?"

And then they got existential on me. "If you could change something in your life, what would it be?"

"What's the meaning of life?"

Lee turned to me, half whispering, "Dude, let's see how you handle this one."

I told them I wouldn't change much. "My life's had its ups and downs, some big ones, but I've been lucky, and I like my path." As for the second question, I admitted, "Still working on that one."

The hardest questions came next, about Israel, Gaza, and US support for Israel's bombing campaign. I tried to offer a different perspective, one I don't often share with my Jewish friends, whom I usually encourage to look beyond our tribe's side of the conflict. I don't know if it changed anything, but several boys asked for a photo afterward. That, at least, felt like some common ground.

What struck me most was Lee. Unsure how he'd adapt, with him having mainly traveled to places like Italy and the Bahamas, I watched him engage with the boys, field their questions, and connect easily. He was completely at ease in this foreign setting and told me, "This trip has already taught me that I need to widen my travel boundaries to have these special experiences."

On the drive to our next stop, I reflected on how well-informed and curious the boys were, especially given their remote setting. The internet had clearly opened the world to them. It was inspiring, but also sobering; this same technology can be used to divide. Not far from here, Malala Yousafzai, Pakistan's Nobel laureate, still can't return to the Swat Valley without risk to her life because of the spread of hate and negative publicity about her desire for change.

Later, we hit traffic near a small village. Curious, we asked Manzoor to stop. A crowd was gathering near a volleyball court. To our surprise, it was a regional *beach volleyball* championship, at ten thousand feet elevation and fifteen hundred miles from the nearest ocean. As a former volleyball player, I had to watch, with an official waving us into a VIP area. The crowd, dressed in flowing shalwar kameez, watched intently. Some looked over at us, not with suspicion but interest, offering a hand-to-heart gesture or a small wave. I couldn't have felt more welcome.

Pakistan was a land of many contrasts, changing its narratives in some ways while reinforcing others. For instance, we experienced the incredible kindness of fully engaging Pakistani men, yet the absence of women in some places was impossible not to notice.

It reminded me, even during a journey along one of the most stunning stretches of Earth, that the world is a complicated place where beauty and unpleasantness coexist. Listening, not just looking, has taught me more than any guidebook ever could. Maybe those boys already understand that better than many adults. Without seeing much of the world, they already grasped something essential: Understanding begins with hearing different sides of the story.

Chapter 32

The Last African Surprise

*We may have different religions, different
languages, different colored skin, but
we all belong to one human race.*
—Kofi Annan

**May 2024
Lesotho**

After six weeks in Asia and barely a week at home, I wasn't thrilled to be flying again, this time through Africa for one of my last multicountry trips of Project 193: São Tomé and Príncipe, Africa's second smallest country, and another former Portuguese colony, Mozambique. I would also be visiting two small, landlocked nations within South Africa, Eswatini and Lesotho. But first, I had an important visit to Ghana.

I walked into an auditorium filled with three hundred people from West Africa, about a third of them graduating students, including the first five recipients of our new Bourse Jackie English-language scholarship program. I had been invited to deliver a commencement speech at the BT Institute in Accra. Standing on that stage, I experienced something I've felt countless times during Project 193: *There is no place I would rather be than where I am right now.* Saying that so often during this journey was the clearest sign I could have that my travels had healed such a painful loss.

Our new Bourse Jackie English-language scholarship program was designed to open doors for talented young women from Francophone West Africa to learn English, a tribute to Jackie's enduring spirit.

During my speech, I described the first steps I'd taken that led me to where I was, there in Accra. After handing out diplomas, Aida from Burkina Faso took the stage to recite her poem, "Vanities of Vanities." Aida was one of our scholarship recipients studying biological sciences. She had always dreamed of working for the World Health Organization but had struggled trying to learn English online. Now, she delivered her speech in powerful, booming English.

"Let's love ourselves. Forgive each other.

"Let's stop marching on the body of the next person, wounding creation.

"Falling to being an animal won't make us bigger.

"Let's travel light . . ."

She paused to look out onto the sea of people before continuing with growing strength:

"May my presence be useful.

"For that, I'll fight with the strength I've got.

"I am a proud African woman, intelligent and sweet, fierce and beautiful.

"I radiate strength and independence."

Thunderous applause echoed throughout the auditorium. Aida's words hit me with unexpected force; George, the founder of the BT Institute, seated beside me, passed me some tissues. It wasn't just her English, powerful and proud; it was the way she stood there, unshaken, fully seen. Jackie would have loved her, and I felt her in that room, not in a vague spiritual sense, but vividly. As if she were sitting beside me, tissues in hand, whispering, "Keep going."

Leaving the hopeful energy of Accra behind, I journeyed to São

Tomé and Príncipe, where the beauty of the islands belied a haunting past.

São Tomé and Príncipe (STP)

My guide, Nilton, took me to Água Izé, a former cacao plantation where descendants of enslaved laborers still worked the land. The village had crumbling tracks and weathered homes, including one large house on a hill that had once overlooked slave quarters. "People who work the cacao still live here," Nilton said.

We walked into a dark alley with rotting wooden shanties on both sides. A few people sat on the ground in the darkness of a closed-in walkway without lights, preparing food. One woman was washing newly picked cacao fruit, which Nilton explained would then be dried for further processing.

In a dimly lit hovel no larger than six by ten feet, a barefoot mother swayed gently with her infant swaddled close. The light filtering through the small window illuminated the deep joy in her eyes, a stark contrast to the harshness surrounding her. The scene was of deep tenderness, and I was mesmerized.

"How old is your baby?" I asked Nilton to translate.

"Eight days," he said. Her husband was in the fields, harvesting cacao. This mother with her infant radiated the profound joy at bringing a beautiful life into this world, no matter the challenging material circumstances.

From the research I did on São Tomé and Príncipe, I had expected it to be beautiful, a little-visited island archipelago with biodiversity so rich it's nicknamed "the Galápagos of Africa." But I was looking for more than beaches. Like Cape Verde, STP was uninhabited before the Portuguese arrived in the late 1400s, using it as a base to grow sugar and later cacao, with Africans and even Jewish children brought in from Portugal as slaves. Independence came in 1975, followed by a brief experiment with Communism, then democracy in the 1990s. Reading about this layered history in São Tomé made me realize that this country's story of colonization, slavery, ideology, and survival was what I came to explore. Meeting the woman and her infant at Água

Izé got me thinking about whether her life was any better than that of previous generations.

We spent the rest of the day immersed in STP's natural splendor, its coastal inlets, lush forests, and jagged volcanic spires rising from land and sea. It was the kind of beauty made for postcards. But as in so many of the world's most breathtaking places, I couldn't shake the contrast between the scenery and the struggles of everyday life.

Over lunch, I shared this with Nilton. "We left Communism not long ago," he said. "Today we're freer, but corruption has grown, and the poor are more exposed. We need a middle path." I've always believed in democracy and capitalism, but no system has all the answers. The woman we met had freedom and her family, but not much more.

Mozambique, Eswatini, and Lesotho

Over many years, I had made at least thirty trips across Africa. And with this trip, I would have visited all fifty-four countries on the continent. Yet Mozambique held a special allure for me, a place rich with Arab, African, and Portuguese cultural influences and over twenty-five hundred kilometers of pristine beaches along the Indian Ocean. Jackie and I had technically passed through Mozambique in 1996 during a grueling twenty-four-hour bus ride from Malawi to Harare, Zimbabwe. Though we had visas, we never stopped; the country was still emerging from a brutal civil war that had claimed more than a million lives, according to the UN. The region we traveled through was unsafe, so all we could do was catch fleeting glimpses through the bus window, brief, tantalizing hints of a country I longed to explore.

I had been fortunate to stay healthy on most trips despite the grueling conditions, long flights, rough roads, and questionable hygiene. Over three years, I'd fallen ill only once, in Afghanistan, yet even then I kept moving. But this time in Mozambique, my body finally caught up with me. I was sidelined for several days, forced to rest on Inhaca Island, a quiet refuge an hour's boat ride from the capital, Maputo. For the second time in a row, I left Mozambique without really knowing it. The country remained a blur, less a destination than a pause in the journey, an unfinished chapter that stirred a sense of absence.

But soon, the itinerary pulled me inland, toward two landlocked kingdoms, Eswatini and Lesotho.

Eswatini felt like an ancient kingdom lifted straight from a timeless fable.

Ruled by Africa's last absolute monarch, King Mswati III, it was renamed from Swaziland in 2018, supposedly to avoid confusion with Switzerland. The king has fifteen wives, a small number compared to his father's seventy, in a country of just over a million. *You can only imagine all the princes and princesses running around.*

Eswatini also has one of the world's highest HIV rates, tied to cultural norms, limited health-care access, and polygamy. Despite high literacy rates, life expectancy here is among the lowest anywhere.

From there, I made my way into the highlands of Lesotho with some similarities but a big contrast in landscape. Known as the Mountain Kingdom, Lesotho is a ruggedly beautiful and mountainous land. Its lowest elevation point is at forty-five hundred feet.

In my travels in Africa throughout the years, with its being the warmest of the seven continents by far, I have rarely needed much more than a short-sleeved shirt, and maybe a light jacket in the mountains. So, imagine my surprise when I woke and saw snow outside my window the day of my return flight to Sausalito. *Wait, what?* Other than on the summit of Kilimanjaro in 1996, I had never seen snow in Africa. Snowflakes drifted down like ash from a volcano, softening the hard edges of the city below. The brown earth turned white in slow motion. I opened the window and let the cold air in, stunned but overjoyed that Africa had one last surprise for me. It was a moment that felt like a blessing, or maybe a farewell. By the time I got into my airport shuttle, the snow had intensified, and I was starting to wonder if we would be snowed in.

Reading my thoughts, my driver, Moseboh, said, "You know, I am fifty-five years old. I have never seen snow like this in the capital. I would not worry about your flight. Surely the snow will stop and turn to slush soon enough." But the snow kept falling, and after a six-hour wait in the departure lounge of one of the world's smallest airports, my flight was canceled. The next morning, by the time I arrived at the airport, the sun was out and there was no sign of what might have been the most significant snowfall in recent Lesotho history. It felt like a gift of nature for visiting my final African country.

Despite its many challenges, corruption, poverty, instability, I remain deeply connected to this continent. It is where Jackie and I had a life-changing journey together in the mid-1990s, and where I later found the purpose that would shape my humanitarian work, made more important with her loss on the African continent. It was where my worldview was forever changed.

I had just visited two of Africa's more mono-ethnic nations, Eswatini, home of the Swazi, and Lesotho, home of the Basotho. Both face daunting issues like low life expectancy, high HIV rates, and limited opportunities for youth, yet they felt relatively safe and socially cohesive. Perhaps their ethnic homogeneity plays a role. In contrast, some of Africa's most fragile states are patchworks of hundreds of ethnic groups: Sudan with over 500, Nigeria with 370, and Chad with 200. In many places, loyalty first flows to the clan, then to religion, and only distantly to the nation, making unity elusive and sometimes impossible.

Though I grew up in a kind of tribal household myself, a Jewish family in Southern California, I've long been cautious about the pull of tribal identity. Still, I can't deny the sense of belonging and strength it can offer. I've seen both its beauty and its limits up close.

Even back home in the US, we're fractured in different ways. It made me wonder how any nation holds together. The continent of Africa, in all its complexity, beauty and struggle, hope and hardship, defies simple conclusions. Flying over the red soil one last time on Project 193, I felt what I'd always felt here: awe, purpose, and connection.

Chapter 33

The Thundering Hordes

I tasted freedom and a way of life from which there could be no recall.
—Wilfred Thesiger, *Arabian Sands*

July 2024
Mongolia

On an early Sunday morning, I landed in Ulaanbaatar, the world's coldest capital. Visiting during Mongolia's *very* short summer, I headed out immediately to Sukhbaatar Square where there are festivals nearly every weekend.

Near a statue of Genghis Khan, a crowd clustered around two pull-up bars. An older man hung on one bar, his arms pulsing, while on the other a young girl hung effortlessly as if suspended in space. The man's face was turning blue, and just as I walked up, he let go with a thud, drawing gasps from the crowd.

Outdoor boxing rings lined the square, with young fighters

cheered on by crowds in traditional dress. I did a double take when I saw a teenage girl pummeling a boy her age, her face flushed. The crowd went wild. Boxing, it turns out, is big in Mongolia, for men and women alike. In only a few hours in Mongolia, I had learned that this was a different place.

But I wasn't here for city life. I was headed to Mongolia's far west, where it borders Russia and China. I joined a Koryo group tour, and after a flight to Khovd, we headed out for a long journey in rugged Soviet-era UAZ trucks. In my vehicle were Karen, the mother of one of Benjamin's high school friends; her daughter Maddy; and talkative Liz, from the UK. Throughout the drive, Maddy made a game of coaxing our stoic driver into smiling. It took a few days until she succeeded, but only after gifting him a bottle of vodka.

Our local guide, Bek, a towering Kazakh-Mongolian, was a rare exception to the reserved demeanor we encountered with the many other locals we met. As we passed a tiny town of one hundred buildings, he shared, "This is where I went to boarding school." Beyond it, no more towns, just valleys, mountains, and sky. "In summer, we set up yurts in the mountains and herded Mongolia's Big Five with my father," he said, referring to horses, goats, camels, yaks, and sheep, the lifeblood of this part of nomadic Mongolia.

Over the next six days camping in one spot more spectacular than the next, circumnavigating the westernmost part of this massive country bouncing up and down along the rocky roads in our UAZ, I began to understand the allure of this place. The impressive landscapes are as stunning as they are endless. On a single day, we traversed at least a dozen immense, jaw-dropping valleys. In one, we came across two weather-beaten men stranded with an empty gas tank. Their glazed eyes and unsteady stance told us they were drunk. Bek offered them some fuel and a ride; they accepted the fuel but declined the ride.

This encounter aside, the valleys unfolded like a vibrant tapestry of raw nature: shimmering rivers and pristine lakes, all framed by the rugged mountains and little yurts scattered across the landscape like tiny white-painted dots. They were alive with a bright pattern of colorful midsummer wildflowers in bloom—yellows, reds, purples, and violets. In the summer, this was the land where the ethnic Kazakh-Mongolians set up yurts as temporary shelter and grazed their herds.

As we crossed bright green fields dotted with nomads' animals, I imagined this untouched land looked much as it might have centuries ago, when Genghis Khan and his Mongol armies swept west across the steppe.

One evening, we stopped at a lakeside yurt. As I began pitching my tent, hail suddenly pelted down. In the middle of summer? This spectacular, and harsh, terrain mirrored the legacy of Genghis Khan (or "Chinggis," as Mongolians say). He united warring clans and, in the early 1200s, conquered the largest contiguous land empire in history, 18 percent of the world's landmass, all on horseback.

I'd always thought of the Mongols as ruthless conquerors, but Bek painted a strikingly different view. "They connected East and West through trade and ideas. They also offered complete religious tolerance and a meritocratic outlook." Having read so much about the devastation they left behind, I found this to be a strikingly different narrative.

Surely there is no figure in history more tied to his country and revered by his people than Genghis Khan. So, I asked Bek, who by then had imbibed a few extra glasses of vodka, "What are the characteristics Mongolians have today that remain from the time of Genghis Kahn?"

He easily responded, "Free, independent, self-sufficient." Then a smirk appeared on his face as he added, "And stubborn."

As we continued west, the culture and landscape deepened their hold on me. The next day, we reached the base of Khüiten Peak, Mongolia's tallest mountain, rising 14,500 feet. Liz and some of the others rode in on horseback while Karen, Maddy, and I hiked. There, a group of eagle hunters appeared, wearing fur hats and hide coats. Eagle hunting, or the art of *berkutchi*, typically passed down from father to son (and to daughter sometimes as chronicled in the movie *The Eagle Huntress*), has long been one of the most important parts of their nomadic traditions as a means of hunting for food and fur. One man carried a majestic golden eagle on his arm. He invited me to mount his horse, then placed the eagle on my gloved arm. The eagle's powerful weight pressed firmly into the thick leather covering my arm, its talons sharp and unyielding. As it spread its vast wings, a surge of awe and connection to this ancient tradition washed over me. It was not lost on me that the last time I had been on a horse, it was Jackie's beloved horse Rosie (though I didn't last on her long before being thrown).

On our next-to-last day in Mongolia, we attended the Naadam festival, Mongolia's celebration of its "Big Three" sports—wrestling, horse racing, and archery. In a wide-open field near Khovd, the smell of roasted meats drifting from nearby tents, crowds gathered to cheer. Wrestlers, wearing their iconic open-chested vests and eagle-feathered hats, grappled directly on the grass. They moved like ancient titans across the steppe, each bout a ritual echo of Mongolia's warrior past, where strength, honor, and the spirits of the land intertwined in every grip and throw. Female archers stood in rainbow-colored robes, firing arrows in unison. *They looked simply bad-ass to me.* Off to the side, men in traditional dress played "ankle-bone shooting," launching sheep ankle bones to knock out their opponents' pieces. When they hit the target, the crowd roared with approval.

Once again, I was struck by the palpable sense of pride that Mongolians have for their past. The Naadam competitions are serious business, less like a show and more like a tradition still beating strong.

. . .

That night, our guide took us to meet someone we had been eagerly anticipating—a shaman. Shamanism in Mongolia goes back a few thousand years. More than a practice, it is an all-encompassing belief system that includes medicine, religion, a reverence for nature, and ancestor worship. Genghis Kahn himself relied on this belief system to make important decisions of conquest.

It was a short, off-grid drive from where we were staying to a meadow with a stream beside a single yurt, the town of Khovd now off in the distance. As we arrived, we could see a woman standing beside the yurt. I admit to being surprised to see a female shaman beckoning us toward her. She was of medium height with an oval, kind face, not one that I would have associated with a shaman. But the rest of her dress gave it away. She wore a long blue robe with various adornments around her neck; beads and shells hung below her chest. A bell dangled from one shoulder, while the other bore what seemed to be an eagle's skull, some feathers still attached. She was holding a flat, octagonal drum in one hand and said something to our translator, Enkhmaa, who shared, "Please sit in a semicircle around her. She wants to know how she can help you."

We settled into a circle on the floor just outside of the shaman's yurt. It was dusk, with the sky casting a long shadow from the mountains in front of us. Looking out into the sweeping valley, we fell into a stillness, magnified by the anticipation that the shaman, who remained standing, was about to enter her spiritual realm.

Someone in our group relayed that we just wanted to know about her life and how she performed her practice. Without speaking to the shaman, Enkhmaa shot back, "She takes the business of healing, whether physical ailments or spiritual, seriously. I am sure that this is what she wants to do with the group, so please tell her about any problems you have. But first, she needs to put herself in a trance." The shaman sat down in front of us and took a big swig from a bottle, which I assumed was some type of strong alcohol. Then she put on a hat with dangling cloth strips that covered her whole face. As she started to sway back and forth, her high-pitched chant grew faster, matching the increasing rhythm of her swaying, until she abruptly stopped. Removing her head covering, she looked at the group and said something to the translator. We were told that she had "summoned the wisdom" of her ancestors and that she was ready to hear our problems.

But as we looked around our circle, no one said anything. After a few moments of silence, Karen spoke up and asked about her future. After the shaman responded, it was my turn. "What do you see in terms of changes in my life in the future?" The question was translated, and the shaman asked me how old I was and what I did. "I am sixty-four years old, and much of what I do is focused on humanitarian work in education."

After a few seconds of reflection, she said something to Enkhmaa that was translated back in not the easiest-to-understand English. "You have something very important to you and some new activities. Keep going with them; keep them close to you." To me, this seemed so general. Yes, we were launching some new programs with Caravan to Class, but that kind of statement could be relevant to just about anyone. I didn't want to question the powers of this shaman, but I needed to see something to believe it.

The next morning, I woke up early and drank some coffee while working on my computer in the small mess hall. Outside were several yurts where my travel mates still slept. From here, you could see the vastness of the countryside we had traveled through the last few days. In one direction, the distant silhouettes of buildings in the city of Khovd, behind me a range of low mountains along the river where we met the shaman, and in another direction, the high desert that stretched for miles. The translator's brother came over to me and asked what I was doing. I told him about my travels and that I was writing a book about my journey. He said, "That is so impressive that you have been to 189 countries, but I already know about your book."

What? I must have looked confused, because he called his sister over to explain. She told me, "Yes, I thought I mentioned that the shaman said that you are *writing* something important to you, a new activity for you. Keep going with it; keep it close to you." *Wow.* That was too specific for me to disbelieve. I had not mentioned anything to the shaman about a writing project. It did make me think about my own spirituality. Did this experience give me more faith in shamanism? In the end, it definitely made me believe in *this* particular shaman.

Our visit with the shaman was a fitting conclusion to a journey through this wonder-filled country. Mongolia left a deep impression: the resilience of its people, their connection to the land, and the living traditions that stretched back to the era of Genghis Khan. That past here wasn't preserved in glass; it really rode through its valleys. Mongolia's heritage remained alive in daily life—in the Naadam games, where ancient skills were still proudly passed from one generation to the next, and in the enduring nomadic lifestyle shaped by the rhythm of seasons and the needs of animals. It felt alive.

In this vast land of yurts, eagles, and open skies, even as this incredible journey I had been on neared its end, I realized that a big takeaway from Project 193 would be a commitment to never stop learning about our vast and varied world.

Chapter 34

Among a Thousand Tongues

Fear is for people who don't get out very much.
—Rick Steves

August 2024
Papua New Guinea

I am normally happy to get back home, but this would be a sad return. I was flying to Dallas to attend the memorial of my brother-in-law Brian, Jackie's brother, who, like his sister, also tragically passed away at age fifty-five. Benjamin was going to join me, but his flight from New York got canceled due to the computer outage impacting flights around the world. I would have to face this difficult event alone.

Seeing Jackie's ninety-year-old parents, who had outlived two of their three children, gutted me, though I had come to accept the idea that life can be cruel at times. The memorial reopened old wounds, a stark reminder that life can shift to year zero overnight. Compounding my grief was my mother's declining health; moving her to a twenty-four-hour-care facility sharpened my sense of mortality and loneliness.

Back in Sausalito, the house was quiet. Daniel was away from home the entire month of July, fighting fires across Northern California. I had not seen him since before I left for Mongolia. *I was in a funk.* In a reflective moment speaking with a close friend on the phone, I said something I'd never voiced before: "I'm no longer anyone's priority." Jackie had made me hers, and for years, I'd been at the heart of my mom's and the boys' lives. But now, my mother could no longer mentally hold me in that way, and my boys were off doing exactly what they should be doing, building their lives. It was a lonely realization, stark and sobering.

Deep down, I knew the answer: After seven years without Jackie, I missed having a partner. I'd been spending time with someone, but it remained a friendship, nothing more. Was I ready to admit that I didn't want to face the rest of my life alone?

And another layer of uncertainty loomed. With only a few countries left, I was about to embark on my final multicountry trip for Project 193, to Solomon Islands and Papua New Guinea. This three-year journey had consumed me, providing purpose and connection, through the extreme-travel community and across the globe. But what would happen when it ended? Could I truly settle in Sausalito, a place I hadn't really lived in since losing Jackie? Or would I just need to keep traveling?

A friend once asked, "Are you running from something by traveling so much?" I had answered, "Maybe." The truth was, I didn't want to think about it. The project gave me structure, excitement, and a sense of mission. But with the finish line in sight, I had to confront what came next, something Jackie and I had never imagined when we dreamed of our empty-nest years. Each passport stamp brought me closer not just to completion, but to a reckoning.

I began to wonder: Does healing ever truly end? Or once I crossed that invisible line, would I finally have to stop running and face what I'd left behind?

Thankfully, as the departure date for my next trip approached, I began feeling better. Planning kicked in, checking logistics, researching countries. As I dove into trip prep, the fog began to lift. Or maybe I just put the funk on hold. *For now.*

Solomon Islands

Just an hour into my flight from San Francisco to Brisbane, I overheard the passenger in front of me telling a flight attendant, "I'm a former US Navy pilot, heading to Solomon Islands where I work for the Australian government."

My curiosity was piqued. Later, while waiting for the restroom, we got to talking.

"I'm heading to Solomon Islands too," I offered.

"You State Department?"

I smiled. "No, just a tourist."

"Why would you want to vacation in that hellhole?"

Sure, some places have deep challenges, but an entire country as a "hellhole"? I certainly wasn't about to explain my travel quest, so I replied, "Surely there must be something interesting?"

"Not a thing," he said flatly.

Conversation over. His negativity only strengthened my resolve to find something good about Solomon Islands.

On arrival in Honiara, I met up with Claire, my travel friend from Yemen who, burka and all, had shocked some Yemeni men in a small village by beating them at their own board game. We were both going to Papua New Guinea (PNG) with Wander Expeditions and decided to hit Solomon Islands along the way. Enter Amanda, our guide. One of only two women in her village to earn a college degree out of nearly a thousand people, she had left a promising legal career to work in tourism and help her family open a jungle lodge.

"What do you enjoy about it?" I asked.

"I get to work with my family, support my village, and meet people from around the world. I learn not from books but from real experiences."

Amanda began by introducing us to Solomons' cultural heritage, part of the Melanesian sub-region of Oceania, known for its immense ethnic, linguistic, and geographic diversity. The country is a constellation of more than one thousand islands, scattered across turquoise waters, and home to seventy-four distinct languages, each a window into a unique worldview.

We hiked through dense jungle, crossed a riverbed, and arrived at a striking waterfall, completely alone. The warm river air carried the scent of damp earth and wild greenery. On the way back, we met a mother and daughter floating timber down the river to sell in their village. The girl, with striking blond hair against deep brown skin, common here due to a rare genetic trait, carried a bouquet of wild ferns and handed them to Amanda.

"What are we doing with these?" I asked.

"We'll cook them for lunch with rice. It tastes better than spinach."

And so it went. One unexpected, rewarding experience after another, from rich scenery to genuine, grounded human connection. At the local market, I saw shell money still used for ceremonial transactions and dowries, a living reminder of the islands' precolonial heritage. The past here wasn't tucked away in museums; it was alive, spoken, traded, worn.

I thought to myself, *How is it that just a short flight from Western modernity, you can find yourself in a place so different, so layered with history and culture?*

I also kept thinking, *What an ass*, about the pilot. But more than that, I was simply glad to prove him wrong. Too often, places are written off by those who never really look. But if you arrive with curiosity instead of judgment, there's an ocean of culture, story, and meaning waiting to meet you.

Papua New Guinea (PNG)

I'd saved a few special trips for the final stretch of Project 193—Bhutan, Pakistan, Mongolia, and Papua New Guinea. I timed my visit to PNG for a special festival. I'm not usually a festival guy, but some events are cultural musts, like Gerewol in Chad or Naadam in Mongolia. And having been to a few now during my journey, I have come to appreciate that there is nothing like them for the liveliness of these large gatherings and seeing culture come truly alive. They are expressed in many ways: color, dress, rhythm, sound that reflect the traditions of ancient communities embodied in profound joy. The Mount Hagen Festival in PNG was one of them. It began in 1961 to encourage peace among enemy tribes. Now, it's a celebration of cultural pride and a living anthropology lesson.

Though I usually prefer traveling solo, my first Project 193 trip had been with WE in Uganda, and I'd promised Alvaro to do one of my last trips with his company. So I chose Wander Expeditions for this one. Plus, going solo to Mount Hagen would have been a logistical headache. Also, Elena, my "roomie" on a Saudi Arabia trip in 2021, was leading the group for Alvaro. We'd stayed in touch since that adventure, and she even met with some Bourse Jackie scholarship recipients in Mali, later texting me, "What impressive young women."

I had enjoyed hanging with Elena a few times along my travel journey. Having spent two decades teaching across four continents, visiting over 150 countries along the way, she's considered one of Spain's most-traveled women.

Meeting the group in Port Moresby, I was back in the whirlwind of Wander youth, eighteen of us, most in their late twenties to early thirties. This was a diverse and fun crew of adventurous, globally minded travelers. Andrea, a Croatian Qatar Airways flight attendant; James, a Macao Chinese polyglot working in Brussels; Andrei, a Russian Ukrainian in Singapore; and Luigi, from Italy, who had even written a book titled *Viaggi Alla Ricerca Di Sé: Perdersi per ritrovarsi* (*Journeys in Search of the Self: Getting Lost to Find Yourself*). His questions—Why travel alone? What are we seeking far from home?—struck a chord.

All of us bonded quickly, thanks to a four-hour delay on our flight to Mount Hagen on Air Niugini, an airline infamous in travel circles for cancellations.

The next day, arriving early to the festival, we saw tribes applying paint and donning traditional dress. At one point, I motioned to a Huli man's paint and my face, jokingly asking, "Can you do that to me?" He took my question seriously. I sat, and twenty minutes later had a painted face with layers of white, yellow, red, and black. Looking in the mirror brought a big smile to my face.

Soon, dozens of tribes, each with ten to fifteen people, began dancing in formation, many in trances from chewing betel nut. I found it captivating—the Asaro Mudmen, coated in clay with oversized mud masks; the Skeleton Tribe, painted to resemble bone structures; and the brightly colored Huli, inspired by birds of paradise. Women from the Dust Shakers wore natural-fiber skirts, painted bodies, and feathered headdresses.

"They mourn through dance," our guide, Florence, explained. "The dust they throw represents ashes. By shaking it off, they symbolically release grief and embrace new beginnings." *Was this what my journey was really about too?*

The Gimi tribe caught me off guard, men wearing only penis sheaths and performing the Moku-Moku dance celebrating reproduction. I was briefly startled by all the nudity, and it did take me a while to get used to it. But as the day wore on, I saw the confidence they had in their bodies, completely unselfconscious. It made me question my own discomfort.

Needing a break from the intensity, loud music, and some very loud bangs that I thought were drumming, I sat with Florence in the shade. I took this moment to ask her how it was possible that 850 languages were spoken in PNG. Florence herself spoke several local languages in addition to English. "Geography explains a lot," she said. "The rivers, mountains, jungles, and islands isolated groups. That's why so many languages." But there had to be more. Many countries are diverse geographically and don't have *this* many separate languages. Later, I read that it takes about a thousand years for one language to evolve into two after a group splits apart physically. And PNG has been inhabited for over forty thousand years.

As we spoke, armed guards patrolled the perimeter, and crowds watched the festivities from outside the fences. I asked why security was so tight. "Locals, mostly men, often get drunk, and fights break out, sometimes violently," Florence said. "There's also been a rise in tribal warfare, especially in cities." PNG ranks second in crime per capita, just behind Venezuela, and the capital, Port Moresby, is considered one of the world's most dangerous. When we boarded the bus to leave, we were held at the gate awaiting a police escort. "Those bangs earlier," Florence told us, "were gunshots outside the grounds."

The next day, we explored villages in the Eastern Highlands. I was happy to get away from the confines of the festival and into some real villages that WE had arranged to visit. In one, women from the

Red Lady tribe performed, painted head to toe in red pigment. I wandered over to check out the villagers who were watching us. A man approached us with a smile. "We're happy to welcome you. Where are you from?"

"I'm from the US," I replied. "But most in the group are European."

As we talked, the conversation slowly drifted into a subject I was not expecting, making me uncomfortable. "In my grandfather's time, there were tribal wars. After battles, they sometimes killed enemies, and even cooked and ate them."

I'd read about cannibalism and headhunting in Papua New Guinea, but hearing it spoken of so openly was jarring.

"Even my parents were involved," he said, his tone more reflective than shocking. "It continued until after the war, when the missionaries came and we converted to Christianity. The Australians helped put an end to it after World War Two."

I was still digesting his words when a crowd gathered, not to join the conversation, but to smile, shake hands, and say hello. These weren't casual smiles. These were deep, ear-to-ear expressions of genuine joy.

Back home, I sometimes wonder why it's so hard for people to say hello on a trail. Would I have even noticed this before losing Jackie? Or was I once someone who didn't say hello, either? It took being in one of the world's most remote places to remember how far a simple hello can go.

I came to Papua New Guinea to witness its famed cultural diversity and to understand why so many languages thrive here. I checked both boxes. But what stayed with me most, what I hadn't expected, was the warmth of the people. Everything I'd read painted PNG as one of the world's most dangerous places. And yet, the kindness I encountered was disarming.

This was my 192nd country, and the connections I made here were among the most touching. I've had moving encounters before, in Syria, in Pakistan, and now I could add Papua New Guinea to the list.

Chapter 35

Conflict Borders

*We realize the importance of our
voices only when we are silenced.*
—Malala Yousafzai

**September 2024
Korea**

Among the roughly fifteen extreme travelers left with only North Korea on their list, rumors of the country's reopening flickered on and off. Yet in the travel community, I was already treated like a UN Master. After I submitted visa stamps, flight tickets, hotel invoices, and photos to NomadMania's verifier, Thomas Buechler, he confirmed, "You've passed the NomadMania 193 verification. Once you visit North Korea, you'll officially join the very small club of travelers who have been to every country in the world."

Being added to the Most Traveled People's UN Masters WhatsApp group reinforced that I was part of a global group that I was happy to belong to. Though one country remained, the goal felt less urgent. I'd come to see that the real reward wasn't the final stamp, but the countless moments along the climb, the stories, the people, the unexpected lessons.

Not knowing when North Korea would open up, I decided to head to the other Korea. Who really knew what was going on in the "Hermit Kingdom"? I wasn't about to pin my hopes on Kim Jong Un, "Rocket Man," as Trump once called him.

Arriving in Seoul, I realized I hadn't been here in over thirty years. Back then, I spent days in smoke-filled conference rooms with a Korean financial firm while at JP Morgan as the country opened its markets to foreign investors. This visit would be very different. I had joined another Koryo tour, *North Korea from a Near Distance*, which would travel along the DMZ, visiting border areas and observation posts inside South Korea.

The first day took us two hours through several military checkpoints to reach the Key observation post. We climbed a steep hill to the command center, a surreal contrast: soldiers, barbed wire, and bunkers against the backdrop of North Korea's lush, quiet, almost dreamlike hills.

I spoke with a young soldier fresh from boot camp. South Korea mandates eighteen months of military service for all able-bodied men before the age of thirty. He looked younger than my sons but came across as disciplined and alert. Wearing a green-brown uniform and a helmet with the South Korean flag, the soldier carried a handgun in one of his vest pouches. The sharp scent of pine mixed with the metallic tang of military gear. His posture was rigid, every movement precise under the watchful eye of commanders nearby.

"Sir," he said respectfully when I greeted him. Before I could ask a question, a loud boom rang out. I instinctively ducked. "What was that?" I asked as I covered my head with my hands.

"Likely a land mine triggered by wildlife," he said. "We know where our land mines are and the North Koreans know theirs, but the animals don't."

"How do you view the North Korean soldiers watching us?" I asked. They were just six hundred meters away.

"Before joining the army, I believed we were one people, sharing language and culture, and would reunite someday," he said. "But last week, I watched them plant land mines across the fence. I realized, they're trained to kill my family." Less than twenty-four hours since arriving, I was beginning to absorb the reality of two different Koreas.

. . .

That night, over our welcome dinner, I met others in the group. Unlike the travelers on past trips with Wander Expeditions or Spiekermann, these travelers weren't chasing countries or adventure; they were drawn to North Korea specifically. The group included diplomats, journalists, military personnel, and academics. One expert, a Russian professor living in South Korea, had studied the North for four decades. Colonel Gee from the South Korean Army joined us too. The tour was led by Greg, a Hungarian North Korea specialist with Koryo Tours. For me, being around all these experts on North Korea was like signing up for introductory French in college and finding myself in an upper-division French literature class with fluent speakers. The learning curve was steep to say the least.

Greg, in his thirties, was personable, and clearly passionate. His grandparents had once visited North Korea when Hungary and the DPRK were allies. Their stories inspired him to travel there in 2016, and he was so moved, he deferred university and joined Koryo. He has since led twenty-seven tours to North Korea.

Korea had grown even more closed in recent years. Kim Jong Un had walked away from the reunification dream and doubled down on control. Officially, the border closure was still blamed on COVID, but the real motive was tighter authoritarianism.

My fate, completing the quest to visit every country, rested in the hands of a dictator.

Later, on a ferry from Incheon to Yeonpyeong Island, I had a chance to talk more with Greg. I'd once been obsessed with South America, Parisian culture, China, even Russia. But Greg had devoted himself to perhaps the most impenetrable country on Earth.

"What made you postpone getting your PhD to be a tour guide for North Korea?" I asked.

"It felt familiar," he said, "like my parents' Hungary, which had

Soviet architecture and state control. But mostly, I saw people living their lives, just trying to get by."

He went on, "I couldn't interact with them, but I felt they were like my grandparents under Communism. It wasn't their fault. If they'd been born a hundred kilometers south, their lives would have been freer, easier."

His words stayed with me. Sometimes, it really is just the luck, or misfortune, of where you're born.

Yeonpyeong Island, in disputed waters, was shelled by North Korea in 2010, killing four South Koreans. The UN called it one of the most serious clashes since the 1953 armistice.

Looking out at many points on the small island, you can see that the long coastline of North Korea is not that far away. One sign on a beach we visited warned not to pick up garbage floating onto the island as "North Korean souvenirs" because it could be unexploded mines.

Back in Seoul the next day, we drove along the DMZ to the Typhoon Observatory. A winding river traced lazy S-curves through green valleys, framed by tiered mountain ridges fading from deep green to steel blue. Through binoculars, I could make out a weathered white building on the North Korean side, a field in front of it where people worked, some walking the fence line, one on a bicycle. They were ordinary people tending to a hard life, earning an average $1,200 a year, thirty times less than their neighbors to the south. But what struck me wasn't the strangeness of seeing North Koreans; it was the humanity of it. Who were they? What were their hopes? Their dreams?

Scanning the hills, I felt the crushing weight of history. Thousands had died for these hilltops, only to see them handed back at the 1953 armistice, negotiations that determined whether your allegiance lay with North or South Korea. The futility was almost tangible.

At nearly all of the DMZ's observation posts, you needed special permits. But the Dora Observatory, where most tourists went, required none. Unlike the isolated, restricted sites we'd seen, this place swarmed with at least twenty massive tour buses. It felt surreal, less like a war zone than a crowded tourist attraction, just steps from the edge of a conflict that never officially ended.

We took a cable car over the Imjin River to Camp Greaves, South

Korea's oldest military base, now a Korean war museum. One exhibit, a letter from a sixteen-year-old soldier, gutted me.

> Dear Mother, I have killed. I threw a grenade. It exploded in a blink, tore my eardrum, ended lives. It was cruel. They are the enemy, but also human. We speak the same language, share the same blood. My heart is heavy.

He died just days later.

Sitting there, I wondered where the blame lies for this kind of dehumanization. Ignorance, yes. Even Greg admitted that, growing up fascinated by North Korea, he once saw its people as robotic products of dictatorship. But the media plays a big part; negative stories sell better than human ones. And leaders exploit fear because it's easier than building bridges.

I'm not naive about the brutality of North Korea's regime. But the regime is not its people, just as our leaders don't always represent us. One thing has become clear to me in the past years: Travel really changes your lens and complicates the stories you thought you understood.

Greg's journey brought that full circle. On our last day, he said, "I just applied to do my PhD on how tourism in North Korea shifts Western narratives about its people."

On my final day in Seoul, I walked around and took in how much had changed in thirty years. The city is now a mix of tradition and modernity, part old village, part futuristic metropolis. South Korea is a global leader in connectivity and smart tech, though it only surpassed the North in development in the 1970s.

Wandering through Ikseon-dong, with its narrow alleys and traditional architecture, I could've sworn I was in a small Korean village. Until I saw a long line outside a café.

"Why are people lining up?" I asked someone nearby.

He smiled and, in accented English, replied, "They have the best avocado toast in Seoul."

On my last night in Seoul, I managed to arrange a one-on-one meeting with a North Korean defector. A poised young woman in a dark green dress and black jacket walked in. "Hello, my name is Yuna," she said. I quickly masked my surprise; whatever image I had of a defector, she wasn't it.

Yuna told me her story. K-pop and South Korean dramas had opened her eyes to the truth: Everything she had been told about life beyond North Korea was a lie.

She had escaped across the frozen Tumen River in 2006, at age eighteen, after stealing money from her father, a high-ranking general. "Despite the famine," she said, looking me straight in the eye, her gravelly voice steady, "I had food, clothes, and studied English and violin. You don't play violin during a famine unless your family has power." From China, she made it to Thailand through Myanmar and Laos. A Korean monk helped her reach the South Korean embassy and claim asylum. "Back then, it cost a few hundred dollars. Now it can cost up to $100,000. That's why defections have dropped from two thousand a year to barely one hundred."

Her escape was riveting, but I wondered what life was like for her now. "How are you perceived, as a defector, in South Korea?"

Her voice softened. "I kept to myself at first. Sure, I was grateful for freedom, a passport, a license. But people saw us as backward, uncultured." She continued, "Sometimes, I didn't even want to speak Korean because my accent was a giveaway."

"What do you think of how North Korea is portrayed in the West?"

She didn't hesitate. "Yes, we were brainwashed. But some in your country are also, by the media and by leaders who use fear to control. All I ever see are headlines about Kim Jong Un and missiles. Never about the people. My people."

I pushed back. "But how can the media report on people it can't access?"

"There are thirty-four thousand of us, North Korean defectors, around the world. Most still talk to family in the North. But no one asks us about their hopes, dreams, or daily lives. To the world, North Korea is just the Kim family and nukes. But we are human beings."

We talked about generational shifts in South Korea. "Older people saw us as family, victims of a system we didn't choose. The younger generation? They don't care. They're too busy chasing careers, or they see us as the enemy."

I thought about the soldier I'd met earlier near the DMZ, expressing the same sentiment about people his own age, same language, now seen as adversaries.

Yuna's final words stayed with me. "Please understand that I am happy I am here in the South. North Korea is a hard place. But hardship also gives you purpose and community. We didn't have depression. South Korea has freedom, yes, but also isolation and serious mental health challenges." She finished with, "In my youth in the North, even in our suffering, we had each other."

There was so much to absorb on this trip—Greg and his passion for understanding North Korea; the South Korean soldier whose enemy was someone his own age, of the same race and language; and Yuna, who moved between both worlds with ease. Reflecting on this, I thought, as someone who deeply believes in our shared humanity, I had learned once again an important lesson: Those we label as enemies are human too. And in seeing their humanity, we rediscover our own.

On my Asiana Airlines flight from Seoul to San Francisco, I kept thinking about how I'd only signed up for this tour because North Korea, my elusive 193rd country, was still closed. At certain points, I was just a few hundred feet away. So close, yet still out of reach.

I hadn't stepped foot in North Korea, hadn't added a new country, and with October already here, I knew I wouldn't finish Project 193 in 2024. But somehow, that no longer felt like the point. This trip to the borderlands of South Korea embodied the deeper spirit of the journey. I'd formed a real bond with a fellow traveler, Greg, and had been moved by Yuna's courage and generosity, leaving me with a deeper understanding of both Koreas.

Chapter 36

Closure

*Don't grieve. Anything you lose
comes round in another form.*
—Rumi

**October 2024
Botswana**

For a time after launching my quest to visit every country in the world, I was unsure if I actually wanted to visit Botswana. The thought was unsettling. The name, a trigger.

Back in the 1990s, Jackie and I had passed through while traveling overland from one African country to the next. But after losing Jackie, my only impression of Botswana was of one thing: *the soul-crushing phone call from the Okavango Delta.*

Many have experienced loss, but few lose a loved one without a clear memory of where it happened. For me, I had come to grips with Jackie being gone forever, but I also carried a lingering sense of something unresolved, a missing piece. This trip felt like a pilgrimage, and I knew instinctively that being in the place where we lost her was that piece.

Though I'd been told the details years ago, I hadn't truly absorbed them. Maybe I wasn't ready. I told myself, *This trip will bring closure.* But what did that even mean? Friends warned, "It will be emotional. Prepare yourself." A deeper fear emerged: *What if it's not emotional?*

Added to this, perhaps my final trip for a while, returning to Botswana wasn't just about finding closure with Jackie. It was also where I'd confront something I'd been avoiding: what comes after. After the nonstop moving around of this journey, I was afraid the finish might unmoor me again, that without a destination, I might lose my way. So much of who I'd become was tied to this journey. Could I exist without it?

Maun, Botswana

I thought about this while flying into Maun. The landscape below reminded me of Timbuktu—dry, sandy, and sparse, save for a few shrubs. When I stepped outside the terminal, the hundred-degree heat slammed into me. Maun is the gateway to the Okavango Delta and Kalahari Desert, drawing safari tourists from all over. At the Duck Café near the airport, it was clear this was safari central, with tourists in khaki, olive, and wide-brimmed hats. I felt out of place in my jeans, Nike sneakers, and the white Unbound Merino T-shirt I'd been wearing for the past two days. Thanks to the fabric being antimicrobial, it didn't smell. *Supposedly.*

Yes, like the other tourists, I was heading to a safari camp, but for a different reason. Almost a year earlier, while planning the trip, I realized I didn't want to just visit the site of Jackie's death and fly home. I wanted to see more of the country, and I planned to arrive at Okavango Horse Safari (OHS) at the end of the trip, on October 22, Jackie's birthday, exactly seven years after our last full day together.

My first stop was the Kalahari Desert. Fueled by another Duck Café espresso, I returned to the terminal. The airstrip teemed with small Mack Air planes and helicopters. I couldn't help wondering which helicopter Jackie had boarded for OHS in her final days. What would life have looked like if she'd made the return flight here, then on to Nairobi to meet me?

My mind drifted back to that day in my hotel room in Dubai. One moment, I was anticipating seeing her beautiful smile. The next moment, I was answering a call that shattered everything—a split second when my life changed forever. But this journey had helped to soften the edges of that trauma.

Camp Kalahari

Our single-prop plane descended into the vast Kalahari Desert, a semi-arid region stretching across Botswana, Namibia, and South Africa, larger than even France. Looking down at the cracked earth, it was hard to believe life thrived here. But unlike other deserts, the Kalahari receives decent rainfall during the wet season, after October's punishing heat.

We landed on a dirt runway, greeted by a jeep. This was the land of the Bushmen, or Khoi-San, known for their "click" language, one of the world's most ancient, unique, and complex speech systems. My guide, DeClerk, shared his real name, Xhlaoxue, which was nearly impossible for outsiders to pronounce. I tried a few times, bringing a hearty laugh from DeClerk.

That evening, we went on a bush walk. DeClerk spoke of how the 2014 hunting ban had changed everything for the Bushmen. "Hunting was who we were," he said. Now, like him, many of his people worked in tourism, sharing their culture. Even without hunting, DeClerk said he would often walk fifty kilometers a day just for the joy of it. "It's what we do."

The Bushmen I met were striking in appearance with lean frames, sun-kissed skin, high cheekbones, and a deep connection to the land.

As we walked, one Bushman picked up a piece of zebra dung. "This is how we make fire," he said. Curious but cautious, I asked, "Why zebra and not elephant?" I was out of my element here.

"Elephant dung is too hard. It burns with a terrible smell, whereas zebras eat soft grasses. Feel how soft this is." After touching it, I discreetly took out my hand sanitizer while another local guide picked up two sticks and rubbed one vertically into the end of the other, twisting it furiously like a spindle. A flame appeared within minutes.

Nearby, another Bushman dug into the sand, revealing a tuber called "devil's claw," used medicinally. As he dug, a scorpion emerged, tail raised in warning. Calmly, he grabbed it, then, with a grin, put it in his mouth, still holding its tail and pincers. After a few moments, he removed it. It lay still in his hand, pacified. "We played with them as kids," he explained.

After my time in the Kalahari, I can now weigh the merits of zebra versus elephant dung for starting a fire and even explain, at least in theory, how to calm a scorpion. *Some lessons are more unexpected than others.*

Though the Bushmen were the highlight, the wildlife didn't disappoint. We saw zebras, wildebeests, kudu, and even a lioness, her coat glistening in the sun as she lay in the grass, visibly full from a recent kill.

But the most magical moment came on a game drive near a patch of burrow holes. "Sit there," DeClerk instructed, pointing to one.

A minute after I'd sat down, a small head emerged, a meerkat. It eyed me, climbed from the hole, and then, astonishingly, into my lap. I froze. The last time I thought of a meerkat was when Jackie and I watched *The Lion King* with our children. Timon the meerkat was always a favorite with the boys. It stood on me like a lookout post, then returned to its burrow. DeClerk explained, "These meerkats are habituated to us. They know that we like them." I smiled, struck by the intimacy of the moment hanging with the cute little guy.

That evening, I watched my last Kalahari sunset in silence, reflecting on all I had seen. Botswana had long symbolized grief. But hanging out with DeClerk and the Bushmen, with their harmony and resilience, gave me something grounding. Their ability to read skies, track wildlife, and interpret animal behavior reminded me how much, in our busy lives, we can be out of step with the natural world.

Maun

Is it ironic to feel the most powerful kindness in the midst of your deepest trauma? Or is it biology, neurotransmitters amplifying moments of compassion during pain? I came to Botswana to stand where Jackie took her last breath, but I also came to thank a man whose words soothed me at the lowest point of my life. Knowing exactly what to say, he had a rare gift.

As I waited at the Thamalakane River Lodge restaurant, I thought about our first conversation seven years earlier. Much time had passed, but his name, Omphile, meaning "gift" in his language, had become a kind of talisman to me, representing the goodness of humanity. A worrisome thought struck me: *What if meeting him now is a letdown?* Maybe I should have preserved the angel-like version I remembered. I knew little about Omphile beyond his role at the Funeral Services Group (FSG) in Maun. He had arranged Jackie's cremation and transport, and said words I've never forgotten: *I can assure you she was as beautiful as when you last saw her.*

Soon, I saw a man my height approaching, in a red shirt and FSG cap. I offered a handshake, but he pulled me into a hug. I gladly accepted, remembering his parting words years ago: *We should never walk with fear of what we may lose, but with love and faith during hard times.*

As we sat outside, looking over the river, ordering a Coke and salad, Omphile told me that after being promoted, he now lived in the capital, Gaborone. He had made a long trek to come and meet me in Maun. I said, "It's strange. I know almost nothing about you, yet I'll never forget you. You gave me some peace when I needed it most." He smiled and with that began telling his story.

Raised in a rural village, one of six siblings, he spent years confused by his father's mistreatment, until he learned the man wasn't his real father. "My grandmother gave me the love I needed," he said. "She only got mad if I skipped church." His passion? Horses. "You know, Jackie had the same passion. Her horse's name was Rosie," I told him.

At twenty-two, tired of his father's abuse, he applied to be an au pair in the US. After selling his horses and buying a one-way ticket, he arrived in Palo Alto with just fifty dollars. For eleven years, he worked odd jobs, eventually landing at a horse ranch in Half Moon Bay, California. On his return to Botswana, the only solid job he could find was at FSG. "It's not what I imagined," he said, "but I realized I'm suited to helping people." His path was unusual, but perhaps that was what shaped his rare empathy.

I asked, "How do you stay positive doing this work?"

"It's a job that must be done. I find meaning in helping people through loss."

He drove me back to the lodge, and at the hotel, we hugged again, this one longer. "Let's stay in touch, my friend."

Okavango Horse Safaris (OHS)

Back at the Duck, I awaited my helicopter ride to OHS, the final leg of my trip. Losing Jackie and longing to reconnect with life had sparked my quest to visit all 193 countries. But as my journey progressed, it became clear that Botswana had to be my final stop, not only to honor Jackie, but to bring closure to this journey.

It was a place that Jackie clearly loved, texting me and the boys only a few days before her tragic death:

> Hey Guys, I miss you all tons and have not had much reception here in the Botswana bush. The place I am at now in the Okavango Delta is spectacular and crazy amazing! It would mean a lot to me if I could bring you all back here soon, like maybe August 2018. Yesterday, my guide and I were cantering with giraffes! Love, Jackie/Mom

About twenty minutes into my helicopter flight, the pilot turned to me and pointed off in the distance. "That is the camp."

As I looked over, I saw a water hole with animals in it. "Are those elephants?"

"Yes, those are the ellies," the pilot said.

We touched down just beyond the camp, and as the rotors whirred to a halt, the pilot circled around to open my door. I stepped out, and a strong wave of sensation hit me. It was neither sorrow nor fear, but something deeper, almost reverence. And with this came a piercing clarity, a powerful feeling of gratitude for the woman whose memory had brought me here. *I was standing on sacred ground.* This was where Jackie took her final breath.

Though the camp was nearby, a safari jeep came to collect me.

A tall man with a warm smile greeted me. "Mr. Barry, I'm Rogers. Welcome to Okavango Horse Safaris." The staff members lined up to shake my hand. Their eyes said they knew why I was here. Barney and her husband, PJ, the owners, were last. I had only spoken to her once, on the day she gave me the terrible news. She offered her hand; I gave her a hug. "Thank you," she said quietly.

We sat around the campfire for a quick briefing about my visit. "Again, I want to express my deep regrets for what happened to your wife. She was a very special woman." Not really wanting to get into it right away, I thanked her and said that in addition to being here for some closure, I was also looking forward to seeing some beautiful animals. Barney offered up, "Why don't you rest a bit, and then Rogers will take you out to see some of the wildlife. And when you return, we can go over whatever you would like to."

I retreated to my tent-cabin and sat outside on the deck, which was raised about six feet off the ground. In the distance, a number of elephants were foraging. As if in a trance, I must have watched them for a good half hour, their movements a blend of power and grace. It felt good to watch them for their beauty and not feel any link between them and Jackie's death. A thought hit me: *A wild animal simply has no control over its instincts. Blaming elephants for what happened, rather than recognizing Jackie's death as a tragic, freak accident, would make no sense.* But the mind can play tricks on you sometimes.

Rogers picked me up for our drive. I'd learned he'd been with OHS since he was fourteen, rising from stable hand to senior guide. He had been here for a few decades. "I prefer the metal horse now," he joked, patting the jeep.

OHS lies in a private concession the size of London. We drove past golden grasses, umbrella-shaped acacias, and skies that stretched forever. The wildlife was stunning, with all that you could possibly want to see. Just minutes into our drive, we saw countless elephants, giraffes, zebras, kudus, warthogs, even a honey badger, but no lions.

Rogers playfully patted me on the back and said, "I am going to find that pride of lions for you." Within half an hour, we saw twenty-four lions in three groupings, some lounging in trees, others on rock outcroppings, or asleep in the grass. "They have just eaten and are tired. See the big bellies of the little ones?"

We stopped at a wide watering hole where about ten hippos lounged in the shallows. After a few moments of silence, I finally worked up the courage to ask, "Did you know Jackie?"

Almost as if he'd been waiting for the question, Rogers nodded solemnly. "I was her horse guide the entire time here. She was so kind, so full of life. We were all devastated. Barney arranged for counseling. Barry, I took it very hard." He paused, searching my face. "Would you like me to continue?"

I met his eyes and saw the sorrow still lingering there. "Please do."

For years, when people asked what had happened, I'd often replied, "It's not something I want to talk about." But the truth was, I'd never really known the full story myself, or if I did, I had blocked it out. And now, I needed to know.

Rogers continued, "It was early morning at about 6:00 a.m. I was in the barn getting the horses ready for her last ride. Her bags were packed. I knew she was to take the helicopter for her onward journey to meet you. She was at breakfast, and mentioned that she needed to go back to her tent. Our assistant guide would not be there when she returned from the ride—I think she wanted to get some money to give him. That was the kind of person Jackie was, so generous and friendly. As she was on her way back to the breakfast area, the accident happened. I heard people yelling and ran over." His voice trailed off.

Seeing that I was overwhelmed, he said, "Barney was there. Maybe she should be the one to tell you more. Elephants, especially males in musth or older barren females, can be dangerously unpredictable."

I nodded, grateful but spent. We continued the drive in silence, the landscape softening the visuals in my mind.

Later, Barney took me for a walk around camp. By the stables, she pointed out Sherife, one of Jackie's horses, and the tent area. "We built this elevated walkway after the accident," she said as I glanced down and saw the old dirt path.

"That's the one she took?" I asked.

Barney nodded, then led me to a small tree with a wire screen. "This is where it happened. We planted this in her honor. It was the staff's idea. Heading back from her tent, she tripped over a log.... The elephant was on her before we could react." She paused. "Paramedics came quickly by helicopter from Maun. But it was too late." Barney looked at me, unsure whether or not to continue.

I said gently, "Thank you." I had heard enough.

Back at my tent, I collapsed onto the deck, stunned and empty. My thoughts spun in relentless circles—Jackie's face, this place, the people who were there, and the cruel, exact sequence of moments that took her from us. So many small moments, one last ride, a quick stop at her tent, tripping, and then she was gone. And for the first time since arriving here, the weight became too much. I broke down and wept; *helplessly, uncontrollably.*

The next day was a bit of a blur, another game drive with Rogers and a bit of hanging out at my tent-cabin, reading and writing. My last night before dinner, I just needed to chill by myself and reflect on what I'd been through the last day and a half. I heard someone walking up the walkway. It was Rogers. "Barry, how about you and I go watch the sunset and have a drink?" Exactly what I needed.

"Perfect," I replied.

As we sat on the jeep, Rogers with a Coke, me with a beer, we toasted Jackie. "She loved the ellies. Got so excited, like my daughter when I bring her a present. You were lucky to have had one like her in your life."

Then, searching my face, he added, "And you may find love again, my friend."

I offered a smile.

Closure was a word I had been using a lot lately. What did that word really mean, and had I found it? For years, I searched for ways to honor Jackie. We created the Jackie Tikkun Olam and Kindness Award at our kids' K-8 school, and there was the Heart and Hope Award from the Alexander Valley Film Festival. We made donations to animal rights organizations she loved. But the most meaningful tribute of all was the Bourse Jackie scholarship program in West Africa. Each gesture helped keep her memory alive and, perhaps, softened the ache of knowing I was the one who got to watch our boys grow up.

But I had come to realize that "closure" was something deeper. It wasn't just the displays of gratitude for Jackie. Part of it was surely seeing that Jackie had spent her final days immersed in beauty, surrounded by wildlife, serenity, and kind souls like Rogers. Now, when

I hear "Botswana," I no longer hear only tragedy. I hear wonder and feel some peace. But there was an added dimension to the meaning of "closure" for me.

Reflecting on the last thing Rogers said, it was also about opening myself to the possibility of love again, the kind of deep, soul-level connection that seemed unimaginable after her death seven years earlier. I thought back to a recent trip, returning home to my mother's declining health and the sudden loss of Jackie's brother. I felt the weight of solitude, the ache of not having someone to turn to. But what I found in Botswana wasn't just closure; it was the continued sign of change taking root and a possible new beginning.

Before I went to bed that night, I emailed my boys about my trip. I focused on the beauty of the place, the incredible wildlife, and Rogers. I ended with, You guys know that Mom really wanted to take us all back with her. We should think about coming back someday soon.

Sausalito

Whether returning from Papua New Guinea, Mongolia, or Botswana, I always noticed the jarring shift between worlds. Just the day before, I was in the Okavango Delta, practicing my Arabic while watching elephants drink from a nearby water hole. Now, I was back in Sausalito, the bay outside my window, waiting for a dinner guest. She and I had started going out for dinners on my trips home over a year ago, just getting to know each other as friends, but recently things had begun to change.

We walked down Caledonia Street toward the local pizza place, but the line was out the door. So, we kept going, landing at a small neighborhood Italian restaurant.

"How about here?" I asked. "They have great food."

She paused. "Are you sure? I know this place holds a lot of memories for you and Jackie." She knew that this was where Jackie and I were married. We'd also celebrated the boys' graduations, our anniversaries, and it was the place we gathered after Jackie's celebration of life.

"I'm okay if you are," I replied. She gave a nod.

We sat, ordered dinner and two glasses of wine. As our glasses met, I offered a toast.

"Thanks for coming to Sausalito tonight. It's really good to see you. And . . . a late happy birthday."

Her birthday had just passed, on October 22, the same day as Jackie's. And I was exactly where I wanted to be.

Epilogue

"Think a moment about the best things that have ever happened in your life, and then ask yourself whether they were planned or happened by chance."

Those were the opening words of my talk to a crowd of over two hundred at the four-day Extraordinary Travel Fest in Bangkok. The audience included some of the most accomplished travelers on the planet. Ric Gazarian of the *Counting Countries* podcast had invited me to speak about the unexpected path that led me, through loss, travel, humanitarian work, and reconnection, to a new sense of purpose.

"We couldn't have the goals we do without caring about the world and its people, many of whom lack what we take for granted. I'm profoundly grateful that a bucket-list trip to Timbuktu in 2010 to celebrate my fiftieth birthday set me on an unintentional path of humanitarian work in West Africa now in my wife's name, Bourse Jackie. Now, the work of Caravan to Class, my travels, and my upcoming book, *Belonging to the World*, have all merged. Most of the best things in my life really did happen by chance."

At the event, I caught up with fellow travelers like Mette Mikkelsen, a fourth-generation female Danish explorer also stuck at 192 countries, and Harry Mitsidis, the founder of NomadMania. I bumped into old friends like Renée and Cameron, and finally met others I'd only known virtually. It struck me how familiar these "strangers" felt. Despite all the time I'd spent abroad, this community grounded me in a new way.

Then I saw a face I instantly recognized, just missing his signature ponytail. "Fadi, what are you doing here? I miss my Syrian friends and family."

"Barry, Syria misses you too," he said with a grin. "My company is one of the sponsors."

As I listened to presentation after presentation, I realized how many of the people in the room had become my friends. These weren't just extreme travelers ticking boxes; they were curious, compassionate global citizens. There was Renée, traveling the world in her wheelchair; Elena, exploring the world with her young kids; Jacquelyn, visiting remote corners solo; Luisa, the oldest UN Master at eighty; and Haley, traveling before losing her eyesight. They shattered stereotypes, each redefining what it means to be a bold traveler.

Then there were the legends: Charles Veley, founder of MTP, who turned out to live ten minutes from me in Marin County (*I guess I am not even the most-traveled guy in my area*); Thor Peterson, who spent nine years visiting every country without stepping on a plane; and Francis Tapon, who climbed the highest peak of each country in Africa and then walked the entire length of Madagascar.

Three years ago, I had no idea this world existed. I had made the decision to visit every country without fully grasping what it might actually entail. But now, standing among this community, I felt I belonged. What started as a personal challenge had become a shared journey, a quest that healed me, transformed me, and taught me about our world.

After Jackie died, I started traveling to avoid home, not yet ready to face a house filled with memories. Then a chance phone call with Alvaro Rojas changed everything. He introduced me to Project 193, and I fully accepted the challenge.

Though I've reached just 192 of 193 countries—North Korea still eludes me—the project feels complete. I used to worry that finishing this journey might reopen the ache, that without a goal, I'd lose my compass. But standing here now, I know this quest gave me something lasting—direction and a new foundation for living. Over the last three years, I've added 72 countries, traveled more than 600,000 miles, and slept in nearly 250 different beds. But those numbers tell only a very tiny part of the story.

This journey awakened something deeper: a love of history, culture, and geography that made my everyday concerns seem small. In the National Museum in Addis Ababa, I stood before Lucy, our

3.2-million-year-old ancestor. In Somaliland, I studied ancient cave paintings at Las Geel. In Eritrea, I visited the Mosque of the Companions, tracing the path of Islam into Africa. And this is all in just the Horn of Africa alone, a place I once never imagined I'd visit. These were more than destinations; they were immersive classrooms.

Being in Iran, Mongolia, and Yemen, I learned to tie historical threads across continents, from Persia and Rome to Genghis Khan to Islam and then to colonial empires. I saw how ideas, faiths, and migrations shaped our modern world. And in that, I found perspective and knowledge.

But above all, I found people.

I've come to realize that I'm very drawn to stories of the people of our world, each one a unique and personal window into the human condition. Many have been shaped over generations. There's nothing more deeply unifying than gaining an understanding of the way lives unfold in the most distant places of our planet. Whether it was the look of grace in a new mother's eyes in São Tomé, truck drivers offering selfies on the Karakoram Highway, or two men in Port Sudan inviting me for coffee in a war zone, what I was really seeking was connection.

There was also that deeply human moment, having a meal with my Lebanese guide, Pierre, and a Syrian refugee family in their humble makeshift abode in the Bekaa Valley in Lebanon. The hospitality, dignity, and warmth shared around that table reminded me that belonging has nothing to do with wealth or power. It has everything to do with presence and mutual respect.

Yes, there is a huge gap of economic inequality around the world. So many countries are so much materially poorer and often more dangerous than where I live. But that is not the only narrative. They are often spiritually richer, driven by their preference of interdependence over independence.

And I have learned, despite the best efforts of the media and our leaders to persuade me otherwise, that the world is not as dangerous as they make it out to be. I wish I had stories to tell of bold escapes or harrowing moments. Certainly, it would make the story of this journey more riveting. But I don't.

Whether or not travel pushes your boundaries, travel definitely rewires the brain. I remember the rush of my first flip-of-a-coin backpacking trip at eighteen, the sensory overload of new smells, currencies, languages. It wasn't just excitement. It stretched the boundaries of everything I knew.

It's kind of like the expansiveness of a Big Bang going on inside your mind trying to sort things out. With neurons firing away, the model in your brain adapts to all the new, real data of previously unknown surroundings. And once the excitement of the newness wears off, the pleasant feeling does not go away. It's not like the excitement of getting a new toy that becomes old and uninteresting after a while. The impressions of travel are long-embracing. They remain with you. They transform into a higher level of confidence that your knowledge of the world has become more complete.

That transformation gave me more than memories. It helped to reshape some of my values.

In a world that today seems increasingly divided, with many leaders leaning on nationalism to divide and conquer, I stand as an unashamed globalist. Not because I dismiss the value of home, but because I've seen firsthand that connection across cultures is not only possible; it's essential. As the founder of the Baha'i religion, Baha'u'llah, conveyed, "The earth is but one country and mankind its citizens."

An important realization along this journey is that I am getting closer to the person I want to be. We have launched our third Bourse Jackie scholarship program, and in sending out information on WhatsApp to our existing scholarship recipients, I received the following reply from Ms. Nana Djenne from Timbuktu:

> I don't have words to describe how I'm feeling right now. You're showing me once again how much you care about us. And no matter what happens, my duty is to not disappoint you. You're showing and giving love around you wherever you go without expecting nothing back. You know what? I learned a lot, and I am still learning from you, and one day, I will also do something for this world. I pray God to let you live as long as possible. Cordially, Nana Djenne.

Of course, hearing something like this from one of our best scholarship recipients made me feel good. But more than that, I realized that this was not something anyone would have told me before. And if they had, I would not have deserved it. There is no doubt in my mind that Jackie's devastating loss and the intense grieving that followed cracked open something deep in my heart and led to an important awakening: *an imperative to be more like her.* Yes, I healed from the tragedy of what happened to Jackie. But through my journey of loss, I have also transformed into becoming a better version of myself.

I will always carry a deep ache, knowing that my boys won't get to share the many treasured years with their mother as I did with mine, my own mother having lived past one hundred. But I hold on to the hope that they'll carry with them the loving memories, lessons, and countless blessings of having the extraordinary mother they had in Jackie.

As for me, I've lost the one person who shared the memories of our travels and raising our family that only the two of us could understand. That absence will always hurt. But I've also begun creating new memories, ones that lift me up and give my life meaning—memories like this journey I've been on that I'll vividly carry with me for whatever time I have left. And I like to believe that somehow, Jackie knows about them.

I think often about the question that the ten-year-old Pakistani boy asked when I was standing in front of his classroom of male students, high up in the Karakoram mountains in the ridiculously beautiful town of Skardu, talking about my travels. "Mr. Barry," he asked, "what is the meaning of life to you?" Despite the initial smirk I shared with my friend Lee accompanying me on that trip, I've thought about the question ever since.

The truth is, the answer has been right in front of me during my travels. For me, it is finding belonging.

After the soul-crushing tragedy of losing Jackie, this magnificent journey led to an emotional and even spiritual enlightenment that has prepared me for a new beginning. I'm not sure what comes next, but I know I'm finally open to it. After many years of solitude, I feel ready, tentatively, hopefully, for love to return. Franz Kafka is said to have written, "Everything you love will probably be lost, but in the end, love will return in another way."

This wasn't the journey I wanted. It was born of heartbreak. But the same grief that once left me hollow became the doorway to something unexpected, something beautiful. What I hadn't anticipated was how much this journey would be shaped by loss, the places I had been before with Jackie, the places she never got to see, the people who have endured hardship along the way. Buried within my loss was not just a challenge to overcome, but something deeper. I've learned that grief is not something to fear. It can hold our deepest love for those we've lost, and, if we allow, it also carries the power to transform. Grief is not the end of a story. Sometimes, it's the beginning of another.

I am not the same man who began this path. Through pain, I rediscovered wonder. Through movement, I found meaning. And through strangers, I found a new kind of home, a place beyond borders.

Maybe the best things in life don't arrive by plan, but by grace, when we're open enough to receive them.

Author's Note

As this book was moving through its final stage of production, life once again reminded me that journeys rarely unfold as we plan. My 104-year-old mother, whose long life began in Baghdad and shaped my desire to see the world, passed away peacefully on August 29, 2025. On that very same day, I received an invitation to visit North Korea (for the Pyongyang International Film Festival), the one country that had long eluded me.

For a fleeting moment, I believed that after so many near attempts, fate itself was finally bending in my favor, that providence had chosen this unlikely hour to open the door to country number 193. But once again, the chance slipped away. As I was preparing for the trip, my visa was denied, and as of October 2025, North Korea remains beyond reach.

Still, I no longer feel the absence as unfinished business. Perhaps one day I will stand in Pyongyang, or perhaps not. Either way, the journey feels whole. Belonging, I've learned, is not about completing a list but about moving forward with life itself by remaining open to connections and trusting that one's story is never truly over.

Acknowledgments

Writing *Belonging to the World* has been a journey in itself: a journey of reflection, healing, and deep gratitude. What began as an ambitious goal to visit every country became a search for meaning after unimaginable loss, and ultimately, a reconnection with the grace of humanity all across this beautiful world. I started this journey simply needing to get away and pour my soul into something substantial. But about a year in, just after returning from Afghanistan, I felt myself changing, opening, deepening. I somehow knew I needed to write about it. That sense was confirmed when a close friend called that very day and said, "Barry, I had a vision that you were going to write a book about your travels."

This book could not exist without the guidance, wisdom, and spirit of so many people who shared a part of that path with me.

First and foremost, I would like to thank my editors at different stages of the manuscript, Doug Wagner of Windword Literary Services for developmental help and Eva Avery of Copilot Publishing all-around editing. Your insights into structure, storytelling, and theme were invaluable. Without your guidance, *Belonging to the World* would not be what it is today, and I have learned so much from you. Thank you.

To my publishing team at Girl Friday Books: Thank you for believing in my vision and treating it with such care. Your support made the daunting process of bringing this work into the world not only possible but deeply fulfilling.

I'm also grateful to a number of people whose advice, ideas, and enthusiasm shaped this project in meaningful ways: Andi Reese Brady of Personal History Productions, and Claire Balsely, my travel friend through Yemen, Solomon Islands, and Papua New Guinea.

To the many travel companies, logistics coordinators, and visa fixers, especially those who handled the complicated and the obscure with patience and persistence, thank you for helping me reach the places I needed to go.

To the local guides across every continent who welcomed me into your countries and lives with grace, humor, and kindness: You were my windows into culture and my bridges to understanding. I carry your stories with me still.

To the friends and companions I met on the road, and to the extreme-travel community, the dreamers and doers who understand what compels someone to cross the world's most remote borders or return to a place simply for closure—thank you. Your camaraderie, wisdom, and shared madness made the journey lighter and infinitely more joyful.

And to the countless individuals I met across 193 countries, those who invited me into your homes, guided me through your cities, offered food, directions, laughter, and kindness, I am forever changed by you. You reminded me that we belong not to places or possessions, but to one another. In a world too often divided, your simple acts of humanity brought me back to life.

Finally, to my sons, Benjamin and Daniel, who gave me the reason to keep going, and to Jackie, my partner, my compass, my North Star, this journey was, and always will be, for you.

Thank you. All of you. You helped me belong to the world.

About the Author

Barry Hoffner believes the best things in life often happen by chance. After earning his MBA from Columbia University, he worked in investment banking across the globe. A midcareer sabbatical transformed his path as he fell in love, traveled the world with his wife, Jackie, and eventually started a family. He left finance to farm wine grapes and olives and to build his life's work: Caravan to Class, a foundation that brings access to education for youth in West Africa. Caravan to Class's anchor program, Bourse Jackie scholarships for young women, is named in honor of his late wife.

After losing Jackie in 2017, Barry devoted himself to this mission and to a new chapter of exploration. He has since traveled to every country in the world. He lives in Sausalito, California, and is the proud father of two adult sons, Benjamin and Daniel.

www.ingramcontent.com/pod-product-compliance
Lightning Source LLC
LaVergne TN
LVHW040039080526
838202LV00045B/3407